Praise for *Effective C#*

"This book really demonstrates Bill's strengths as a writer and programmer. In a very short amount of time, he is able to present an issue, fix it, and conclude it; each chapter is tight, succinct, and to the point."

—Josh Holmes, independent contractor

"The book provides a good introduction to the C# language elements from a pragmatic point of view, identifying best practices along the way and following a clear and logical progression from the basic syntax to creating components to improving your code-writing skills. Since each topic is covered in short entries, it is very easy to read and you'll quickly realize the benefits of the book."

—Tomas Restrepo, Microsoft MVP

"The book covers the basics well, especially with respect to the decisions needed when deriving classes from System.Object. It is easy to read with examples that are clear, concise, and solid. I think it will bring good value to most readers."

—Rob Steele, Central Region Integration COE and Lead Architect, Microsoft

"*Effective C#* provides the C# developer with the tools they need to rapidly grow their experience in Visual C# 2003 while also providing insight into the many improvements to the language that will be hitting a desktop near you in the form of Visual C# 2005."

—Doug Holland, Precision Objects

"Part of the point of the .NET Framework—and the C# Language, in particular—is to let the developer focus on solving customer problems and delivering a product, rather than spending hours (or even weeks) writing plumbing code. Bill Wagner's *Effective C#* not only shows you what's going on behind the scenes, but also shows you how to take advantage of particular C# code constructs. Written in a dispassionate style that focuses on the facts—and just the facts—of writing effective C# code, Wagner's book drills down into practices that will let you write C# applications and components that are easier to maintain as well as faster to run. I'm recommending *Effective C#* to all students of my "NET Boot-Camp" and other C#-related courses."

—Richard Hale Shaw, www.RichardHaleShawGroup.com

"*Effective C#* is very well organized and easy to read with a good mix of code and explanations that give the reader deep understanding of the topic. The author is an authority on C# and the .NET runtime, but keeps the content accessible and easy to read through a conversational tone while still imparting expert knowledge to the reader."

—Brian Noyes, Principal Software Architect, IDesign, Inc.

Effective C#

Bill Wagn

Sept 2005

Effective SOFTWARE DEVELOPMENT SERIES
Scott Meyers, Consulting Editor

The **Effective Software Development Series** provides expert advice on all aspects of modern software development. Books in the series are well written, technically sound, of lasting value, and tractable length. Each describes the critical things the experts almost always do—or almost always avoid doing—to produce outstanding software.

Scott Meyers (author of the *Effective C++* books and CD) conceived of the series and acts as its consulting editor. Authors in the series work with Meyers and with Addison-Wesley Professional's editorial staff to create essential reading for software developers of every stripe.

TITLES IN THE SERIES

Effective C#

50 Specific Ways to Improve Your C#

Bill Wagner

✦ Addison-Wesley

Boston • San Francisco • New York • Toronto • Montreal
London • Munich • Paris • Madrid
Capetown • Sydney • Tokyo • Singapore • Mexico City

Many of the designations used by manufacturers and sellers to distinguish their products are claimed as trademarks. Where those designations appear in this book, and the publisher was aware of a trademark claim, the designations have been printed with initial capital letters or in all capitals.

The author and publisher have taken care in the preparation of this book, but make no expressed or implied warranty of any kind and assume no responsibility for errors or omissions. No liability is assumed for incidental or consequential damages in connection with or arising out of the use of the information or programs contained herein.

The publisher offers excellent discounts on this book when ordered in quantity for bulk purchases or special sales, which may include electronic versions and/or custom covers and content particular to your business, training goals, marketing focus, and branding interests. For more information, please contact:

U. S. Corporate and Government Sales
(800) 382-3419
corpsales@pearsontechgroup.com

For sales outside the U. S., please contact:

International Sales
international@pearsoned.com

Visit us on the Web: www.awprofessional.com

Library of Congress Cataloging-in-Publication Data:
2004111537

ISBN 0-321-24566-0

Printed in the United States on recycled paper at *RR Donnelley, Crawfordsville, Indiana*

10 9 8 7 6 5 4 3

Contents at a Glance

Contents

Chapter 4   Creating Binary Components   177

Chapter 5   Working with the Framework   205

Chapter 6   Miscellaneous   265

Index   295

Introduction

This book is designed to offer practical advice for the programmer on how to improve productivity when using the C# language and the .NET libraries. In it, I have comprised 50 key items, or minitopics, related to the most–frequently-asked questions that I (and other C# consultants) have encountered while working with the C# community.

I started using C# after more than 10 years of C++ development, and it seems that many C# developers are following suit. Throughout the book, I discuss where following C++ practices may cause problems in using C#. Other C# developers are coming to the language with a strong Java background; they may find some of these passages rather obvious. Because some of the best practices change from Java to C#, I encourage Java developers to pay special attention to the discussions on value types (see Chapter 1, "C# Language Elements"). In addition, the .NET Garbage Collector behaves differently than the JVM Garbage Collector (see Chapter 2, ".NET Resource Management").

The items in this book are the collection of recommendations that I most often give developers. Although not all items are universal, most of the items can be easily applied to everyday programming scenarios. These include discussions on Properties (Item 1), Conditional Compilation (Item 4), Immutable Types (Item 7), Equality (Item 9), ICloneable (Item 27), and the new Modifier (Item 29). It has been my experience that, in most situations, decreasing development time and writing good code are the primary goals of the programmer. Certain scientific and engineering applications may place the highest premium on the overall performance of the system. Still, for others, it's all about the scalability. Depending on your goals, you might find particular information more (or less) relevant under certain circumstances. To address this, I have tried to explain the goals in detail. My discussions on readonly and const (Item 2), Serializable Types (Item 25), CLS Compliance (Item 31), Web Methods

(Item 34), and DataSets (Item 41) assume certain design goals. Those goals are spelled out in these items, so that you can decide what is most applicable for you in your given situation.

Although each item in *Effective C#* stands alone, it is important to understand that the items have been organized around major topics, such as C# language syntax, resource management, and object and component design. This is no accident. My goal is to maximize learning the material covered in the book by leveraging and building each item on earlier items. Don't let that keep you from using it as a reference, though. If you have specific questions, this book functions well as the ideal "ask-me" tool.

Please keep in mind that this is not a tutorial or a guide to the language, nor is it going to teach you C# syntax or structure. My goal is to provide guidance on the best constructs to use in different situations.

Who Should Read this Book?

Effective C# is written for professional developers, those programmers who use C# in their daily work lives. It assumes that you have some experience with object-oriented programming and at least one language in the C family: C, C++, C#, or Java. Developers with a Visual Basic 6 background should be familiar with both the C# syntax and object-oriented design before reading this book.

Additionally, you should have some experience with the major areas of .NET: Web Services, ADO.NET, Web forms, and Windows Forms. I reference these concepts throughout the book.

To fully take advantage of this book, you should understand the way the .NET environment handles assemblies, the Microsoft Intermediate Language (MSIL), and executable code. The C# compiler produces assemblies that contain MSIL, which I often abbreviate as IL. When an assembly is loaded, the Just In Time (JIT) Compiler converts that MSIL into machine-executable code. The C# compiler does perform some optimizations, but the JIT compiler is responsible for many more effective optimizations, such as inlining. Throughout the book, I've explained which process is involved in which optimizations. This two-step compilation process has a significant effect on which constructs perform best in different situations.

About the Content

Chapter 1, "C# Language Elements," discusses the C# syntax elements and the core methods of `System.Object` that are part of every type you write. These are the topics that you must remember every day when you write C# code: declarations, statements, algorithms, and the `System.Object` interface. In addition, all the items that directly relate to the distinction between value types and reference types are in this chapter. Many items have some differences, depending on whether you are using a reference type (class) or a value type (struct). I strongly encourage you to read the discussions on value and reference types (Items 6 through 8) before reading deeper into the book.

Chapter 2, ".NET Resource Management," covers resource management with C# and .NET. You'll learn how to optimize your resource allocation and usage patterns for the .NET managed execution environment. Yes, the .NET Garbage Collector makes your life much simpler. Memory management is the environment's responsibility, not yours. But, your actions can have a big impact on how well the Garbage Collector performs for your application. And even if memory is not your problem, nonmemory resources are still your responsibility; they can be handled through `IDisposable`. You'll learn the best practices for resource management in .NET here.

Chapter 3, "Expressing Designs with C#," covers object-oriented design from a C# perspective. C# provides a rich palette of tools for your use. Sometimes, the same problems can be solved in many ways: using interfaces, delegates, events, or attributes and reflection. Which one you pick will have a huge impact on the future maintainability of your system. Choosing the best representation of your design will help to make it easier for the programmers using your types. The most natural representation will make your intent clearer. Your types will be easier to use and harder to misuse. The items in Chapter 3 focus on the design decisions you will make and when each C# idiom is most appropriate.

Chapter 4, "Creating Binary Components," covers components and language interoperability. You'll learn how to write components that can be consumed by other .NET languages, without sacrificing your favorite C# features. You'll also learn how to subdivide your classes into components in order to upgrade pieces of your application. You should be able to release new versions of a component without redistributing the entire application.

Chapter 5, "Working with the Framework," covers underutilized portions of the .NET Framework. I see a strong desire in many developers to create their own software rather than use what's already been built. Maybe it's the size of the .NET Framework that causes this; maybe it's that the framework is completely new. These items cover the parts of the framework where I have seen developers reinvent the wheel rather than use what they've been given. Save yourself the time by learning how to use the framework more efficiently.

Chapter 6, "Miscellaneous," finishes with items that did not fit in the other categories and with a look forward. Look here for C# 2.0 information, standards information, exception-safe code, security, and interop.

A Word About the Items

My vision for these items is to provide you with clear and succinct advice for writing C# software. Some guidelines in the book are universal because they affect the correctness of a program, such as initializing data members properly (see Chapter 2). Others are not so obvious and have generated much debate in the .NET community, such as whether to use ADO.NET `DataSets`. While I personally believe that using them is a great timesaver (see Item 41), other professional programmers, whom I highly respect, disagree. It really depends on what you're building. My position comes from a timesaving stance. For others who write a great deal of software that transfer information between .NET- and Java-based systems, `DataSets` are a bad idea. Throughout the book, I support and have given justification for all the suggestions I make. If the justification does not apply to your situation, neither does the advice. When the advice is universal, I usually omit the obvious justification, which is this: Your program won't work otherwise.

Styles and Code Conventions

One difficulty in writing a book about a programming language is that language designers give real English words a very specific new meaning. This makes for passages that can be tough to understand: "Develop interfaces with interfaces" is an example. Any time I use a specific language keyword, it is in the `code` style. When I discuss general topics with specific C# concepts, the specific C# topic is capitalized, as in: "Create

`Interfaces` to represent the interface supported by your classes." It's still not perfect, but it should make many of these passages easier to read.

Many related C# terms are used in this book. When I refer to a member of type, it refers to any definition that can be part of a type: methods, properties, fields, indexers, events, enums, or delegates. When only one applies, I use a more specific term. A number of terms in this book might or might not already be familiar to you. When these terms first appear in the text, they are set in **bold** and defined.

The samples in this book are short, focused sections of code that are meant to demonstrate the advice of that particular item. They are designed to highlight the advantages of following the advice. They are not complete samples to incorporate into your current programs. You cannot just copy the listings and compile them. I've omitted many details from each listing. In all cases, you should assume the presence of common `using` clauses:

```
using System;
using System.IO;
using System.Collections;
using System.Data;
```

When I use less common namespaces, I make sure that you can see the relevant namespace. Short samples use the fully qualified class names, and long samples include the less common `using` statements.

I take similar liberties with code inside the samples. For example, when I show this:

```
string s1 = GetMessage( );
```

I might not show the body of the `GetMessage()` routine if it's not relevant to the discussion. Whenever I omit code, you can assume that the missing method does something obvious and reasonable. My purpose in this is to keep us focused on the particular topic. By omitting code that is not part of that topic, we don't become distracted. It also keeps each item short enough that you should be able to finish an item in one sitting.

Regarding C# 2.0

I say little about the upcoming C# 2.0 release; there are two reasons for this. First and foremost, most of the advice in this book applies just as well for C# 2.0 as it does for the current version. Although C# 2.0 is a significant upgrade, it is built on C# 1.0 and does not invalidate most of today's advice. Where the best practices will likely change, I've noted that in the text.

The second reason is that it's too early to write the most effective uses of the new C# 2.0 features. This book is based on the experience I've had—and the experience my colleagues have had—using C# 1.0. None of us has enough experience with the new features in C# 2.0 to know the best ways to incorporate them into our daily tasks. I'd rather not mislead you when the simple fact is that the time to cover the new C# 2.0 features in an Effective book has not yet arrived.

Making Suggestions, Providing Feedback, and Getting Book Updates

This book is based on my experiences and many conversations with colleagues. If your experience is different, or if you have any questions or comments, I want to hear about it. Please contact me via email: `wwagner@srtsolutions.com`. I'll be posting those comments online as an extension to the book. See `www.srtsolutions.com/EffectiveCSharp` for the current discussion.

Acknowledgments

Although writing seems like a solitary activity, this book is the product of a large team of people. I was lucky enough to have two wonderful editors, Stephane Nakib and Joan Murray. Stephane Nakib first approached me about writing for Addison Wesley a little more than a year ago. I was skeptical. The bookstore shelves are filled with .NET and C# books. Until C# 2.0 has been around long enough to cover thoroughly, I could not see the need for another reference, tutorial, or programming book about C# and .NET. We discussed several ideas and kept coming back to a book on C# best practices. During those discussions, Stephane told me that Scott Meyers had begun an Effective series, modeled after his Effective C++ books. My own copies of Scott's three books are very well worn. I've also recommended them to every professional C++ developer I know. His style is clear and focused. Each item of advice has solid justifications. The Effective books are a great resource, and the format makes it easy to remember the advice. I know many C++ developers who have copied the table of contents and tacked it to the cubicle wall as a constant reminder. As soon as Stephane mentioned the idea of writing *Effective C#*, I jumped at the opportunity. This book contains in one place all the advice I've been giving to C# developers. I am honored to be a part of this series. Working with Scott has taught me a great deal. I only hope this book improves your C# skills as much as Scott's books improved my C++ skills.

Stephane helped pitch the idea of an *Effective C#* book, reviewed outlines and manuscripts, and graciously championed the book through the early writing process. When she moved out of acquisitions, Joan Murray picked up and shepherded the manuscript through production without missing a beat. Ebony Haight provided a constant presence as an editorial assistant through the entire process. Krista Hansing did all the copyediting, turning programmer jargon into English. Christy Hackerd did all the work to turn the word documents into the finished book you now hold.

Any errors that remain are mine. But the vast majority of errors, omissions, and unclear descriptions were caught by a wonderful team of reviewers. Most notably, Brian Noyes, Rob Steel, Josh Holmes, and Doug Holland made the text you have in front of you more correct and more useful than the earlier drafts. Also, thank you to all the members of the Ann Arbor Computing Society, the Great Lakes Area .NET User Group, the Greater Lansing User Group, and the West Michigan .NET User Group, who all heard talks based on these items and offered great feedback.

Most of all, Scott Meyers' participation had a huge, positive impact on the final version of this book. Discussing early drafts of this book with him made me clearly understand why my copies of the *Effective C++* books are so worn. Very little, if anything, escapes his reviews.

I want to thank Andy Seidl and Bill French from MyST Technology Partners (`myst-technology.com`). I used a secure MyST-based blogsite to publish early drafts of each item for reviewers. The process was much more efficient and shortened the cycle between drafts of the book. We've since opened parts of the site for the public so you can see parts of the book in an online format. See `www.srtsolutions.com/EffectiveCSharp` for the online version.

I've been writing magazine articles for several years now and I need to publicly thank the person who got me started: Richard Hale Shaw. He gave me (as an untested author) a column in the original *Visual C++ Developer's Journal* he helped found. I would not have discovered how much I enjoy writing without his help. I also would not have had the opportunity to write for *Visual Studio Magazine, C# Pro*, or *ASP.NET Pro* without the initial help he gave.

Along the way, I've been fortunate to work with many wonderful editors at different magazines. I'd like to list them all, but space does not permit it. One does deserve a special mention: Elden Nelson. I've enjoyed all our time working together and he has had a strong positive effect on my writing style.

My business partners, Josh Holmes and Dianne Marsh, put up with my limited involvement in the company while taking the time to write this book. They also helped review manuscripts, ideas, and thoughts on items.

Throughout the long process of writing, the guidance of my parents, Bill and Alice Wagner, to always finish what I start could be the only reason you are now holding a completed book.

Finally, the most important thanks go to my family: Marlene, Lara, Sarah, and Scott. Writing a book takes an incredible amount of time from all those activities we enjoy. And after all this time on the book, their continued patience has never wavered.

1 | C# Language Elements

Why should you change what you are doing today if it works? The answer is that you can be better. You change tools or languages because you can be more productive. You don't realize the expected gains if you don't change your habits. This is harder when the new language, C#, has so much in common with a familiar language, such as C++ or Java. It's easy to fall back on old habits. Most of these old habits are fine. The C# language designers want you to be able to leverage your knowledge in these languages. However, they also added and changed some elements to provide better integration with the Common Language Runtime (CLR), and provide better support for component-oriented development. This chapter discusses those habits that you should change—and what you should do instead.

Item 1: Always Use Properties Instead of Accessible Data Members

The C# language promoted properties from an ad-hoc convention to a first-class language feature. If you're still creating public variables in your types, stop now. If you're still creating get and set methods by hand, stop now. Properties let you expose data members as part of your public interface and still provide the encapsulation you want in an object-oriented environment. **Properties** are language elements that are accessed as though they are data members, but they are implemented as methods.

Some members of a type really are best represented as data: the name of a customer, the x,y location of a point, or last year's revenue. Properties enable you to create an interface that acts like data access but still has all the benefits of a function. Client code accesses properties as though they are accessing public variables. But the actual implementation uses methods, in which you define the behavior of property accessors.

The .NET Framework assumes that you'll use properties for your public data members. In fact, the data binding code classes in the .NET Framework support properties, not public data members. Data binding ties a property of an object to a user interface control, either a web control or a Windows Forms control. The data binding mechanism uses reflection to find a named property in a type:

```
textBoxCity.DataBindings.Add( "Text",
  address, "City" );
```

The previous code binds the `Text` property of the `textBoxCity` control to the `City` property of the `address` object. (See Item 38 for more details.) It will not work with a public data member named `City`; the Framework Class Library designers did not support that practice. Public data members are bad practice, so support for them was not added. Their decision simply gives you yet another reason to follow the proper object-oriented techniques. Let me add a quick note for the grizzled C++ and Java programmers: The data binding code does not look for `get` and `set` functions, either. You should be using properties instead of the convention of `get_` and `set_` functions in those languages.

Yes, data binding applies only to those classes that contain elements that are displayed in your user interface logic. But that doesn't mean properties should be used exclusively in UI logic. You should still be using properties for other classes and structures. Properties are far easier to change as you discover new requirements or behaviors over time. You might soon decide that your customer type should never have a blank name. If you used a public property for `Name`, that's easy to fix in one location:

```
public class Customer
{
  private string _name;
  public string Name
  {
    get
    {
      return _name;
    }
    set
    {
      if (( value == null ) ||
```

```
      ( value.Length == 0 ))
      throw new ArgumentException( "Name cannot be blank",
        "Name" );
    _name = value;
    }
  }

  // ...
}
```

If you had used public data members, you're stuck looking for every bit of code that sets a customer's name and fixing it there. That takes more time—much more time.

Because properties are implemented with methods, adding multi-threaded support is easier. Simply enhance the implementation of the get and set methods to provide synchronized access to the data:

```
public string Name
{
  get
  {
    lock( this )
    {
      return _name;
    }
  }
  set
  {
    lock( this )
    {
      _name = value;
    }
  }
}
```

Properties have all the language features of methods. Properties can be virtual:

```
public class Customer
{
  private string _name;
```

```
   public virtual string Name
   {
     get
     {
       return _name;
     }
     set
     {
       _name = value;
     }
   }


   // remaining implementation omitted
}
```

It's also easy to see that you can extend properties to be abstract or even part of an interface definition:

```
public interface INameValuePair
{
   object Name
   {
     get;
   }

   object Value
   {
     get;
     set;
   }
}
```

Last, but certainly not least, you can use interfaces to create `const` and nonconst versions of an interface:

```
public interface IConstNameValuePair
{
   object Name
   {
     get;
   }
```

```csharp
  object Value
  {
    get;
  }
}
public interface INameValuePair
{
  object Value
  {
    get;
    set;
  }
}

// Usage:
public class Stuff : IConstNameValuePair, INameValuePair
{
  private string _name;
  private object _value;

  #region IConstNameValuePair Members
  public object Name
  {
    get
    {
      return _name;
    }
  }

  object IConstNameValuePair.Value
  {
    get
    {
      return _value;
    }
  }

  #endregion

  #region INameValuePair Members
```

```
public object Value
{
  get
  {
    return _value;
  }
  set
  {
    _value = value;
  }
}
#endregion
}
```

Properties are full-fledged, first-class language elements that are an extension of methods that access or modify internal data. Anything you can do with member functions, you can do with properties.

The accessors for a property are two separate methods that get compiled into your type. You can specify different accessibility modifiers to the `get` and `set` accessors in a property in C# 2.0. This gives you even greater control over the visibility of those data elements you expose as properties:

```
// Legal C# 2.0:
public class Customer
{
  private string _name;
  public virtual string Name
  {
    get
    {
      return _name;
    }
    protected set
    {
      _name = value;
    }
  }

  // remaining implementation omitted
}
```

The property syntax extends beyond simple data fields. If your type should contain indexed items as part of its interface, you can use **indexers** (which are parameterized properties). It's a useful way to create a property that returns the items in a sequence:

```
public int this [ int index ]
{
  get
  {
    return _theValues [ index ] ;
  }
  set
  {
    _theValues[ index ] = value;
  }
}


// Accessing an indexer:
int val = MyObject[ i ];
```

Indexers have all the same language support as single-item properties: They are implemented as methods you write, so you can apply any verification or computation inside the indexer. Indexers can be virtual or abstract, can be declared in interfaces, and can be read-only or read-write. Single-dimension indexers with numeric parameters can participate in data binding. Other indexers can use noninteger parameters to define maps and dictionaries:

```
public Address this [ string name ]
{
  get
  {
    return _theValues[ name ] ;
  }
  set
  {
    _theValues[ name ] = value;
  }
}
```

In keeping with the multidimensional arrays in C#, you can create multidimensional indexers, with similar or different types on each axis:

```
public int this [ int x, int y ]
{
  get
  {
    return ComputeValue( x, y );
  }
}

public int this[ int x, string name ]
{
  get
  {
    return ComputeValue( x, name );
  }
}
```

Notice that all indexers are declared with the `this` keyword. You cannot name an indexer. Therefore, you can have, at most, one indexer with the same parameter list in each type.

This property functionality is all well and good, and it's a nice improvement. But you might still be tempted to create an initial implementation using data members and then replace the data members with properties later when you need one of those benefits. That sounds like a reasonable strategy—but it's wrong. Consider this portion of a class definition:

```
// using public data members, bad practice:
public class Customer
{
  public string Name;

  // remaining implementation omitted
}
```

It describes a customer, with a name. You can get or set the name using the familiar member notation:

```
string name = customerOne.Name;
customerOne.Name = "This Company, Inc.";
```

That's simple and straightforward. You are thinking that you could later replace the `Name` data member with a property, and the code would keep working without any change. Well, that's sort of true.

Properties are meant to look like data members when accessed. That's the purpose behind the new syntax. But properties are not data. A property access generates different MSIL than a data access. The previous customer type generates the following MSIL for the Name field:

```
.field public string Name
```

Accessing the field generates these statements:

```
ldloc.0
ldfld       string NameSpace.Customer::Name
stloc.1
```

Storing a value in the field generates this:

```
ldloc.0
ldstr       "This Company, Inc."
stfld       string NameSpace.Customer::Name
```

Don't worry—we're not going to look at IL all day. But here, it is important because we are about to see how changing between data members and properties breaks binary compatibility. Consider this version of the customer type, which is created by using properties:

```
public class Customer
{
  private string _name;
  public string Name
  {
    get
    {
      return _name;
    }
    set
    {
      _name = value;
    }
  }

  // remaining implementation omitted
}
```

When you write C# code, you access the name property using the exact same syntax:

```
string name = customerOne.Name;
customerOne.Name = "This Company, Inc.";
```

But the C# compiler generates completely different MSIL for this version. The Customer type has this:

```
.property instance string Name()
{
  .get instance string NameSpace.Customer::get_Name()
  .set instance void NameSpace.Customer::set_Name(string)
} // end of property Customer::Name


.method public hidebysig specialname instance string
        get_Name() cil managed
{
  // Code size        11 (0xb)
  .maxstack   1
  .locals init ([0] string CS$00000003$00000000)
  IL_0000:  ldarg.0
  IL_0001:  ldfld       string NameSpace.Customer::_name
  IL_0006:  stloc.0
  IL_0007:  br.s        IL_0009
  IL_0009:  ldloc.0
  IL_000a:  ret
} // end of method Customer::get_Name
.method public hidebysig specialname instance void
        set_Name(string 'value') cil managed
{
  // Code size        8 (0x8)
  .maxstack   2
  IL_0000:  ldarg.0
  IL_0001:  ldarg.1
  IL_0002:  stfld       string NameSpace.Customer::_name
  IL_0007:  ret
} // end of method Customer::set_Name
```

Two major points must be understood about how property definitions translate into MSIL. First, the .property directive defines the type of the property and the functions that implement the get and set accessors of the property. The two functions are marked with `hidebysig` and `specialname`. For our purposes, those designations mean that these functions are not called directly in C# source code, and they are not to be considered part of the formal type definition. Instead, you access them through the property.

Sure, you expected different MSIL to be generated for the property definition. More important to this discussion, there are changes to the MSIL generated for the `get` and `set` access to the property as well:

```
// get
ldloc.0
callvirt    instance string NameSpace.Customer::get_Name()
stloc.1

// set
ldloc.0
ldstr       "This Company, Inc."
callvirt    instance void NameSpace.Customer::set_Name(string)
```

The same C# source to access the name of a customer compiles to very different MSIL instructions, depending on whether the `Name` member is a property or a data member. Accessing a property and accessing a data member use the same C# source. It's the work of the C# compiler to translate the source into different IL necessary for properties or data members.

Although properties and data members are source compatible, they are not binary compatible. In the obvious case, this means that when you change from a public data member to the equivalent public property, you must recompile all code that uses the public data member. Chapter 4, "Creating Binary Components," discusses binary components in detail, but remember that the simple act of changing a data member to a property breaks binary compatibility. It makes upgrading single assemblies that have been deployed much more difficult.

While looking at the IL for a property, you probably wonder about the relative performance of properties and data members. Properties will not be faster than data member access, but they might not be any slower. The JIT compiler does inline some method calls, including property accessors. When the JIT compiler does inline property accessors, the performance of data members and properties is the same. Even when a property accessor has not been inlined, the actual performance difference is the negligible cost of one function call. That is measurable only in a small number of situations.

Whenever you expose data in your type's public or protected interfaces, use properties. Use an indexer for sequences or dictionaries. All data members should be private, without exception. You immediately get support for data binding, and you make it much easier to make any changes to the implementation of the methods in the future. The extra typing to encapsulate any variable in a property amounts to one or two minutes of your day. Finding that you need to use properties later to correctly express your designs will take hours. Spend a little time now, and save yourself lots of time later.

Item 2: Prefer `readonly` to `const`

C# has two different versions of constants: **compile-time** constants and **runtime** constants. They have very different behaviors, and using the wrong one will cost you performance or correctness. Neither problem is a good one to have, but if you must pick one, a slower, correct program is better than a faster, broken program. For that reason, you should prefer runtime constants over compile-time constants. Compile-time constants are slightly faster, but far less flexible, than runtime constants. Reserve the compile-time constants for when performance is critical and the value of the constant will never change over time.

You declare runtime constants with the `readonly` keyword. Compile-time constants are declared with the `const` keyword:

```
// Compile time constant:
public const int _Millennium = 2000;
```

```
// Runtime constant:
public static readonly int _ThisYear = 2004;
```

The differences in the behavior of compile-time and runtime constants follow from how they are accessed. A compile-time constant is replaced with the value of that constant in your object code. This construct:

```
if ( myDateTime.Year == _Millennium )
```

compiles to the same IL as if you had written this:

```
if ( myDateTime.Year == 2000 )
```

Runtime constants are evaluated at runtime. The IL generated when you reference a read-only constant references the `readonly` variable, not the value.

This distinction places several restrictions on when you are allowed to use either type of constant. Compile-time constants can be used only for primitive types (built-in integral and floating-point types), enums, or strings. These are the only types that enable you to assign meaningful constant values in initializers. These primitive types are the only ones that can be replaced with literal values in the compiler-generated IL. The following construct does not compile. You cannot initialize a compile-time constant using the `new` operator, even when the type being initialized is a value type:

```
// Does not compile, use readonly instead:
private const DateTime _classCreation = new
  DateTime( 2000, 1, 1, 0, 0, 0 );
```

Compile-time constants are limited to numbers and strings. Read-only values are also constants, in that they cannot be modified after the constructor has executed. But read-only values are different, in that they are assigned at runtime. You have much more flexibility in working with runtime constants. For one thing, runtime constants can be any type. You must initialize them in a constructor, or you can use an initializer. You can make `readonly` values of the `DateTime` structures; you cannot create `DateTime` values with `const`.

You can use `readonly` values for instance constants, storing different values for each instance of a class type. Compile-time constants are, by definition, static constants.

The most important distinction is that `readonly` values are resolved at runtime. The IL generated when you reference a `readonly` constant references the `readonly` variable, not the value. This difference has far-reaching implications on maintenance over time. Compile-time constants generate the same IL as though you've used the numeric constants in your code, even across assemblies: A constant in one assembly is still replaced with the value when used in another assembly.

The way in which compile-time and runtime constants are evaluated affects runtime compatibility. Suppose you have defined both const and readonly fields in an assembly named Infrastructure:

```
public class UsefulValues
{
  public static readonly int StartValue = 5;

  public const int EndValue = 10;
}
```

In another assembly, you reference these values:

```
for ( int i = UsefulValues.StartValue;
  i < UsefulValues.EndValue;
  i++ )
  Console.WriteLine( "value is {0}", i );
```

If you run your little test, you see the following obvious output:

```
Value is 5
Value is 6
...
Value is 9
```

Time passes, and you release a new version of the Infrastructure assembly with the following changes:

```
public class UsefulValues
{
  public static readonly int StartValue = 105;

  public const int EndValue = 120;
}
```

You distribute the Infrastructure assembly without rebuilding your Application assembly. You expect to get this:

```
Value is 105
Value is 106
...
Value is 119
```

In fact, you get no output at all. The loop now uses the value 105 for its start and 10 for its end condition. The C# compiler placed the const value of 10 into the Application assembly instead of a reference to the storage used by EndValue. Contrast that with the StartValue value. It was declared as readonly: It gets resolved at runtime. Therefore, the Application assembly makes use of the new value without even recompiling the Application assembly; simply installing an updated version of the Infrastructure assembly is enough to change the behavior of all clients using that value. Updating the value of a public constant should be viewed as an interface change. You must recompile all code that references that constant. Updating the value of a read-only constant is an implementation change; it is binary compatible with existing client code. Examining the MSIL for the previous loop shows you exactly why this happens:

```
IL_0000:   ldsfld      int32 Chapter1.UsefulValues::StartValue
IL_0005:   stloc.0
IL_0006:   br.s        IL_001c
IL_0008:   ldstr       "value is {0}"
IL_000d:   ldloc.0
IL_000e:   box         [mscorlib]System.Int32
IL_0013:   call        void [mscorlib]System.Console::WriteLine
      (string,object)
IL_0018:   ldloc.0
IL_0019:   ldc.i4.1
IL_001a:   add
IL_001b:   stloc.0
IL_001c:   ldloc.0
IL_001d:   ldc.i4.s    10
IL_001f:   blt.s       IL_0008
```

You can see that the StartValue is loaded dynamically at the top of the MSIL listing. But the end condition, at the end of the MSIL, is hard-coded at 10.

On the other hand, sometimes you really mean for a value to be determined at compile time. For example, consider a set of constants to mark different versions of an object in its serialized form (see Item 25). Persistent values that mark specific versions should be compile-time constants; they never change. The current version should be a runtime constant, changing with each release.

```
private const int VERSION_1_0 = 0x0100;
private const int VERSION_1_1 = 0x0101;
private const int VERSION_1_2 = 0x0102;
// major release:
private const int VERSION_2_0 = 0x0200;

// check for the current version:
private static readonly int CURRENT_VERSION =
  VERSION_2_0;
```

You use the runtime version to store the current version in each saved file:

```
// Read from persistent storage, check
// stored version against compile-time constant:
protected MyType( SerializationInfo info,
  StreamingContext cntxt )
{
  int storedVersion = info.GetInt32( "VERSION" );
  switch ( storedVersion )
  {
  case VERSION_2_0:
    readVersion2( info, cntxt );
    break;
  case VERSION_1_1:
    readVersion1Dot1( info, cntxt );
    break;

  // etc.
  }
}


// Write the current version:
[ SecurityPermissionAttribute( SecurityAction.Demand,
  SerializationFormatter =true ) ]
void ISerializable.GetObjectData( SerializationInfo inf,
    StreamingContext cxt )
{
  // use runtime constant for current version:
  inf.AddValue( "VERSION", CURRENT_VERSION );

  // write remaining elements...
}
```

The final advantage of using `const` over `readonly` is performance: Known constant values can generate slightly more efficient code than the variable accesses necessary for `readonly` values. However, any gains are slight and should be weighed against the decreased flexibility. Be sure to profile performance differences before giving up the flexibility.

`const` must be used when the value must be available at compile times: attribute parameters and enum definitions, and those rare times when you mean to define a value that does not change from release to release. For everything else, prefer the increased flexibility of `readonly` constants.

Item 3: Prefer the `is` or `as` Operators to Casts

C# is a strongly typed language. Good programming practice means that we all try to avoid coercing one type into another when we can avoid it. But sometimes, runtime type checking is simply unavoidable. Many times in C#, you write functions that take `System.Object` parameters because the framework defines the method signature for you. You likely need to attempt to downcast those objects to other types, either classes or interfaces. You've got two choices: Use the `as` operator or use that old C standby, the cast. You also have a defensive variant: You can test a conversion with `is` and then use `as` or casts to convert it.

The correct choice is to use the `as` operator whenever you can because it is safer than blindly casting and is more efficient at runtime. The `as` and `is` operators do not perform any user-defined conversions. They succeed only if the runtime type matches the sought type; they never construct a new object to satisfy a request.

Take a look at an example. You write a piece of code that needs to convert an arbitrary object into an instance of `MyType`. You could write it this way:

```
object o = Factory.GetObject( );

// Version one:
MyType t = o as MyType;

if ( t != null )
{
```

```
      // work with t, it's a MyType.
   } else
   {
      // report the failure.
   }
```

Or, you could write this:

```
object o = Factory.GetObject( );

// Version two:
try {
   MyType t;
   t = ( MyType ) o;
   if ( t != null )
   {
      // work with T, it's a MyType.
   } else
   {
      // Report a null reference failure.
   }
} catch
{
   // report the conversion failure.
}
```

You'll agree that the first version is simpler and easier to read. It does not have the try/catch clause, so you avoid both the overhead and the code. Notice that the cast version must check null in addition to catching exceptions. null can be converted to any reference type using a cast, but the as operator returns null when used on a null reference. So, with casts, you need to check null and catch exceptions. Using as, you simply check the returned reference against null.

The biggest difference between the as operator and the cast operator is how user-defined conversions are treated. The as and is operators examine the runtime type of the object being converted; they do not perform any other operations. If a particular object is not the requested type or is derived from the requested type, they fail. Casts, on the other hand, can use conversion operators to convert an object to the requested type. This includes any built-in numeric conversions. Casting a long to a short can lose information.

The same problems are lurking when you cast user-defined types. Consider this type:

```
public class SecondType
{
  private MyType _value;

  // other details elided

  // Conversion operator.
  // This converts a SecondType to
  // a MyType, see item 29.
  public static implicit operator
    MyType( SecondType t )
  {
    return t._value;
  }
}
```

Suppose an object of `SecondType` is returned by the `Factory.GetObject()` function in the first code snippet:

```
object o = Factory.GetObject( );

// o is a SecondType:
MyType t = o as MyType; // Fails. o is not MyType

if ( t != null )
{
  // work with t, it's a MyType.
} else
{
  // report the failure.
}

// Version two:
try {
  MyType t1;
  t = ( MyType ) o; // Fails. o is not MyType
  if ( t1 != null )
  {
```

```
    // work with t1, it's a MyType.
  } else
  {
    // Report a null reference failure.
  }
} catch
{
  // report the conversion failure.
}
```

Both versions fail. But I told you that casts will perform user-defined conversions. You'd think the cast would succeed. You're right—it should succeed if you think that way. But it fails because your compiler is generating code based on the compile-time type of the object, o. The compiler knows nothing about the runtime type of o; it views o as an instance of System. Object. The compiler sees that there is no user-defined conversion from System.Object to MyType. It checks the definitions of System.Object and MyType. Lacking any user-defined conversion, the compiler generates the code to examine the runtime type of o and checks whether that type is a MyType. Because o is a SecondType object, that fails. The compiler does not check to see whether the actual runtime type of o can be converted to a MyType object.

You could make the conversion from SecondType to MyType succeed if you wrote the code snippet like this:

```
object o = Factory.GetObject( );

// Version three:
SecondType st = o as SecondType;
try {
  MyType t;
  t = ( MyType ) st;
  if ( t != null )
  {
    // work with T, it's a MyType.
  } else
  {
    // Report a null reference failure.
  }
} catch
```

```
{
  // report the failure.
}
```

You should never write this ugly code, but it does illustrate a common problem. Although you would never write this, you can use a System. Object parameter to a function that expects the proper conversions:

```
object o = Factory.GetObject( );

DoStuffWithObject( o );

private void DoStuffWithObject( object o2 )
{
  try {
    MyType t;
    t = ( MyType ) o2; // Fails. o is not MyType
    if ( t != null )
    {
      // work with T, it's a MyType.
    } else
    {
      // Report a null reference failure.
    }
  } catch
  {
    // report the conversion failure.
  }
}
```

Remember that user-defined conversion operators operate only on the compile-time type of an object, not on the runtime type. It does not matter that a conversion between the runtime type of o2 and MyType exists. The compiler just doesn't know or care. This statement has different behavior, depending on the declared type of st:

```
  t = ( MyType ) st;
```

This next statement returns the same result, no matter what the declared type of st is. So, you should prefer as to casts—it's more consistent. In fact, if the types are not related by inheritance, but a user-defined conversion operator exists, the following statement will generate a compiler error:

```
t = st as MyType;
```

Now that you know to use as when possible, let's discuss when you can't use it. The as operator does not work on value types. This statement won't compile:

```
object o = Factory.GetValue( );
int i = o as int; // Does not compile.
```

That's because ints are value types and can never be null. What value of int should be stored in i if o is not an integer? Any value you pick might also be a valid integer. Therefore, as can't be used. You're stuck with a cast:

```
object o = Factory.GetValue( );
int i = 0;
try {
  i = ( int ) o;
} catch
{
  i = 0;
}
```

But you're not necessarily stuck with the behaviors of casts. You can use the is statement to remove the chance of exceptions or conversions:

```
object o = Factory.GetValue( );
int i = 0;
if ( o is int )
  i = ( int ) o;
```

If o is some other type that can be converted to an int, such as a double, the is operator returns false. The is operator always returns false for null arguments.

The is operator should be used only when you cannot convert the type using as. Otherwise, it's simply redundant:

```
// correct, but redundant:
object o = Factory.GetObject( );
```

```
MyType t = null;
if ( o is MyType )
  t = o as MyType;
```

The previous code is the same as if you had written the following:

```
// correct, but redundant:
object o = Factory.GetObject( );

MyType t = null;
if ( ( o as MyType ) != null )
  t = o as MyType;
```

That's inefficient and redundant. If you're about to convert a type using as, the is check is simply not necessary. Check the return from `as` against null; it's simpler.

Now that you know the difference among is, as, and casts, which operator do you suppose the `foreach` loop uses?

```
public void UseCollection( IEnumerable theCollection )
{
  foreach ( MyType t in theCollection )
    t.DoStuff( );
}
```

`foreach` uses a cast operation to perform conversions from an object to the type used in the loop. The code generated by the `foreach` statement equates to this hand-coded version:

```
public void UseCollection( IEnumerable theCollection )
{
  IEnumerator it = theCollection.GetEnumerator( );
  while ( it.MoveNext( ) )
  {
    MyType t = ( MyType ) it.Current;
    t.DoStuff( );
  }
}
```

`foreach` needs to use casts to support both value types and reference types. By choosing the `cast` operator, the `foreach` statement exhibits the same behavior, no matter what the destination type is. However, because a cast is used, `foreach` loops can generateBadCastExceptions.

Because `IEnumerator.Current` returns a `System.Object`, which has no conversion operators, none is eligible for this test. A collection of `SecondType` objects cannot be used in the previous `UseCollection()` function because the conversion fails, as you already saw. The `foreach` statement (which uses a cast) does not examine the casts that are available in the runtime type of the objects in the collection. It examines only the conversions available in the `System.Object` class (the type returned by `IEnumerator.Current`) and the declared type of the loop variable (in this case, `MyType`).

Finally, sometimes you want to know the exact type of an object, not just whether the current type can be converted to a target type. The `as` operator returns `true` for any type derived from the target type. The `GetType()` method gets the runtime type of an object. It is a more strict test than the `is` or `as` statement provides. `GetType()` returns the type of the object and can be compared to a specific type.

Consider this function again:

```
public void UseCollection( IEnumerable theCollection )
{
  foreach ( MyType t in theCollection )
    t.DoStuff( );
}
```

If you made a create a `NewType` class derived from `MyType`, a collection of `NewType` objects would work just fine in the `UseCollection` function:

```
public class NewType : MyType
{
  // contents elided.
}
```

If you mean to write a function that works with all objects that are instances of `MyType`, that's fine. If you mean to write a function that works only with `MyType` objects exactly, you should use the exact type for comparison. Here, you would do that inside the `foreach` loop. The most common time when the exact runtime type is important is when doing equality tests (see Item 9). In most other comparisons, the `.isinst` comparisons provided by `as` and `is` are semantically correct.

Good object-oriented practice says that you should avoid converting types, but sometimes there are no alternatives. When you can't avoid the conversions, use the language's as and is operators to express your intent more clearly. Different ways of coercing types have different rules. The is and as statements are almost always the correct semantics, and they succeed only when the object being tested is the correct type. Prefer those statements to cast operators, which can have unintended side effects and succeed or fail when you least expect it.

Item 4: Use Conditional Attributes Instead of `#if`

`#if/#endif` blocks have been used to produce different builds from the same source, most often debug and release variants. But these have never been a tool we were happy to use. `#if/#endif` blocks are too easily abused, creating code that is hard to understand and harder to debug. Language designers have responded by creating better tools to produce different machine code for different environments. C# has added the Conditional attribute to indicate whether a method should be called based on an environment setting. It's a cleaner way to describe conditional compilation than `#if/#endif`. The compiler understands the Conditional attribute, so it can do a better job of verifying code when conditional attributes are applied. The conditional attribute is applied at the method level, so it forces you to separate conditional code into distinct methods. Use the Conditional attribute instead of `#if/#endif` blocks when you create conditional code blocks.

Most veteran programmers have used conditional compilation to check pre- and post-conditions in an object. You would write a private method to check all the class and object invariants. That method would be conditionally compiled so that it appeared only in your debug builds.

```
private void CheckState( )
{
// The Old way:
#if DEBUG
  Trace.WriteLine( "Entering CheckState for Person" );

  // Grab the name of the calling routine:
  string methodName =
    new StackTrace( ).GetFrame( 1 ).GetMethod( ).Name;
```

```
    Debug.Assert( _lastName != null,
      methodName,
      "Last Name cannot be null" );

    Debug.Assert( _lastName.Length > 0,
      methodName,
      "Last Name cannot be blank" );

    Debug.Assert( _firstName != null,
      methodName,
      "First Name cannot be null" );

    Debug.Assert( _firstName.Length > 0,
      methodName,
      "First Name cannot be blank" );

  Trace.WriteLine( "Exiting CheckState for Person" );
#endif
}
```

Using the `#if` and `#endif` pragmas, you've created an empty method in your release builds. The `CheckState()` method gets called in all builds, release and debug. It doesn't do anything in the release builds, but you pay for the method call. You also pay a small cost to load and JIT the empty routine.

This practice works fine, but can lead to subtle bugs that appear only in release builds. The following common mistake shows what can happen when you use pragmas for conditional compilation:

```
public void Func( )
{
  string msg = null;

#if DEBUG
  msg = GetDiagnostics( );
#endif
  Console.WriteLine( msg );
}
```

Everything works fine in your debug build, but the release builds print a blank line. Your release builds happily print a blank message. That's not your intent. You goofed, but the compiler couldn't help you. You have code that is fundamental to your logic inside a conditional block. Sprinkling your source code with #if/#endif blocks makes it hard to diagnose the differences in behavior with the different builds.

C# has a better alternative: the Conditional attribute. Using the Conditional attribute, you can isolate functions that should be part of your classes only when a particular environment variable is defined or set to a certain value. The most common use of this feature is to instrument your code with debugging statements. The .NET Framework library already has the basic functionality you need for this use. This example shows how to use the debugging capabilities in the .NET Framework Library, to show you how Conditional attributes work and when to add them to your code.

When you build the Person object, you add a method to verify the object invariants:

```
private void CheckState( )
{
  // Grab the name of the calling routine:
  string methodName =
    new StackTrace( ).GetFrame( 1 ).GetMethod( ).Name;

  Trace.WriteLine( "Entering CheckState for Person:" );
  Trace.Write( "\tcalled by " );
  Trace.WriteLine( methodName );

  Debug.Assert( _lastName != null,
    methodName,
    "Last Name cannot be null" );

  Debug.Assert( _lastName.Length > 0,
    methodName,
    "Last Name cannot be blank" );

  Debug.Assert( _firstName != null,
    methodName,
    "First Name cannot be null" );
```

```
Debug.Assert( _firstName.Length > 0,
  methodName,
  "First Name cannot be blank" );


Trace.WriteLine( "Exiting CheckState for Person" );
}
```

You might not have encountered many library functions in this method, so let's go over them briefly. The StackTrace class gets the name of the calling method using Reflection (see Item 43). It's rather expensive, but it greatly simplifies tasks, such as generating information about program flow. Here, it determines the name of the method that called Check-State. The remaining methods are part of the System.Diagnostics. Debug class or the System.Diagnostics.Trace class. The Debug. Assert method tests a condition and stops the program if that condition is false. The remaining parameters define messages that will be printed if the condition is false. Trace.WriteLine writes diagnostic messages to the debug console. So, this method writes messages and stops the program if a person object is invalid. You would call this method in all your public methods and properties as a precondition and a post-condition:

```
public string LastName
{
  get
  {
    CheckState( );
    return _lastName;
  }
  set
  {
    CheckState( );
    _lastName = value;
    CheckState( );
  }
}
```

CheckState fires an assert the first time someone tries to set the last name to the empty string, or null. Then you fix your set accessor to check the parameter used for LastName. It's doing just what you want.

But this extra checking in each public routine takes time. You'll want to include this extra checking only when creating debug builds. That's where the `Conditional` attribute comes in:

```
[ Conditional( "DEBUG" ) ]
private void CheckState( )
{
  // same code as above
}
```

The `Conditional` attribute tells the C# compiler that this method should be called only when the compiler detects the DEBUG environment variable. The `Conditional` attribute does not affect the code generated for the `CheckState()` function; it modifies the calls to the function. If the DEBUG symbol is defined, you get this:

```
public string LastName
{
  get
  {
    CheckState( );
    return _lastName;
  }
  set
  {
    CheckState( );
    _lastName = value;
    CheckState( );
  }
}
```

If not, you get this:

```
public string LastName
{
  get
  {
    return _lastName;
  }
  set
```

```
    {
      _lastName = value;
    }
}
```

The body of the `CheckState()` function is the same, regardless of the state of the environment variable. This is one example of why you need to understand the distinction made between the compilation and JIT steps in .NET. Whether the DEBUG environment variable is defined or not, the `CheckState()` method is compiled and delivered with the assembly. That might seem inefficient, but the only cost is disk space. The `Check-State()` function does not get loaded into memory and JITed unless it is called. Its presence in the assembly file is immaterial. This strategy increases flexibility and does so with minimal performance costs. You can get a deeper understanding by looking at the `Debug` class in the .NET Framework. On any machine with the .NET Framework installed, the `System.dll` assembly does have all the code for all the methods in the `Debug` class. Environment variables control whether they get called when callers are compiled.

You can also create methods that depend on more than one environment variable. When you apply multiple conditional attributes, they are combined with OR. For example, this version of `CheckState` would be called when either DEBUG or TRACE is `true`:

```
[ Conditional( "DEBUG" ),
  Conditional( "TRACE" ) ]
private void CheckState( )
```

To create a construct using AND, you need to define the preprocessor symbol yourself using preprocessor directives in your source code:

```
#if ( VAR1 && VAR2 )
#define BOTH
#endif
```

Yes, to create a conditional routine that relies on the presence of more than one environment variable, you must fall back on your old practice of `#if`. All `#if` does is create a new symbol for you. But avoid putting any executable code inside that pragma.

The `Conditional` attribute can be applied only to entire methods. In addition, any method with a `Conditional` attribute must have a return type of void. You cannot use the Conditional attribute for blocks of code inside methods or with methods that return values. Instead, create carefully constructed conditional methods and isolate the conditional behavior to those functions. You still need to review those conditional methods for side effects to the object state, but the Conditional attribute localizes those points much better than #if/#endif. With #if and #endif blocks, you can mistakenly remove important method calls or assignments.

The previous examples use the predefined DEBUG or TRACE symbols. But you can extend this technique for any symbols you define. The Conditional attribute can be controlled by symbols defined in a variety of ways. You can define symbols from the compiler command line, from environment variables in the operating system shell, or from pragmas in the source code.

The Conditional attribute generates more efficient IL than #if/#endif does. It also has the advantage of being applicable only at the function level, which forces you to better structure your conditional code. The compiler uses the Conditional attribute to help you avoid the common errors we've all made by placing the #if or #endif in the wrong spot. The Conditional attribute provides better support for you to cleanly separate conditional code than the preprocessor did.

Item 5: Always Provide ToString()

System.Object.ToString() is one of the most used methods in the .NET environment. You should write a reasonable version for all the clients of your class. Otherwise, you force every user of your class to use the properties in your class and create a reasonable human-readable representation. This string representation of your type can be used to easily display information about an object to users: in Windows Forms, web forms, or console output. The string representation can also be useful for debugging. Every type that you create should provide a reasonable override of this method. When you create more complicated types, you should implement the more sophisticated IFormattable.ToString(). Face it: If you don't override this routine, or if you write a poor one, your clients are forced to fix it for you.

The System.Object version returns the name of the type. It's useless information: "Rect", "Point", "Size" is not what you want to display to your users. But that's what you get when you don't override ToString() in your classes. You write a class once, but your clients use it many times. A little more work when you write the class pays off every time you or someone else uses it.

Let's consider the simplest requirement: overriding System.Object. ToString(). Every type you create should override ToString() to provide the most common textual representation of the type. Consider a Customer class with three fields:

```
public class Customer
{
  private string    _name;
  private decimal   _revenue;
  private string    _contactPhone;
}
```

The inherited version of Object.ToString() returns "Customer". That is never useful to anyone. Even if ToString() will be used only for debugging purposes, it should be more sophisticated than that. Your override of Object.ToString() should return the textual representation most likely to be used by clients of that class. In the Customer example, that's the name:

```
public override string ToString()
{
  return _name;
}
```

If you don't follow any of the other recommendations in this item, follow that exercise for all the types you define. It will save everyone time immediately. When you provide a reasonable implementation for the Object.ToString() method, objects of this class can be more easily added to Windows Forms controls, web form controls, or printed output. The .NET FCL uses the override of Object.ToString() to display objects in any of the controls: combo boxes, list boxes, text boxes, and other controls. If you create a list of customer objects in a Windows Form or a web form, you get the name displayed as the text. System. Console.WriteLine() and System.String.Format(), as well as ToString() internally. Anytime the .NET FCL wants to get the string representation of a customer, your customer type supplies that customer's name. One simple three-line method handles all those basic requirements.

This one simple method, `ToString()`, satisfies many of the requirements for displaying user-defined types as text. But sometimes, you need more. The previous customer type has three fields: the name, the revenue, and a contact phone. The `System.ToString()` override uses only the name. You can address that deficiency by implementing the `IFormattable` interface on your type. `IFormattable` contains an overloaded `ToString()` method that lets you specify formatting information for your type. It's the interface you use when you need to create different forms of string output. The customer class is one of those instances. Users will want to create a report that contains the customer name and last year's revenue in a tabular format. The `IFormattable.ToString()` method provides the means for you to let users format string output from your type. The `IFormattable.ToString()` method signature contains a format string and a format provider:

```
string System.IFormattable.ToString( string format,
  IFormatProvider formatProvider )
```

You can use the format string to specify your own formats for the types you create. You can specify your own key characters for the format strings. In the customer example, you could specify n to mean the name, r for the revenue, and p for the phone. By allowing the user to specify combinations as well, you would create this version of `IFormattable.ToString()`:

```
#region IFormattable Members
// supported formats:
// substitute n for name.
// substitute r for revenue
// substitute p for contact phone.
// Combos are supported:  nr, np, npr, etc
// "G" is general.
string System.IFormattable.ToString( string format,
  IFormatProvider formatProvider )
{
  if ( formatProvider != null )
  {
    ICustomFormatter fmt = formatProvider.GetFormat(
      this.GetType( ) )
      as ICustomFormatter;
    if ( fmt != null )
```

```
        return fmt.Format( format, this, formatProvider );
}

switch ( format )
{
  case "r":
    return _revenue.ToString( );
  case "p":
    return _contactPhone;
  case "nr":
    return string.Format( "{0,20}, {1,10:C}",
      _name, _revenue );
  case "np":
    return string.Format( "{0,20}, {1,15}",
      _name, _contactPhone );
  case "pr":
    return string.Format( "{0,15}, {1,10:C}",
      _contactPhone, _revenue );
  case "pn":
    return string.Format( "{0,15}, {1,20}",
      _contactPhone, _name );
  case "rn":
    return string.Format( "{0,10:C}, {1,20}",
      _revenue, _name );
  case "rp":
    return string.Format( "{0,10:C}, {1,20}",
      _revenue, _contactPhone );
  case "nrp":
    return string.Format( "{0,20}, {1,10:C}, {2,15}",
      _name, _revenue, _contactPhone );
  case "npr":
    return string.Format( "{0,20}, {1,15}, {2,10:C}",
      _name, _contactPhone, _revenue );
  case "pnr":
    return string.Format( "{0,15}, {1,20}, {2,10:C}",
      _contactPhone, _name, _revenue );
  case "prn":
    return string.Format( "{0,15}, {1,10:C}, {2,15}",
      _contactPhone, _revenue, _name );
  case "rpn":
```

```
      return string.Format( "{0,10:C}, {1,15}, {2,20}",
        _revenue, _contactPhone, _name );
    case "rnp":
      return string.Format( "{0,10:C}, {1,20}, {2,15}",
        _revenue, _name, _contactPhone );
    case "n":
    case "G":
    default:
      return _name;
  }
}
#endregion
```

Adding this function gives your clients the capability to specify the presentation of their customer data:

```
IFormattable c1 = new Customer();
Console.WriteLine( "Customer record: {0}",
  c1.ToString( "nrp", null ) );
```

Any implementation of IFormattable.ToString() is specific to the type, but you must handle certain cases whenever you implement the IFormattable interface. First, you must support the general format, "G". Second, you must support the empty format in both variations: "" and null. All three format specifiers must return the same string as your override of the Object.ToString() method. The .NET FCL calls IFormattable.ToString() instead of Object.ToString() for every type that implements IFormattable. The .NET FCL usually calls IFormattable.ToString() with a null format string , but a few locations use the "G" format string, to indicate the general format. If you add support for the IFormattable interface and do not support these standard formats, you've broken the automatic string conversions in the FCL.

The second parameter to IFormattable.ToString() is an object that implements the IFormatProvider interface. This object lets clients provide formatting options that you did not anticipate. If you look at the previous implementation of IFormattable.ToString(), you will undoubtedly come up with any number of format options that you would like but that you find lacking. That's the nature of providing human-readable output. No matter how many different formats you support, your users will one day want some format that you did not anticipate. That's why the first few lines of the method look for an object that implements IFormatProvider and delegate the job to its ICustom-Formatter.

Shift your focus now from class author to class consumer. You find that you want a format that is not supported. For example, you have customers whose names are longer than 20 characters, and you want to modify the format to provide a 50-character width for the customer name. That's why the IFormatProvider interface is there. You create a class that implements IFormatProvider and a companion class that implements ICustomFormatter to create your custom output formats. The IFormatProvider interface defines one method: GetFormat(). GetFormat() returns an object that implements the ICustomFormatter interface. The ICustomFormatter interface specifies the method that does the actual formatting. The following pair creates modified output that uses 50 columns for the customer name:

```csharp
// Example IFormatProvider:
public class CustomFormatter : IFormatProvider
{
  #region IFormatProvider Members
  // IFormatProvider contains one method.
  // This method returns an object that
  // formats using the requested interface.
  // Typically, only the ICustomFormatter
  // is implemented
  public object GetFormat( Type formatType )
  {
    if ( formatType == typeof( ICustomFormatter ))
      return new CustomerFormatProvider( );
    return null;
  }
  #endregion

  // Nested class to provide the
  // custom formatting for the Customer class.
  private class CustomerFormatProvider : ICustomFormatter
  {
    #region ICustomFormatter Members
    public string Format( string format, object arg,
```

```
        IFormatProvider formatProvider )
    {
      Customer c = arg as Customer;
      if ( c == null )
        return arg.ToString( );
      return string.Format( "{0,50}, {1,15}, {2,10:C}",
        c.Name, c.ContactPhone, c.Revenue );
    }
    #endregion
  }
}
```

The `GetFormat()` method creates the object that implements the `ICus-tomFormatter` interface. The `ICustomFormatter.Format()` method does the actual work of formatting the output in the requested manner. That one method translates the object into a string format. You can define the format strings for `ICustomFormatter.Format()` so that you can specify multiple formats in one routine. The `FormatProvider` will be the `IFormatProvider` object from the `GetFormat()` method.

To specify your custom format, you need to explicitly call `string.Format()` with the `IFormatProvider` object:

```
Console.WriteLine( string.Format( new CustomFormatter(),
  "", c1 ));
```

You can create `IFormatProvider` and `ICustomFormatter` implementations for classes whether or not the class implemented the `IFormattable` interface. So, even if the class author didn't provide reasonable `ToString()` behavior, you can make your own. Of course, from outside the class, you have access to only the public properties and data members to construct your strings. Writing two classes, `IFormatProvider` and `IcustomFormatter`, is a lot of work just to get text output. But implementing your specific text output using this form means that it is supported everywhere in the .NET Framework.

So now step back into the role of class author again. Overriding `Object.ToString()` is the simplest way to provide a string representation of your classes. You should provide that every time you create a type. It should be the most obvious, most common representation of your type. On those rarer occasions when your type is expected to provide more sophisticated output, you should take advantage of implementing the IFormattable interface. It provides the standard way for users of your class to customize the text output for your type. If you leave these out, your users are left with implementing custom formatters. Those solutions require more code, and because users are outside of your class, they cannot examine the internal state of the object.

Eventually, people consume the information in your types. People understand text output. Provide it in the simplest fashion possible: Override ToString() in all your types.

Item 6: Distinguish Between Value Types and Reference Types

Value types or reference types? Structs or classes? When should you use each? This isn't C++, in which you define all types as value types and can create references to them. This isn't Java, in which everything is a reference type. You must decide how all instances of your type will behave when you create it. It's an important decision to get right the first time. You must live with the consequences of your decision because changing later can cause quite a bit of code to break in subtle ways. It's a simple matter of choosing the struct or class keyword when you create the type, but it's much more work to update all the clients using your type if you change it later.

It's not as simple as preferring one over the other. The right choice depends on how you expect to use the new type. Value types are not polymorphic. They are better suited to storing the data that your application manipulates. Reference types can be polymorphic and should be used to define the behavior of your application. Consider the expected responsibilities of your new type, and from those responsibilities, decide which type to create. Structs store data. Classes define behavior.

The distinction between value types and reference types was added to .NET and C# because of common problems that occurred in C++ and Java. In C++, all parameters and return values were passed by value. Passing by value is very efficient, but it suffers from one problem: partial copying (sometimes called slicing the object). If you use a derived object where a base object is expected, only the base portion of the object gets copied. You have effectively lost all knowledge that a derived object was ever there. Even calls to virtual functions are sent to the base class version.

The Java language responded by more or less removing value types from the language. All user-defined types are reference types. In the Java language, all parameters and return values are passed by reference. This strategy has the advantage of being consistent, but it's a drain on performance. Let's face it, some types are not polymorphic—they were not intended to be. Java programmers pay a heap allocation and an eventual garbage collection for every variable. They also pay an extra time cost to dereference every variable. All variables are references. In C#, you declare whether a new type should be a value type or a reference type using the `struct` or `class` keywords. Value types should be small, lightweight types. Reference types form your class hierarchy. This section examines different uses for a type so that you understand all the distinctions between value types and reference types.

To start, this type is used as the return value from a method:

```
private MyData _myData;
public MyData Foo()
{
 return _myData;
}


// call it:
MyData v = Foo();
TotalSum += v.Value;
```

If `MyData` is a value type, the return value gets copied into the storage for v. Furthermore, v is on the stack. However, if `MyData` is a reference type, you've exported a reference to an internal variable. You've violated the principle of encapsulation (see Item 23).

Or, consider this variant:

```
private MyData _myData;
public MyData Foo()
{
 return _myData.Clone( ) as MyData;
}


// call it:
MyData v = Foo();
TotalSum += v.Value;
```

Now, v is a copy of the original _myData. As a reference type, two objects are created on the heap. You don't have the problem of exposing internal data. Instead, you've created an extra object on the heap. If v is a local variable, it quickly becomes garbage and Clone forces you to use runtime type checking. All in all, it's inefficient.

Types that are used to export data through public methods and properties should be value types. But that's not to say that every type returned from a public member should be a value type. There was an assumption in the earlier code snippet that MyData stores values. Its responsibility is to store those values.

But, consider this alternative code snippet:

```
private MyType _myType;
public IMyInterface Foo()
{
 return _myType as IMyInterface;
}


// call it:
IMyInterface iMe = Foo();
iMe.DoWork( );
```

The _myType variable is still returned from the Foo method. But this time, instead of accessing the data inside the returned value, the object is accessed to invoke a method through a defined interface. You're accessing the MyType object not for its data contents, but for its behavior. That behavior is expressed through the IMyInterface, which can be implemented by multiple different types. For this example, MyType should be a reference type, not a value type. MyType's responsibilities revolve around its behavior, not its data members.

That simple code snippet starts to show you the distinction: Value types store values, and reference types define behavior. Now look a little deeper at how those types are stored in memory and the performance considerations related to the storage models. Consider this class:

```
public class C
{
  private MyType _a = new MyType( );
  private MyType _b = new MyType( );
```

```
    // Remaining implementation removed.
}


C var = new C();
```

How many objects are created? How big are they? It depends. If MyType is a value type, you've made one allocation. The size of that allocation is twice the size of MyType. However, if MyType is a reference type, you've made three allocations: one for the C object, which is 8 bytes (assuming 32-bit pointers), and two more for each of the MyType objects that are contained in a C object. The difference results because value types are stored inline in an object, whereas reference types are not. Each variable of a reference type holds a reference, and the storage requires extra allocation.

To drive this point home, consider this allocation:

```
MyType [] var = new MyType[ 100 ];
```

If MyType is a value type, one allocation of 100 times the size of a MyType object occurs. However, if MyType is a reference type, one allocation just occurred. Every element of the array is null. When you initialize each element in the array, you will have performed 101 allocations—and 101 allocations take more time than 1 allocation. Allocating a large number of reference types fragments the heap and slows you down. If you are creating types that are meant to store data values, value types are the way to go.

The decision to make a value type or a reference type is an important one. It is a far-reaching change to turn a value type into a class type. Consider this type:

```
public struct Employee
{
    private string  _name;
    private int      _ID;
    private decimal _salary;

    // Properties elided

    public void Pay( BankAccount b )
    {
```

```
    b.Balance += _salary;
  }
}
```

This fairly simple type contains one method to let you pay your employees. Time passes, and the system runs fairly well. Then you decide that there are different classes of `Employees`: Salespeople get commissions, and managers get bonuses. You decide to change the `Employee` type into a class:

```csharp
public class Employee
{
  private string  _name;
  private int     _ID;
  private decimal _salary;

  // Properties elided

  public virtual void Pay( BankAccount b )
  {
    b.Balance += _salary;
  }
}
```

That breaks much of the existing code that uses your customer struct. Return by value becomes return by reference. Parameters that were passed by value are now passed by reference. The behavior of this little snippet changed drastically:

```csharp
Employee e1 = Employees.Find( "CEO" );
e1.Salary += Bonus; // Add one time bonus.
e1.Pay( CEOBankAccount );
```

What was a one-time bump in pay to add a bonus just became a permanent raise. Where a copy by value had been used, a reference is now in place. The compiler happily makes the changes for you. The CEO is probably happy, too. The CFO, on the other hand, will report the bug. You just can't change your mind about value and reference types after the fact: It changes behavior.

This problem occurred because the `Employee` type no longer follow the guidelines for a value type. In addition to storing the data elements that define an employee, you've added responsibilities—in this example, paying the employee. Responsibilities are the domain of class types. Classes can define polymorphic implementations of common responsibilities easily; structs cannot and should be limited to storing values.

The documentation for .NET recommends that you consider the size of a type as a determining factor between value types and reference types. In reality, a much better factor is the use of the type. Types that are simple structures or data carriers are excellent candidates for value types. It's true that value types are more efficient in terms of memory management: There is less heap fragmentation, less garbage, and less indirection. More important, value types are copied when they are returned from methods or properties. There is no danger of exposing references to internal structures. But you pay in terms of features. Value types have very limited support for common object-oriented techniques. You cannot create object hierarchies of value types. You should consider all value types as though they were sealed. You can create value types that implement interfaces, but that requires boxing, which Item 17 shows causes performance degradation. Think of value types as storage containers, not objects in the OO sense.

You'll create more reference types than value types. If you answer yes to all these questions, you should create a value type. Compare these to the previous `Employee` example:

1. Is this type's principal responsibility data storage?
2. Is its public interface defined entirely by properties that access or modify its data members?
3. Am I confident that this type will never have subclasses?
4. Am I confident that this type will never be treated polymorphically?

Build low-level data storage types as value types. Build the behavior of your application using reference types. You get the safety of copying data that gets exported from your class objects. You get the memory usage benefits that come with stack-based and inline value storage, and you can utilize standard object-oriented techniques to create the logic of your application. When in doubt about the expected use, use a reference type.

Item 7: Prefer Immutable Atomic Value Types

Immutable types are simple: After they are created, they are constant. If you validate the parameters used to construct the object, you know that it is in a valid state from that point forward. You cannot change the object's internal state to make it invalid. You save yourself a lot of otherwise necessary error checking by disallowing any state changes after an object has been constructed. Immutable types are inherently thread safe: Multiple readers can access the same contents. If the internal state cannot change, there is no chance for different threads to see inconsistent views of the data. Immutable types can be exported from your objects safely. The caller cannot modify the internal state of your objects. Immutable types work better in hash-based collections. The value returned by `Object.GetHashCode()` must be an instance invariant (see Item 10); that's always true for immutable types.

Not every type can be immutable. If it were, you would need to clone objects to modify any program state. That's why this recommendation is for both atomic and immutable value types. Decompose your types to the structures that naturally form a single entity. An `Address` type does. An address is a single thing, composed of multiple related fields. A change in one field likely means changes to other fields. A customer type is not an atomic type. A customer type will likely contain many pieces of information: an address, a name, and one or more phone numbers. Any of these independent pieces of information might change. A customer might change phone numbers without moving. A customer might move, yet still keep the same phone number. A customer might change his or her name without moving or changing phone numbers. A customer object is not atomic; it is built from many different immutable types using composition: an address, a name, or a collection of phone number/type pairs. Atomic types are single entities: You would naturally replace the entire contents of an atomic type. The exception would be to change one of its component fields.

Here is a typical implementation of an address that is mutable:

```
// Mutable Address structure.
public struct Address
{
  private string _line1;
  private string _line2;
  private string _city;
```

```csharp
private string _state;
private int    _zipCode;

// Rely on the default system-generated
// constructor.

public string Line1
{
  get { return _line1; }
  set { _line1 = value; }
}
public string Line2
{
  get { return _line2; }
  set { _line2 = value; }
}
public string City
{
  get { return _city; }
  set { _city= value; }
}
public string State
{
  get { return _state; }
  set
  {
    ValidateState(value);
    _state = value;
  }
}
public int ZipCode
{
  get { return _zipCode; }
  set
  {
    ValidateZip( value );
    _zipCode = value;
  }
}
```

```
    // other details omitted.
}

// Example usage:
Address a1 = new Address( );
a1.Line1 = "111 S. Main";
a1.City = "Anytown";
a1.State = "IL";
a1.ZipCode = 61111 ;
// Modify:
a1.City = "Ann Arbor"; // Zip, State invalid now.
a1.ZipCode = 48103; // State still invalid now.
a1.State = "MI"; // Now fine.
```

Internal state changes means that it's possible to violate object invariants, at least temporarily. After you have replaced the City field, you have placed a1 in an invalid state. The city has changed and no longer matches the state or ZIP code fields. The code looks harmless enough, but suppose that this fragment is part of a multithreaded program. Any context switch after the city changes and before the state changes would leave the potential for another thread to see an inconsistent view of the data.

Okay, so you're not writing a multithreaded program. You can still get into trouble. Imagine that the ZIP code was invalid and the set threw an exception. You've made only some of the changes you intended, and you've left the system in an invalid state. To fix this problem, you would need to add considerable internal validation code to the address structure. That validation code would add considerable size and complexity. To fully implement exception safety, you would need to create defensive copies around any code block in which you change more than one field. Thread safety would require adding significant thread-synchronization checks on each property accessor, both sets and gets. All in all, it would be a significant undertaking—and one that would likely be extended over time as you add new features.

Instead, make the Address structure an immutable type. Start by changing all instance fields to read-only:

```
public struct Address
{
    private readonly string _line1;
    private readonly string _line2;
```

```
private readonly string  _city;
private readonly string  _state;
private readonly int     _zipCode;

// remaining details elided
}
```

You'll also want to remove all set accessors to each property:

```
public struct Address
{
  // ...
  public string Line1
  {
    get { return _line1; }
  }
  public string Line2
  {
    get { return _line2; }
  }
  public string City
  {
    get { return _city; }
  }
  public string State
  {
    get { return _state; }
  }
  public int ZipCode
  {
    get { return _zipCode; }
  }
}
```

Now you have an immutable type. To make it useful, you need to add all necessary constructors to initialize the Address structure completely. The Address structure needs only one additional constructor, specifying each field. A copy constructor is not needed because the assignment operator is just as efficient. Remember that the default constructor is still accessible. There is a default address where all the strings are null, and the ZIP code is 0:

```
public struct Address
{
  private readonly string  _line1;
  private readonly string  _line2;
  private readonly string  _city;
  private readonly string  _state;
  private readonly int      _zipCode;

  public Address( string line1,
    string line2,
    string city,
    string state,
    int zipCode)
  {
    _line1 = line1;
    _line2 = line2;
    _city = city;
    _state = state;
    _zipCode = zipCode;
    ValidateState( state );
    ValidateZip( zipCode );
  }

  // etc.
}
```

Using the immutable type requires a slightly different calling sequence to modify its state. You create a new object rather than modify the existing instance:

```
// Create an address:
Address a1 = new Address( "111 S. Main",
  "", "Anytown", "IL", 61111 );

// To change, re-initialize:
a1 = new Address( a1.Line1,
  a1.Line2, "Ann Arbor", "MI", 48103 );
```

The value of a1 is in one of two states: its original location in Anytown, or its updated location in Ann Arbor. You do not modify the existing address to create any of the invalid temporary states from the previous example. Those interim states exist only during the execution of the Address constructor and are not visible outside of that constructor. As soon as a new Address object is constructed, its value is fixed for all time. It's exception safe: a1 has either its original value or its new value. If an exception is thrown during the construction of the new Address object, the original value of a1 is unchanged.

To create an immutable type, you need to ensure that there are no holes that would allow clients to change your internal state. Value types do not support derived types, so you do not need to defend against derived types modifying fields. But you do need to watch for any fields in an immutable type that are mutable reference types. When you implement your constructors for these types, you need to make a defensive copy of that mutable type. All these examples assume that Phone is an immutable value type because we're concerned only with immutability in value types:

```
// Almost immutable: there are holes that would
// allow state changes.
public struct PhoneList
{
  private readonly Phone[] _phones;

  public PhoneList( Phone[] ph )
  {
    _phones = ph;
  }

  public IEnumerator Phones
  {
    get
    {
      return _phones.GetEnumerator();
    }
  }
}

Phone[] phones = new Phone[10];
```

```
// initialize phones
PhoneList pl = new PhoneList( phones );

// Modify the phone list:
// also modifies the internals of the (supposedly)
// immutable object.
phones[5] = Phone.GeneratePhoneNumber( );
```

The array class is a reference type. The array referenced inside the `PhoneList` structure refers to the same array storage (phones) allocated outside of the object. Developers can modify your immutable structure through another variable that refers to the same storage. To remove this possibility, you need to make a defensive copy of the array. The previous example shows the pitfalls of a mutable collection. Even more possibilities for mischief exist if the `Phone` type is a mutable reference type. Clients could modify the values in the collection, even if the collection is protected against any modification. This defensive copy should be made in all constructors whenever your immutable type contains a mutable reference type:

```
// Immutable: A copy is made at construction.
public struct PhoneList
{
  private readonly Phone[] _phones;

  public PhoneList( Phone[] ph )
  {
    _phones = new Phone[ ph.Length ];
    // Copies values because Phone is a value type.
    ph.CopyTo( _phones, 0 );
  }

  public IEnumerator Phones
  {
    get
    {
      return _phones.GetEnumerator();
    }
  }
}
```

```
Phone[] phones = new Phone[10];
// initialize phones
PhoneList pl = new PhoneList( phones );

// Modify the phone list:
// Does not modify the copy in pl.
phones[5] = Phone.GeneratePhoneNumber( );
```

You need to follow the same rules when you return a mutable reference type. If you add a property to retrieve the entire array from the `PhoneList` struct, that accessor would also need to create a defensive copy. See Item 23 for more details.

The complexity of a type dictates which of three strategies you will use to initialize your immutable type. The `Address` structure defined one constructor to allow clients to initialize an address. Defining the reasonable set of constructors is often the simplest approach.

You can also create factory methods to initialize the structure. Factories make it easier to create common values. The .NET Framework `Color` type follows this strategy to initialize system colors. The static methods `Color.FromKnownColor()` and `Color.FromName()` return a copy of a color value that represents the current value for a given system color.

Third, you can create a mutable companion class for those instances in which multistep operations are necessary to fully construct an immutable type. The .NET string class follows this strategy with the `System.Text.StringBuilder` class. You use the `StringBuilder` class to create a string using multiple operations. After performing all the operations necessary to build the string, you retrieve the immutable string from the `StringBuilder`.

Immutable types are simpler to code and easier to maintain. Don't blindly create `get` and `set` accessors for every property in your type. Your first choice for types that store data should be immutable, atomic value types. You easily can build more complicated structures from these entities.

Item 8: Ensure That 0 Is a Valid State for Value Types

The default .NET system initialization sets all objects to all 0s. There is no way for you to prevent other programmers from creating an instance of a value type that is initialized to all 0s. Make that the default value for your type.

One special case is enums. Never create an enum that does not include 0 as a valid choice. All enums are derived from `System.ValueType`. The values for the enumeration start at 0, but you can modify that behavior:

```
public enum Planet
{
  // Explicitly assign values.
  // Default starts at 0 otherwise.
  Mercury = 1,
  Venus = 2,
  Earth = 3,
  Mars = 4,
  Jupiter = 5,
  Saturn = 6,
  Neptune = 7,
  Uranus = 8,
  Pluto = 9
}


Planet sphere = new Planet();
```

sphere is 0, which is not a valid value. Any code that relies on the (normal) fact that enums are restricted to the defined set of enumerated values won't work. When you create your own values for an enum, make sure that 0 is one of them. If you use bit patterns in your enum, define 0 to be the absence of all the other properties.

As it stands now, you force all users to explicitly initialize the value:

```
Planet sphere = Planet.Mars;
```

That makes it harder to build other value types that contain this type:

```
public struct ObservationData
{
  Planet   _whichPlanet; //what am I looking at?
  Double   _magnitude; // perceived brightness.
}
```

Users who create a new ObservationData object will create an invalid Planet field:

```
ObservationData d = new ObservationData();
```

The newly created ObservationData has a 0 magnitude, which is reasonable. But the planet is invalid. You need to make 0 a valid state. If possible, pick the best default as the value 0. The Planet enum does not have an obvious default. It doesn't make any sense to pick some arbitrary planet whenever the user does not. When you run into that situation, use the 0 case for an uninitialized value that can be updated later:

```
public enum Planet
{
  None = 0,
  Mercury = 1,
  Venus = 2,
  Earth = 3,
  Mars = 4,
  Jupiter = 5,
  Saturn = 6,
  Neptune = 7,
  Uranus = 8,
  Pluto = 9
}

Planet sphere = new Planet();
```

sphere now contains a value for None. Adding this uninitialized default to the Planet enum ripples up to the ObservationData structure. Newly created ObservationData objects have a 0 magnitude and None for the target. Add an explicit constructor to let users of your type initialize all the fields explicitly:

```
public struct ObservationData
{
  Planet    _whichPlanet; //what am I looking at?
  Double  _magnitude; // perceived brightness.

  ObservationData( Planet target,
    Double mag )
  {
```

```
        _whichPlanet = target;
        _magnitude = mag;
    }
}
```

But remember that the default constructor is still visible and part of the structure. Users can still create the system-initialized variant, and you can't stop them.

Before leaving enums to discuss other value types, you need to understand a few special rules for enums used as flags. Enums that use the Flags attribute should always set the None value to 0:

```
[Flags]
public enum Styles
{
    None = 0,
    Flat = 1,
    Sunken = 2,
    Raised = 4,
}
```

Many developers use flags enumerations with the bitwise AND operator. 0 values cause serious problems with bitflags. The following test will never work if Flat has the value of 0:

```
if ( ( flag & Styles.Flat ) != 0 ) // Never true if Flat == 0.
    DoFlatThings( );
```

If you use Flags, ensure that 0 is valid and that it means "the absence of all flags."

Another common initialization problem involves value types that contain references. Strings are a common example:

```
public struct LogMessage
{
    private int _ErrLevel;
    private string _msg;
}


LogMessage MyMessage = new LogMessage( );
```

`MyMessage` contains a null reference in its _Msg field. There is no way to force a different initialization, but you can localize the problem using properties. You created a property to export the value of _Msg to all your clients. Add logic to that property to return the empty string instead of null:

```
public struct LogMessage
{
  private int _ErrLevel;
  private string _msg;

  public string Message
  {
    get
    {
      return (_msg != null ) ?
        _msg : string.Empty;
    }
    set
    {
      _msg = value;
    }
  }
}
```

You should use this property inside your own type. Doing so localizes the null reference check to one location. The `Message` accessor is almost certainly inlined as well, when called from inside your assembly. You'll get efficient code and minimize errors.

The system initializes all instances of value typess to 0. There is no way to prevent users from creating instances of value types that are all 0s. If possible, make the all 0 case the natural default. As a special case, enums used as flags should ensure that 0 is the absence of all flags.

Item 9: Understand the Relationships Among `ReferenceEquals()`, static `Equals()`, instance `Equals()`, and `operator==`

When you create your own types (either classes or structs), you define what equality means for that type. C# provides four different functions that determine whether two different objects are "equal":

```
public static bool ReferenceEquals
  ( object left, object right );
public static bool Equals
  ( object left, object right );
public virtual bool Equals( object right);
public static bool operator==( MyClass left, MyClass right );
```

The language enables you to create your own versions of all four of these methods. But just because you can doesn't mean that you should. You should never redefine the first two static functions. You'll often create your own instance `Equals()` method to define the semantics of your type, and you'll occasionally override `operator==()`, but only for performance reasons in value types. Furthermore, there are relationships among these four functions, so when you change one, you can affect the behavior of the others. Yes, needing four functions to test equality is complicated. But don't worry—you can simplify it.

Like so many of the complicated elements in C#, this one follows from the fact that C# enables you to create both value types and reference types. Two variables of a reference type are equal if they refer to the same object, referred to as object identity. Two variables of a value type are equal if they are the same type and they contain the same contents. That's why equality tests need so many different methods.

Let's start with the two functions you should never change. `Object.ReferenceEquals()` returns `true` if two variables refer to the same object—that is, the two variables have the same object identity. Whether the types being compared are reference types or value types, this method always tests object identity, not object contents. Yes, that means that `ReferenceEquals()` always returns `false` when you use it to test equality for value types. Even when you compare a value type to itself, `ReferenceEquals()` returns `false`. This is due to boxing, which is covered in Item 16.

```
int i = 5;
int j = 5;
if ( Object.ReferenceEquals( i, j ))
  Console.WriteLine( "Never happens." );
else
  Console.WriteLine( "Always happens." );

if ( Object.ReferenceEquals( i, i ))
  Console.WriteLine( "Never happens." );
else
  Console.WriteLine( "Always happens." );
```

You'll never redefine `Object.ReferenceEquals()` because it does exactly what it is supposed to do: test the object identity of two different variables.

The second function you'll never redefine is static `Object.Equals()`. This method tests whether two variables are equal when you don't know the runtime type of the two arguments. Remember that `System.Object` is the ultimate base class for everything in C#. Anytime you compare two variables, they are instances of `System.Object`. Value types and reference types are instances of `System.Object`. So how does this method test the equality of two variables, without knowing their type, when equality changes its meaning depending on the type? The answer is simple: This method delegates that responsibility to one of the types in question. The static `Object.Equals()` method is implemented something like this:

```
public static bool Equals( object left, object right )
{
  // Check object identity
  if (left == right )
    return true;
  // both null references handled above
  if ((left == null) || (right == null))
    return false;
  return left.Equals (right);
}
```

This example code introduces both of the methods I have not discussed yet: `operator==()` and the instance `Equals()` method. I'll explain both in detail, but I'm not ready to end my discussion of the static `Equals()`

just yet. For right now, I want you to understand that static `Equals()` uses the instance `Equals()` method of the left argument to determine whether two objects are equal.

As with `ReferenceEquals()`, you'll never redefine the static `Object.Equals()` method because it already does exactly what it needs to do: determines whether two objects are the same when you don't know the runtime type. Because the static `Equals()` method delegates to the left argument's instance `Equals()`, it uses the rules for that type.

Now you understand why you never need to redefine the static `ReferenceEquals()` and static `Equals()` methods. It's time to discuss the methods you will override. But first, let's briefly discuss the mathematical properties of an equality relation. You need to make sure that your definition and implementation are consistent with other programmers' expectations. This means that you need to keep in mind the mathematical properties of equality: Equality is **reflexive**, **symmetric**, and **transitive**. The reflexive property means that any object is equal to itself. No matter what type is involved, a `==` a is always true. The symmetric property means that order does not matter: If a `==` b is true, b `==` a is also true. If a `==` b is false, b `==` a is also false. The last property is that if a `==` b and b `==` c are both true, then a `==` c must also be true. That's the transitive property.

Now it's time to discuss the instance `Object.Equals()` function, including when and how you override it. You create your own instance version of `Equals()` when the default behavior is inconsistent with your type. The `Object.Equals()` method uses object identity to determine whether two variables are equal. The default `Object.Equals()` function behaves exactly the same as `Object.ReferenceEquals()`. But wait—value types are different. `System.ValueType` does override `Object.Equals()`. Remember that `ValueType` is the base class for all value types that you create (using the `struct` keyword). Two variables of a value type are equal if they are the same type and they have the same contents. `ValueType.Equals()` implements that behavior. Unfortunately, `ValueType.Equals()` does not have an efficient implementation. `ValueType.Equals()` is the base class for all value types. To provide the correct behavior, it must compare all the member variables in any derived type, without knowing the runtime type of the object. In C#, that means using reflection. As you'll see in Item 44, there are many disadvantages to reflection, especially when performance is a goal. Equality is one of those fundamental constructs that gets called frequently in programs, so performance is a worthy goal. Under almost all circumstances, you can write a much faster override of `Equals()` for any value type. The recommendation for value types is simple: Always create an override of `ValueType.Equals()` whenever you create a value type.

You should override the instance `Equals()` function only when you want to change the defined semantics for a reference type. A number of classes in the .NET Framework Class Library use value semantics instead of reference semantics for equality. Two string objects are equal if they contain the same contents. Two `DataRowView` objects are equal if they refer to the same `DataRow`. The point is that if your type should follow value semantics (comparing contents) instead of reference semantics (comparing object identity), you should write your own override of instance `Object.Equals()`.

Now that you know when to write your own override of `Object.Equals()`, you must understand how you should implement it. The equality relationship for value types has many implications for boxing and is discussed in Item 17. For reference types, your instance method needs to follow predefined behavior to avoid strange surprises for users of your class. Here is the standard pattern:

```
public class Foo
{
  public override bool Equals( object right )
  {
    // check null:
    // the this pointer is never null in C# methods.
    if (right == null)
      return false;

    if (object.ReferenceEquals( this, right ))
      return true;

    // Discussed below.
    if (this.GetType() != right.GetType())
      return false;

    // Compare this type's contents here:
    return CompareFooMembers(
```

```
        this, right as Foo );
  }
}
```

First, `Equals()` should never throw exceptions—it doesn't make much sense. Two variables are or are not equal; there's not much room for other failures. Just return `false` for all failure conditions, such as null references or the wrong argument types. Now, let's go through this method in detail so you understand why each check is there and why some checks can be left out. The first check determines whether the right-side object is null. There is no check on this reference. In C#, this is never null. The CLR throws an exception before calling any instance method through a null reference. The next check determines whether the two object references are the same, testing object identity. It's a very efficient test, and equal object identity guarantees equal contents.

The next check determines whether the two objects being compared are the same type. The exact form is important. First, notice that it does not assume that this is of type Foo; it calls `this.GetType()`. The actual type might be a class derived from Foo. Second, the code checks the exact type of objects being compared. It is not enough to ensure that you can convert the right-side parameter to the current type. That test can cause two subtle bugs. Consider the following example involving a small inheritance hierarchy:

```
public class B
{
  public override bool Equals( object right )
  {
    // check null:
    if (right == null)
      return false;

    // Check reference equality:
    if (object.ReferenceEquals( this, right ))
      return true;

    // Problems here, discussed below.
    B rightAsB = right as B;
    if (rightAsB == null)
      return false;
```

```
      return CompareBMembers( this, rightAsB );
  }
}

public class D : B
{
  // etc.
  public override bool Equals( object right )
  {
    // check null:
    if (right == null)
      return false;

    if (object.ReferenceEquals( this, right ))
      return true;

    // Problems here.
    D rightAsD = right as D;
    if (rightAsD == null)
      return false;

    if (base.Equals( rightAsD ) == false)
      return false;

    return CompareDMembers( this, rightAsD );
  }

}

//Test:
B baseObject = new B();
D derivedObject = new D();

// Comparison 1.
if (baseObject.Equals(derivedObject))
  Console.WriteLine( "Equals" );
else
  Console.WriteLine( "Not Equal" );
```

```
// Comparison 2.
if (derivedObject.Equals(baseObject))
  Console.WriteLine( "Equals" );
else
  Console.WriteLine( "Not Equal" );
```

Under any possible circumstances, you would expect to see either Equals or Not Equal printed twice. Because of some errors, this is not the case with the previous code. The second comparison will never return true. The base object, of type B, can never be converted into a D. However, the first comparison might evaluate to true. The derived object, of type D, can be implicitly converted to a type B. If the B members of the right-side argument match the B members of the left-side argument, B.Equals() considers the objects equal. Even though the two objects are different types, your method has considered them equal. You've broken the symmetric property of Equals. This construct broke because of the automatic conversions that take place up and down the inheritance hierarchy.

When you write this, the D object is explicitly converted to a B:

```
baseObject.Equals( derived )
```

If baseObject.Equals() determines that the fields defined in its type match, the two objects are equal. On the other hand, when you write this, the B object cannot be converted to a D object:

```
derivedObject.Equals( base )
```

The B object cannot be converted to a D object. The derivedObject.Equals() method always returns false. If you don't check the object types exactly, you can easily get into this situation, in which the order of the comparison matters.

There is another practice to follow when you override Equals(). You should call the base class only if the base version is not provided by System.Object or System.ValueType. The previous code provides an example. Class D calls the Equals() method defined in its base class, Class B. However, Class B does not call baseObject.Equals(). It calls the version defined in System.Object, which returns true only when the two arguments refer to the same object. That's not what you want, or you wouldn't have written your own method in the first place.

The rule is to override `Equals()` whenever you create a value type, and to override `Equals()` on reference types when you do not want your reference type to obey reference semantics, as defined by `System.Object`. When you write your own `Equals()`, follow the implementation just outlined. Overriding `Equals()` means that you should write an override for `GetHashCode()`. See Item 10 for details.

Three down, one to go: `operator==()`. Anytime you create a value type, redefine `operator==()`. The reason is exactly the same as with the instance `Equals()` function. The default version uses reflection to compare the contents of two value types. That's far less efficient than any implementation that you would write, so write your own. Follow the recommendations in Item 17 to avoid boxing when you compare value types.

Notice that I didn't say that you should write `operator==()` whenever you override instance `Equals()`. I said to write `operator==()` when you create value types. You should rarely override `operator==()`when you create reference types. The .NET Framework classes expect `operator==()` to follow reference semantics for all reference types.

C# gives you four ways to test equality, but you need to consider providing your own definitions for only two of them. You never override the static `Object.ReferenceEquals()` and static `Object.Equals()` because they provide the correct tests, regardless of the runtime type. You always override instance `Equals()` and `operator==()` for value types to provide better performance. You override instance `Equals()` for reference types when you want equality to mean something other than object identity. Simple, right?

Item 10: Understand the Pitfalls of `GetHashCode()`

This is the only item in this book dedicated to one function that you should avoid writing. `GetHashCode()` is used in one place only: to define the hash value for keys in a hash-based collection, typically the `Hashtable` or `Dictionary` containers. That's good because there are a number of problems with the base class implementation of `GetHash-Code()`. For reference types, it works but is inefficient. For value types, the base class version is often incorrect. But it gets worse. It's entirely possible that you cannot write `GetHashCode()` so that it is both efficient and correct. No single function generates more discussion and more confusion than GetHashCode(). Read on to remove all that confusion.

If you're defining a type that won't ever be used as the key in a container, this won't matter. Types that represent window controls, web page controls, or database connections are unlikely to be used as keys in a collection. In those cases, do nothing. All reference types will have a hash code that is correct, even if it is very inefficient. Value types should be immutable (see Item 7), in which case, the default implementation always works, although it is also inefficient. In most types that you create, the best approach is to avoid the existence of GetHashCode() entirely.

One day, you'll create a type that is meant to be used as a hashtable key, and you'll need to write your own implementation of GetHashCode(), so read on. Hash-based containers use hash codes to optimize searches. Every object generates an integer value called a hash code. Objects are stored in buckets based on the value of that hash code. To search for an object, you request its key and search just that one bucket. In .NET, everyobject has a hash code, determined by System.Object.GetHash-Code(). Any overload of GetHashCode() must follow these three rules:

1. If two objects are equal (as defined by operator==), they must generate the same hash value. Otherwise, hash codes can't be used to find objects in containers.
2. For any object A, A.GetHashCode() must be an instance invariant. No matter what methods are called on A, A.GetHashCode() must always return the same value. That ensures that an object placed in a bucket is always in the right bucket.
3. The hash function should generate a random distribution among all integers for all inputs. That's how you get efficiency from a hash-based container.

Writing a correct and efficient hash function requires extensive knowledge of the type to ensure that rule 3 is followed. The versions defined in System.Object and System.ValueType do not have that advantage. These versions must provide the best default behavior with almost no knowledge of your particular type. Object.GetHashCode() uses an internal field in the System.Object class to generate the hash value. Each object created is assigned a unique object key, stored as an integer, when it is created. These keys start at 1 and increment every time a new object of any type gets created. The object identity field is set in the `System.Object` constructor and cannot be modified later. `Object.GetHashCode()` returns this value as the hash code for a given object.

Now examine `Object.GetHashCode()` in light of those three rules. If two objects are equal, `Object.GetHashCode()` returns the same hash value, unless you've overridden `operator==`. `System.Object`'s version of `operator==()` tests object identity. `GetHashCode()` returns the internal object identity field. It works. However, if you've supplied your own version of `operator==`, you must also supply your own version of `GetHashCode()` to ensure that the first rule is followed. See Item 9 for details on equality.

The second rule is followed: After an object is created, its hash code never changes.

The third rule, a random distribution among all integers for all inputs, does not hold. A numeric sequence is not a random distribution among all integers unless you create an enormous number of objects. The hash codes generated by `Object.GetHashCode()` are concentrated at the low end of the range of integers.

This means that `Object.GetHashCode()` is correct but not efficient. If you create a hashtable based on a reference type that you define, the default behavior from `System.Object` is a working, but slow, hashtable. When you create reference types that are meant to be hash keys, you should override `GetHashCode()` to get a better distribution of the hash values across all integers for your specific type.

Before covering how to write your own override of `GetHashCode`, this section examines `ValueType.GetHashCode()` with respect to those same three rules. `System.ValueType` overrides `GetHashCode()`, providing the default behavior for all value types. Its version returns the hash code from the first field defined in the type. Consider this example:

```
public struct MyStruct
{
    private string   _msg;
    private int      _id;
    private DateTime _epoch;
}
```

The hash code returned from a `MyStruct` object is the hash code generated by the `_msg` field. The following code snippet always returns `true`:

```
MyStruct s = new MyStruct( );
return s.GetHashCode( ) == s._msg.GetHashCode( );
```

The first rule says that two objects that are equal (as defined by `operator==()`) must have the same hash code. This rule is followed for value types under most conditions, but you can break it, just as you could with for reference types. `ValueType.operator==()` compares the first field in the struct, along with every other field. That satisfies rule 1. As long as any override that you define for `operator==` uses the first field, it will work. Any struct whose first field does not participate in the equality of the type violates this rule, breaking `GetHashCode()`.

The second rule states that the hash code must be an instance invariant. That rule is followed only when the first field in the struct is an immutable field. If the value of the first field can change, so can the hash code. That breaks the rules. Yes, `GetHashCode()` is broken for any struct that you create when the first field can be modified during the lifetime of the object. It's yet another reason why immutable value types are your best bet (see Item 7).

The third rule depends on the type of the first field and how it is used. If the first field generates a random distribution across all integers, and the first field is distributed across all values of the struct, then the struct generates an even distribution as well. However, if the first field often has the same value, this rule is violated. Consider a small change to the earlier struct:

```
public struct MyStruct
{
  private DateTime _epoch;
  private string   _msg;
  private int      _id;
}
```

If the `_epoch` field is set to the current date (not including the time), all `MyStruct` objects created in a given date will have the same hash code. That prevents an even distribution among all hash code values.

Summarizing the default behavior, Object.GetHashCode() works correctly for reference types, although it does not necessarily generate an efficient distribution. (If you have overridden Object.operator==(), you can break GetHashCode()). ValueType.GetHashCode() works only if the first field in your struct is read-only. ValueType.GetHashCode() generates an efficient hash code only when the first field in your struct contains values across a meaningful subset of its inputs.

If you're going to build a better hash code, you need to place some constraints on your type. Examine the three rules again, this time in the context of building a working implementation of GetHashCode().

First, if two objects are equal, as defined by operator==(), they must return the same hash value. Any property or data value used to generate the hash code must also participate in the equality test for the type. Obviously, this means that the same properties used for equality are used for hash code generation. It's possible to have properties participate in equality that are not used in the hash code computation. The default behavior for System.ValueType does just that, but it often means that rule 3 usually gets violated. The same data elements should participate in both computations.

The second rule is that the return value of GetHashCode() must be an instance invariant. Imagine that you defined a reference type, Customer:

```
public class Customer
{
  private string _name;
  private decimal _revenue;

  public Customer( string name )
  {
    _name = name;
  }

  public string Name
  {
    get { return _name; }
    set { _name = value; }
  }
}
```

```
public override int GetHashCode()
{
  return _name.GetHashCode();
}
}
```

Suppose that you execute the following code snippet:

```
Customer c1 = new Customer( "Acme Products" );
myHashMap.Add( c1, orders );
// Oops, the name is wrong:
c1.Name = "Acme Software";
```

c1 is lost somewhere in the hash map. When you placed c1 in the map, the hash code was generated from the string "Acme Products". After you change the name of the customer to "Acme Software", the hash code value changed. It's now being generated from the new name: "Acme Software". C1 is stored in the bucket defined by "Acme Products", but it should be in the bucket defined for "Acme Software". You've lost that customer in your own collection. It's lost because the hash code is not an object invariant. You've changed the correct bucket after storing the object.

The earlier situation can occur only if Customer is a reference type. Value types misbehave differently, but they still cause problems. If customer is a value type, a copy of c1 gets stored in the hashmap. The last line changing the value of the name has no effect on the copy stored in the hashmap. Because boxing and unboxing make copies as well, it's very unlikely that you can change the members of a value type after that object has been added to a collection.

The only way to address rule 2 is to define the hash code function to return a value based on some invariant property or properties of the object. System.Object abides by this rule using the object identity, which does not change. System.ValueType hopes that the first field in your type does not change. You can't do better without making your type immutable. When you define a value type that is intended for use as a key type in a hash container, it must be an immutable type. Violate this recommendation, and the users of your type will find a way to break hashtables that use your type as keys. Revisiting the `Customer` class, you can modify it so that the customer name is immutable:

```
public class Customer
{
  private readonly string _name;
  private decimal _revenue;

  public Customer( string name ) :
    this ( name, 0 )
  {
  }

  public Customer( string name, decimal revenue )
  {
    _name = name;
    _revenue = revenue;
  }

  public string Name
  {
    get { return _name; }
  }

  // Change the name, returning a new object:
  public Customer ChangeName( string newName )
  {
    return new Customer( newName, _revenue );
  }

  public override int GetHashCode()
  {
    return _name.GetHashCode();
  }
}
```

Making the name immutable changes how you must work with customer objects to modify the name:

```
Customer c1 = new Customer( "Acme Products" );
myHashMap.Add( c1,orders );
// Oops, the name is wrong:
Customer c2 = c1.ChangeName( "Acme Software" );
Order o = myHashMap[ c1 ] as Order;
myHashMap.Remove( c1 );
myHashMap.Add( c2, o );
```

You have to remove the original customer, change the name, and add the new customer object to the hashtable. It looks more cumbersome than the first version, but it works. The previous version allowed programmers to write incorrect code. By enforcing the immutability of the properties used to calculate the hash code, you enforce correct behavior. Users of your type can't go wrong. Yes, this version is more work. You're forcing developers to write more code, but only because it's the only way to write the correct code. Make certain that any data members used to calculate the hash value are immutable.

The third rule says that `GetHashCode()` should generate a random distribution among all integers for all inputs. Satisfying this requirement depends on the specifics of the types you create. If a magic formula existed, it would be implemented in `System.Object` and this item would not exist. A common and successful algorithm is to XOR all the return values from `GetHashCode()` on all fields in a type. If your type contains some mutable fields, exclude those fields from the calculations.

`GetHashCode()` has very specific requirements: Equal objects must produce equal hash codes, and hash codes must be object invariants and must produce an even distribution to be efficient. All three can be satisfied only for immutable types. For other types, rely on the default behavior, but understand the pitfalls.

Item 11: Prefer `foreach` Loops

The C# `foreach` statement is more than just a variation of the `do`, `while`, or `for` loops. It generates the best iteration code for any collection you have. Its definition is tied to the collection interfaces in the .NET Framework, and the C# compiler generates the best code for the particular type of collection. When you iterate collections, use foreach instead of other looping constructs. Examine these three loops:

```
int [] foo = new int[100];

// Loop 1:
foreach ( int i in foo)
  Console.WriteLine( i.ToString( ));

// Loop 2:
for ( int index = 0;
  index < foo.Length;
  index++ )
  Console.WriteLine( foo[index].ToString( ));

// Loop 3:
int len = foo.Length;
for ( int index = 0;
  index < len;
  index++ )
  Console.WriteLine( foo[index].ToString( ));
```

For the current and future C# compilers (version 1.1 and up), loop 1 is best. It's even less typing, so your personal productivity goes up. (The C# 1.0 compiler produced much slower code for loop 1, so loop 2 is best in that version.) Loop 3, the construct most C and C++ programmers would view as most efficient, is the worst option. By hoisting the Length variable out of the loop, you make a change that hinders the JIT compiler's chance to remove range checking inside the loop.

C# code runs in a safe, managed environment. Every memory location is checked, including array indexes. Taking a few liberties, the actual code for loop 3 is something like this:

```
// Loop 3, as generated by compiler:
int len = foo.Length;
for ( int index = 0;
  index < len;
  index++ )
{
  if ( index < foo.Length )
```

```
      Console.WriteLine( foo[index].ToString( ));
   else
      throw new IndexOutOfRangeException( );
}
```

The JIT C# compiler just doesn't like you trying to help it this way. Your attempt to hoist the Length property access out of the loop just made the JIT compiler do more work to generate even slower code. One of the CLR guarantees is that you cannot write code that overruns the memory that your variables own. The runtime generates a test of the actual array bounds (not your len variable) before accessing each particular array element. You get one bounds check for the price of two.

You still pay to check the array index on every iteration of the loop, and you do so twice. The reason loops 1 and 2 are faster is that the C# compiler and the JIT compiler can verify that the bounds of the loop are guaranteed to be safe. Anytime the loop variable is not the length of the array, the bounds check is performed on each iteration.

The reason that foreach and arrays generated very slow code in the original C# compiler concerns boxing, which is covered extensively in Item 17. Arrays are type safe. foreach now generates different IL for arrays than other collections. The array version does not use the IEnumerator interface, which would require boxing and unboxing:

```
IEnumerator it = foo.GetEnumerator( );
while( it.MoveNext( ))
{
  int i = (int) it.Current; // box and unbox here.
  Console.WriteLine( i.ToString( ) );
}
```

Instead, the foreach statement generates this construct for arrays:

```
for ( int index = 0;
  index < foo.Length;
  index++ )
  Console.WriteLine( foo[index].ToString( ));
```

foreach always generates the best code. You don't need to remember which construct generates the most efficient looping construct: foreach and the compiler will do it for you.

If efficiency isn't enough for you, consider language interop. Some folks in the world (yes, most of them use other programming languages) strongly believe that index variables start at 1, not 0. No matter how much we try, we won't break them of this habit. The .NET team tried. You have to write this kind of initialization in C# to get an array that starts at something other than 0:

```
// Create a single dimension array.
// Its range is [ 1 .. 5 ]
Array test = Array.CreateInstance( typeof( int ),
new int[ ]{ 5 }, new int[ ]{ 1 });
```

This code should be enough to make anybody cringe and just write arrays that start at 0. But some people are stubborn. Try as you might, they will start counting at 1. Luckily, this is one of those problems that you can foist off on the compiler. Iterate the test array using `foreach`:

```
foreach( int j in test )
  Console.WriteLine ( j );
```

The `foreach` statement knows how to check the upper and lower bounds on the array, so you don't have to—and it's just as fast as a hand-coded `for` loop, no matter what different lower bound someone decides to use.

`foreach` adds other language benefits for you. The `loop` variable is read-only: You can't replace the objects in a collection using `foreach`. Also, there is explicit casting to the correct type. If the collection contains the wrong type of objects, the iteration throws an exception.

`foreach` gives you similar benefits for multidimensional arrays. Suppose that you are creating a chess board. You would write these two fragments:

```
private Square[,] _theBoard = new Square[ 8, 8 ];

// elsewhere in code:
for ( int i = 0; i < _theBoard.GetLength( 0 ); i++ )
  for( int j = 0; j < _theBoard.GetLength( 1 ); j++ )
    _theBoard[ i, j ].PaintSquare( );
```

Instead, you can simplify painting the board this way:

```
foreach( Square sq in _theBoard )
  sq.PaintSquare( );
```

The foreach statement generates the proper code to iterate across all dimensions in the array. If you make a 3D chessboard in the future, the foreach loop just works. The other loop needs modification:

```
for ( int i = 0; i < _theBoard.GetLength( 0 ); i++ )
  for( int j = 0; j < _theBoard.GetLength( 1 ); j++ )
    for( int k = 0; k < _theBoard.GetLength( 2 ); k++ )
      _theBoard[ i, j, k ].PaintSquare( );
```

In fact, the foreach loop would work on a multidimensional array that had different lower bounds in each direction. I don't want to write that kind of code, even as an example. But when someone else codes that kind of collection, foreach can handle it.

foreach also gives you the flexibility to keep much of the code intact if you find later that you need to change the underlying data structure from an array. We started this discussion with a simple array:

```
int [] foo = new int[100];
```

Suppose that, at some later point, you realize that you need capabilities that are not easily handled by the array class. You can simply change the array to an ArrayList:

```
// Set the initial size:
ArrayList foo = new ArrayList( 100 );
```

Any hand-coded for loops are broken:

```
int sum = 0;
for ( int index = 0;
  // won't compile: ArrayList uses Count, not Length
  index < foo.Length;
  index++ )
  // won't compile: foo[ index ] is object, not int.
  sum += foo[ index ];
```

However, the foreach loop compiles to different code that automatically casts each operand to the proper type. No changes are needed. It's not just changing to standard collections classes, either—any collection type can be used with foreach.

Users of your types can use foreach to iterate across members if you support the .NET environment's rules for a collection. For the foreach statement to consider it a collection type, a class must have one of a number of properties. The presence of a public `GetEnumerator()` method makes a collection class. Explicitly implementing the `IEnumerable` interface creates a collection type. Implementing the `IEnumerator` interface creates a collection type. `foreach` works with any of them.

`foreach` has one added benefit regarding resource management. The `IEnumerable` interface contains one method: `GetEnumerator()`. The `foreach` statement on an enumerable type generates the following, with some optimizations:

```
IEnumerator it = foo.GetEnumerator( ) as IEnumerator;
using ( IDisposable disp = it as IDisposable )
{
  while ( it.MoveNext( ))
  {
    int elem = ( int ) it.Current;
    sum += elem;
  }
}
```

The compiler automatically optimizes the code in the `finally` clause if it can determine for certain whether the enumerator implements `IDisposable`. But for you, it's more important to see that, no matter what, `foreach` generates correct code.

`foreach` is a very versatile statement. It generates the right code for upper and lower bounds in arrays, iterates multidimensional arrays, coerces the operands into the proper type (using the most efficient construct), and, on top of that, generates the most efficient looping constructs. It's the best way to iterate collections. With it, you'll create code that is more likely to last, and it's simpler for you to write in the first place. It's a small productivity improvement, but it adds up over time.

2 | .NET Resource Management

The simple fact that .NET programs run in a managed environment has a big impact on the kinds of designs that create effective C#. Taking utmost advantage of that environment requires changing your thinking from native environments to the .NET CLR. It means understanding the .NET Garbage Collector. An overview of the .NET memory management environment is necessary to understand the specific recommendations in this chapter, so let's get on with the overview.

The Garbage Collector (GC) controls managed memory for you. Unlike native environments, you are not responsible for memory leaks, dangling pointers, uninitialized pointers, or a host of other memory-management issues. But the Garbage Collector is not magic: You need to clean up after yourself, too. You are responsible for unmanaged resources such as file handles, database connections, GDI+ objects, COM objects, and other system objects.

Here's the good news: Because the GC controls memory, certain design idioms are much easier to implement. Circular references, both simple relationships and complex webs of objects, are much easier. The GC's Mark and Compact algorithm efficiently detects these relationships and removes unreachable webs of objects in their entirety. The GC determines whether an object is reachable by walking the object tree from the application's root object instead of forcing each object to keep track of references to it, as in COM. The `DataSet` class provides an example of how this algorithm simplifies object ownership decisions. A `DataSet` is a collection of `DataTables`. Each `DataTable` is a collection of `DataRows`. Each `DataRow` is a collection of `DataItems`. Each `DataTable` also contains a collection of `DataColumns`. `DataColumns` define the types associated with each column of data. There are other references from the `DataItems` to its appropriate column. Every `DataItem` also contains a reference to its container, the `DataRow`. `DataRows` contain references back to the `DataTable`, and everything contains a reference back to the containing `DataSet`.

If that's not complicated enough, you can create `DataViews` that provide access to filtered sequences of a data table. Those are all managed by a `DataViewManager`. There are references all through the web of objects that make up a `DataSet`. Releasing memory is the GC's responsibility. Because the .NET Framework designers did not need to free these objects, the complicated web of object references did not pose a problem. No decision needed to be made regarding the proper sequence of freeing this web of objects; it's the GC's job. The GC's design simplifies the problem of identifying this kind of web of objects as garbage. After the application releases its reference to the dataset, none of the subordinate objects can be reached. It does not matter that there are still circular references to the `DataSet`, `DataTables`, and other objects in the web. Because these objects cannot be reached from the application, they are all garbage.

The Garbage Collector runs in its own thread to remove unused memory from your program. It also compacts the managed heap each time it runs. Compacting the heap moves each live object in the managed heap so that the free space is located in one contiguous block of memory. Figure 2.1 shows two snapshots of the heap before and after a garbage collection. All free memory is placed in one contiguous block after each GC operation.

Figure 2.1 contents:

Left heap (before): F, E (F), D, C, B, Main Form (C, E)

Right heap (after): F, E (F), C, Main Form (C, E)

Letters in parentheses indicate owned references.
Hashed objects are visible from application.

(B, D) has been removed from memory.
Heap has been compacted.

Figure 2.1   The Garbage Collector not only removes unused memory, but it moves other objects in memory to compact used memory and maximize free space.

As you've just learned, memory management is completely the responsibility of the Garbage Collector. All other system resources are your responsibility. You can guarantee that you free other system resources by defining a finalizer in your type. Finalizers are called by the system before an object that is garbage is removed from memory. You can—and must—use these methods to release any unmanaged resources that an object owns. The finalizer for an object is called at some time after it becomes garbage and before the system reclaims its memory. This nondeterministic finalization means that you cannot control the relationship between when you stop using an object and when its finalizer executes. That is a big change from C++, and it has important ramifications for your designs. Experienced C++ programmers wrote classes that allocated a critical resource in its constructor and released it in its destructor:

```
// Good C++, bad C#:
class CriticalSection
{
public:
  // Constructor acquires the system resource.
  CriticalSection( )
  {
    EnterCriticalSection( );
  }

  // Destructor releases system resource.
  ~CriticalSection( )
  {
    ExitCriticalSection( );
  }
};

// usage:
void Func( )
{
  // The lifetime of s controls access to
  // the system resource.
  CriticalSection s;
  // Do work.

  //...
```

```
    // compiler generates call to destructor.
    // code exits critical section.
}
```

This common C++ idiom ensures that resource deallocation is exception-proof. This doesn't work in C#, however—at least, not in the same way. Deterministic finalization is not part of the .NET environment or the C# language. Trying to force the C++ idiom of deterministic finalization into the C# language won't work well. In C#, the finalizer eventually executes, but it doesn't execute in a timely fashion. In the previous example, the code eventually exits the critical section, but, in C#, it doesn't exit the critical section when the function exits. That happens at some unknown time later. You don't know when. You can't know when.

Relying on finalizers also introduces performance penalties. Objects that require finalization put a performance drag on the Garbage Collector. When the GC finds that an object is garbage but also requires finalization, it cannot remove that item from memory just yet. First, it calls the finalizer. Finalizers are not executed by the same thread that collects garbage. Instead, the GC places each object that is ready for finalization in a queue and spawns yet another thread to execute all the finalizers. It continues with its business, removing other garbage from memory. On the next GC cycle, those objects that have been finalized are removed from memory. Figure 2.2 shows three different GC operations and the difference in memory usage. Notice that the objects that require finalizers stay in memory for extra cycles.

This might lead you to believe that an object that requires finalization lives in memory for one GC cycle more than necessary. But I simplified things. It's more complicated than that because of another GC design decision. The .NET Garbage Collector defines **generations** to optimize its work. Generations help the GC identify the likeliest garbage candidates more quickly. Any object created since the last garbage collection operation is a generation 0 object. Any object that has survived one GC operation is a generation 1 object. Any object that has survived two or more GC operations is a generation 2 object. The purpose of generations is to separate local variables and objects that stay around for the life of the application. Generation 0 objects are mostly local variables. Member variables and global variables quickly enter generation 1 and eventually enter generation 2.

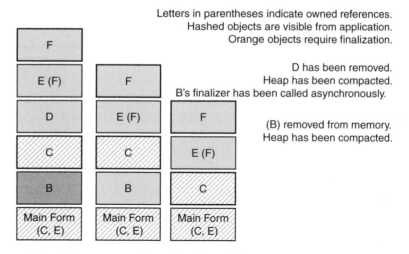

Figure 2.2   This sequence shows the effect of finalizers on the Garbage Collector. Objects stay in memory longer, and an extra thread needs to be spawned to run the Garbage Collector.

The GC optimizes its work by limiting how often it examines first- and second-generation objects. Every GC cycle examines generation 0 objects. Roughly 1 GC out of 10 examines the generation 0 and 1 objects. Roughly 1 GC cycle out of 100 examines all objects. Think about finalization and its cost again: An object that requires finalization might stay in memory for nine GC cycles more than it would if it did not require finalization. If it still has not been finalized, it moves to generation 2. In generation 2, an object lives for an extra 100 GC cycles until the next generation 2 collection.

To close, remember that a managed environment, where the Garbage Collector takes the responsibility for memory management, is a big plus: Memory leaks and a host of other pointer-related problems are no longer your problem. Nonmemory resources force you to create finalizers to ensure proper cleanup of those nonmemory resources. Finalizers can have a serious impact on the performance of your program, but you must write them to avoid resource leaks. Implementing and using the IDisposable interface avoids the performance drain on the Garbage Collector that finalizers introduce. The next section moves on to the specific items that will help you create programs that use this environment more effectively.

Item 12: Prefer Variable Initializers to Assignment Statements

Classes often have more than one constructor. Over time, it's easy for the member variables and the constructors to get out of synch. The best way to make sure this doesn't happen is to initialize variables where you declare them instead of in the body of every constructor. You should utilize the initializer syntax for both static and instance variables.

Constructing member variables when you declare that variable is natural in C#. Just assign a value:

```
public class MyClass
{
  // declare the collection, and initialize it.
  private ArrayList _coll = new ArrayList( );
}
```

Regardless of the number of constructors you eventually add to the `MyClass` type, `_coll` will be initialized properly. The compiler generates code at the beginning of each constructor to execute all the initializers you have defined for your instance member variables. When you add a new constructor, `_coll` gets initialized. Similarly, if you add a new member variable, you do not need to add initialization code to every constructor; initializing the variable where you define it is sufficient. Equally important, the initializers are added to the compiler-generated default constructor. The C# compiler creates a default constructor for your types whenever you don't explicitly define any constructors.

Initializers are more than a convenient shortcut for statements in a constructor body. The statements generated by initializers are placed in object code before the body of your constructors. Initializers execute before the base class constructor for your type executes, and they are executed in the order the variables are declared in your class.

Using initializers is the simplest way to avoid uninitialized variables in your types, but it's not perfect. In three cases, you should not use the initializer syntax. The first is when you are initializing the object to 0, or null. The default system initialization sets everything to 0 for you before any of your code executes. The system-generated 0 initialization is done at a very low level using the CPU instructions to set the entire block of memory to 0. Any extra 0 initialization on your part is superfluous. The C# compiler dutifully adds the extra instructions to set memory to 0 again. It's not wrong—it's just inefficient. In fact, when value types are involved, it's very inefficient.

```
MyValType _MyVal1;  // initialized to 0
MyValType _MyVal2 = new MyValType(); // also 0
```

Both statements initialize the variable to all 0s. The first does so by setting the memory containing MyVal1 to 0. The second uses the IL instruction initobj, which causes both a box and an unbox operation on the _MyVal2 variable. This takes quite a bit of extra time (see Item 17).

The second inefficiency comes when you create multiple initializations for the same object. You should use the initializer syntax only for variables that receive the same initialization in all constructors. This version of MyClass has a path that creates two different ArrayList objects as part of its construction:

```
public class MyClass
{
  // declare the collection, and initialize it.
  private ArrayList _coll = new ArrayList( );

  MyClass( )
  {
  }

  MyClass( int size )
  {
    _coll = new ArrayList( size );
  }
}
```

When you create a new MyClass, specifying the size of the collection, you create two array lists. One is immediately garbage. The variable initializer executes before every constructor. The constructor body creates the second array list. The compiler creates this version of MyClass, which you would never code by hand. (For the proper way to handle this situation, see Item 14.)

```
public class MyClass
{
  // declare the collection, and initialize it.
  private ArrayList _coll;
```

```
MyClass( )
{
  _coll = new ArrayList( );
}

MyClass( int size )
{
  _coll = new ArrayList( );
  _coll = new ArrayList( size );
}
}
```

The final reason to move initialization into the body of a constructor is to facilitate exception handling. You cannot wrap the initializers in a `try` block. Any exceptions that might be generated during the construction of your member variables get propagated outside of your object. You cannot attempt any recovery inside your class. You should move that initialization code into the body of your constructors so that you implement the proper recovery code to create your type and gracefully handle the exception (see Item 45).

Variable initializers are the simplest way to ensure that the member variables in your type are initialized regardless of which constructor is called. The initializers are executed before each constructor you make for your type. Using this syntax means that you cannot forget to add the proper initialization when you add new constructors for a future release. Use initializers when all constructors create the member variable the same way; it's simpler to read and easier to maintain.

Item 13: Initialize Static Class Members with Static Constructors

You know that you should initialize static member variables in a type before you create any instances of that type. C# lets you use static initializers and a static constructor for this purpose. A static constructor is a special function that executes before any other methods, variables, or properties defined in that class are accessed. You use this function to initialize static variables, enforce the singleton pattern, or perform any other necessary work before a class is usable. You should not use your instance constructors, some special private function, or any other idiom to initialize static variables.

As with instance initialization, you can use the initializer syntax as an alternative to the static constructor. If you simply need to allocate a static member, use the initializer syntax. When you have more complicated logic to initialize static member variables, create a static constructor.

Implementing the singleton pattern in C# is the most frequent use of a static constructor. Make your instance constructor private, and add an initializer:

```csharp
public class MySingleton
{
  private static readonly MySingleton _theOneAndOnly =
    new MySingleton( );

  public static MySingleton TheOnly
  {
    get
    {
      return _theOneAndOnly;
    }
  }

  private MySingleton( )
  {
  }

  // remainder elided
}
```

The singleton pattern can just as easily be written this way, in case you have more complicated logic to initialize the singleton:

```csharp
public class MySingleton
{
  private static readonly MySingleton _theOneAndOnly;

  static MySingleton( )
  {
    _theOneAndOnly = new MySingleton( );
```

```
  }

  public static MySingleton TheOnly
  {
    get
    {
      return _theOneAndOnly;
    }
  }

  private MySingleton( )
  {
  }

  // remainder elided
}
```

As with instance initializers, the static initializers are called before any static constructors are called. And, yes, your static initializers execute before the base class's static constructor.

The CLR calls your static constructor automatically when your type is first loaded into an application space. You can define only one static constructor, and it must not take any arguments. Because static constructors are called by the CLR, you must be careful about exceptions generated in them. If you let an exception escape a static constructor, the CLR will terminate your program. Exceptions are the most common reason to use the static constructor instead of static initializers. If you use static initializers, you cannot catch the exceptions yourself. With a static constructor, you can (see Item 45):

```
static MySingleton( )
{
  try {
    _theOneAndOnly = new MySingleton( );
  } catch
  {
    // Attempt recovery here.
  }
}
```

Static initializers and static constructors provide the cleanest, clearest way to initialize static members of your class. They are easy to read and easy to get correct. They were added to the language to specifically address the difficulties involved with initializing static members in other languages.

Item 14: Utilize Constructor Chaining

Writing constructors is often a repetitive task. Many developers write the first constructor and then copy and paste the code into other constructors, to satisfy the multiple overrides defined in the class interface. Hopefully, you're not one of those. If you are, stop it. Veteran C++ programmers would factor the common algorithms into a private helper method. Stop that, too. When you find that multiple constructors contain the same logic, factor that logic into a common constructor instead. You'll get the benefits of avoiding code duplication, and constructor initializers generate much more efficient object code. The C# compiler recognizes the constructor initializer as special syntax and removes the duplicated variable initializers and the duplicated base class constructor calls. The result is that your final object executes the minimum amount of code to properly initialize the object. You also write the least code by delegating responsibilities to a common constructor.

Constructor initializers allow one constructor to call another constructor. This example shows a simple usage:

```
public class MyClass
{
  // collection of data
  private ArrayList _coll;
  // Name of the instance:
  private string  _name;

  public MyClass() :
    this( 0, "" )
  {
  }

  public MyClass( int initialCount ) :
    this( initialCount, "" )
  {
  }
```

```
public MyClass( int initialCount, string name )
{
  _coll = ( initialCount > 0 ) ?
    new ArrayList( initialCount ) :
    new ArrayList();
  _name = name;
}
}
```

C# does not support default parameters, which would be the preferred C++ solution to this problem. You must write each constructor that you support as a separate function. With constructors, that can mean a lot of duplicated code. Use constructor chaining instead of creating a common utility routine. Several inefficiencies are present in this alternative method of factoring out common constructor logic:

```
public class MyClass
{
  // collection of data
  private ArrayList _coll;
  // Name of the instance:
  private string  _name;

  public MyClass()
  {
    commonConstructor( 0, "" );
  }

  public MyClass( int initialCount )
  {
    commonConstructor( initialCount, "" );
  }

  public MyClass( int initialCount, string Name )
  {
    commonConstructor( initialCount, Name );
  }

  private void commonConstructor( int count,
    string name )
```

```
  {
    _coll = (count > 0 ) ?
      new ArrayList(count) :
      new ArrayList();
    _name = name;
  }
}
```

That version looks the same, but it generates far less efficient object code. The compiler adds code to perform several functions on your behalf in constructors. It adds statements for all variable initializers (see Item 12). It calls the base class constructor. When you write your own common utility function, the compiler cannot factor out this duplicated code. The IL for the second version is the same as if you'd written this:

```
// Not legal, illustrates IL generated:
public MyClass()
{
  private ArrayList _coll;
  private string  _name;

  public MyClass( )
  {
    // Instance Initializers would go here.
    object(); // Not legal, illustrative only.
    commonConstructor( 0, "" );
  }

  public MyClass (int initialCount)
  {
    // Instance Initializers would go here.
    object(); // Not legal, illustrative only.
    commonConstructor( initialCount, "" );
  }

  public MyClass( int initialCount, string Name )
  {
    // Instance Initializers would go here.
    object(); // Not legal, illustrative only.
    commonConstructor( initialCount, Name );
  }
```

```
    private void commonConstructor( int count,
      string name )
    {
      _coll = (count > 0 ) ?
        new ArrayList(count) :
        new ArrayList();
      _name = name;
    }
}
```

If you could write the construction code for the first version the way the compiler sees it, you'd write this:

```
// Not legal, illustrates IL generated:
public MyClass()
{
  private ArrayList _coll;
  private string   _name;

  public MyClass( )
  {
    // No variable initializers here.
    // Call the third constructor, shown below.
    this( 0, "" ); // Not legal, illustrative only.
  }

  public MyClass (int initialCount)
  {
    // No variable initializers here.
    // Call the third constructor, shown below.
    this( initialCount, "" );
  }

  public MyClass( int initialCount, string Name )
  {
    // Instance Initializers would go here.
    object(); // Not legal, illustrative only.
    _counter = initialCount;
    _name = Name;
  }
}
```

The difference is that the compiler does not generate multiple calls to the base class constructor, nor does it copy the instance variable initializers into each constructor body. The fact that the base class constructor is called only from the last constructor is also significant: You cannot include more than one constructor initializer in a constructor definition. You can delegate to another constructor in this class using `this()`, or you can call a base class constructor using `base()`. You cannot do both.

Still don't buy the case for constructor initializers? Then think about read-only constants. In this example, the name of the object should not change during its lifetime. This means that you should make it read-only. That causes the common utility function to generate compiler errors:

```
public class MyClass
{
  // collection of data
  private ArrayList _coll;
  // Number for this instance
  private int        _counter;
  // Name of the instance:
  private readonly string  _name;

  public MyClass()
  {
    commonConstructor( 0, "" );
  }

  public MyClass( int initialCount )
  {
    commonConstructor( initialCount, "" );
  }

  public MyClass( int initialCount, string Name )
  {
    commonConstructor( initialCount, Name );
  }

  private void commonConstructor( int count,
    string name )
  {
    _coll = (count > 0 ) ?
```

```
          new ArrayList(count) :
          new ArrayList();
        // ERROR changing the name outside of a constructor.
        _name = name;
    }
}
```

C++ programmers just live with this and initialize _name in all constructors, or they cast away constness in the utility routine. C#'s constructor
initializers provide a better alternative. All but the most trivial classes contain more than one constructor. Their job is to initialize all the members
of an object. By their very nature, these functions have similar or, ideally,
shared logic. Use the C# constructor initializer to factor out those common algorithms so that you write them once and they execute once.

This is the last item about object initialization in C#. That makes it a good
time to review the entire sequence of events for constructing an instance
of a type. You should understand both the order of operations and the
default initialization of an object. You should strive to initialize every
member variable exactly once during construction. The best way for you
to accomplish this is to initialize values as early as possible. Here is the
order of operations for constructing the first instance of a type:

1. Static variable storage is set to 0.
2. Static variable initializers execute.
3. Static constructors for the base class execute.
4. The static constructor executes.
5. Instance variable storage is set to 0.
6. Instance variable initializers execute.
7. The appropriate base class instance constructor executes.
8. The instance constructor executes.

Subsequent instances of the same type start at step 5 because the class initializers execute only once. Also, steps 6 and 7 are optimized so that constructor initializers cause the compiler to remove duplicate instructions.

The C# language compiler guarantees that everything gets initialized in
some way when an object gets created. At a minimum, you are guaranteed
that all memory your object uses has been set to 0 when an instance is created. This is true for both static members and instance members. Your
goal is to make sure that you initialize all the values the way you want
and execute that initialization code only once. Use initializers to initialize

simple resources. Use constructors to initialize members that require more sophisticated logic. Also factor calls to other constructors, to minimize duplication.

Item 15: Utilize `using` and `try/finally` for Resource Cleanup

Types that use unmanaged system resources should be explicitly released using the `Dispose()` method of the `IDisposable` interface. The rules of the .NET environment make that the responsibility of the code that uses the type, not the responsibility of the type or the system. Therefore, anytime you use types that have a `Dispose()` method, it's your responsibility to release those resources by calling `Dispose()`. The best way to ensure that `Dispose()` always gets called is to utilize the `using` statement or a `try/finally` block.

All types that own unmanaged resources implement the `IDisposable` interface. In addition, they defensively create a finalizer for those times when you forget to dispose properly. If you forget to dispose of those items, those nonmemory resources are freed later, when finalizers get their chance to execute. All those objects then stay in memory that much longer, and your application becomes a slowly executing resource hog.

Luckily for you, the C# language designers knew that explicitly releasing resources would be a common task. They added keywords to the language that make it easy.

Suppose you wrote this code:

```
public void ExecuteCommand( string connString,
  string commandString )
{
  SqlConnection myConnection = new SqlConnection(
    connString );
  SqlCommand mySqlCommand = new SqlCommand( commandString,
    myConnection );

  myConnection.Open();
  mySqlCommand.ExecuteNonQuery();
}
```

Two disposable objects are not properly cleaned up in this example: `SqlConnection` and `SqlCommand`. Both of these objects remain in memory until their finalizers are called. (Both of these classes inherit their finalizer from `System.ComponentModel.Component`.)

You fix this problem by calling `Dispose` when you are finished with the command and the connection:

```
public void ExecuteCommand( string connString,
  string commandString )
{
  SqlConnection myConnection = new SqlConnection(
    connString );
  SqlCommand mySqlCommand = new SqlCommand( commandString,
    myConnection );

  myConnection.Open();
  mySqlCommand.ExecuteNonQuery();

  mySqlCommand.Dispose( );
  myConnection.Dispose( );
}
```

That's fine, unless any exceptions get thrown while the SQL command executes. In that case, your calls to `Dispose()` never happen. The `using` statement ensures that `Dispose()` is called. You allocate an object inside a `using` statement, and the C# compiler generates a `try/finally` block around each object:

```
public void ExecuteCommand( string connString,
  string commandString )
{
  using ( SqlConnection myConnection = new
    SqlConnection( connString ))
  {
    using ( SqlCommand mySqlCommand = new
      SqlCommand( commandString,
      myConnection ))
    {
      myConnection.Open();
      mySqlCommand.ExecuteNonQuery();
```

```
      }
   }
}
```

Whenever you use one `Disposable` object in a function, the `using` clause is the simplest method to use to ensure that objects get disposed of properly. The `using` statement generates a `try`/`finally` block around the object being allocated. These two blocks generate exactly the same IL:

```
SqlConnection myConnection = null;

// Example Using clause:
using ( myConnection = new SqlConnection( connString ))
{
  myConnection.Open();
}

// example Try / Catch block:
try {
  myConnection = new SqlConnection( connString );
  myConnection.Open();
}
finally {
  myConnection.Dispose( );
}
```

If you use the `using` statement with a variable of a type that does not support the `IDisposable` interface, the C# compiler generates an error. For example:

```
// Does not compile:
// String is sealed, and does not support IDisposable.
using( string msg = "This is a message" )
  Console.WriteLine( msg );
```

The `using` statement works only if the compile-time type supports the `IDisposable` interface. You cannot use it with arbitrary objects:

```
// Does not compile.
// Object does not support IDisposable.
using ( object obj = Factory.CreateResource( ))
  Console.WriteLine( obj.ToString( ));
```

A quick defensive as clause is all you need to safely dispose of objects that might or might not implement IDisposable:

```
// The correct fix.
// Object may or may not support IDisposable.
object obj = Factory.CreateResource( );
using ( obj as IDisposable )
  Console.WriteLine( obj.ToString( ));
```

If obj implements IDisposable, the using statement generates the cleanup code. If not, the using statement degenerates to using(null), which is safe but doesn't do anything. If you're not sure whether you should wrap an object in a using block, err on the side of safety: Assume that it does and wrap it in the using clause shown earlier.

That covers the simple case: Whenever you use one disposable object that is local to a method, wrap that one object in a using statement. Now you can look at a few more complicated usages. Two different objects need to be disposed in that first example: the connection and the command. The example I showed you creates two different using statements, one wrapping each of the two objects that need to be disposed. Each using statement generates a different try/finally block. In effect, you have written this construct:

```
public void ExecuteCommand( string connString,
  string commandString )
{
  SqlConnection myConnection = null;
  SqlCommand mySqlCommand = null;
  try
  {
    myConnection = new SqlConnection( connString );
    try
    {
      mySqlCommand = new SqlCommand( commandString,
      myConnection );

      myConnection.Open();
      mySqlCommand.ExecuteNonQuery();
    }
```

```
      finally
      {
        if ( mySqlCommand != null )
          mySqlCommand.Dispose( );
      }
    }
    finally
    {
      if ( myConnection != null )
        myConnection.Dispose( );
    }
  }
```

Every using statement creates a new nested try/finally block. I find that an ugly construct, so when I allocate multiple objects that implement IDisposable, I prefer to write my own try/finally blocks:

```
public void ExecuteCommand( string connString,
  string commandString )
{
  SqlConnection myConnection = null;
  SqlCommand mySqlCommand = null;
  try {
    myConnection = new SqlConnection( connString );
    mySqlCommand = new SqlCommand( commandString,
      myConnection );

    myConnection.Open();
    mySqlCommand.ExecuteNonQuery();
  }
  finally
  {
    if ( mySqlCommand != null )
      mySqlCommand.Dispose();
    if ( myConnection != null )
      myConnection.Dispose();
  }
}
```

However, don't get too cute and try to build one using clause with as statements:

```
public void ExecuteCommand( string connString,
  string commandString )
{
  // Bad idea. Potential resource leak lurks!
  SqlConnection myConnection =
    new SqlConnection( connString );
  SqlCommand mySqlCommand = new SqlCommand( commandString,
      myConnection );
      using ( myConnection as IDisposable )
      using (mySqlCommand as IDisposable )
      {
        myConnection.Open();
        mySqlCommand.ExecuteNonQuery();
      }


}
```

It looks cleaner, but it has a subtle bug. The SqlConnection object never gets disposed if the SqlCommand() constructor throws an exception. You must make sure that any objects that implement IDisposable are allocated inside the scope of a using block or a try block. Otherwise, resource leaks can occur.

So far, you've handled the two most obvious cases. Whenever you allocate one disposable object in a method, the using statement is the best way to ensure that the resources you've allocated are freed in all cases. When you allocate multiple objects in the same method, create multiple using blocks or write your own single try/finally block.

There is one more nuance to freeing disposable objects. Some types support both a Dispose method and a Close method to free resources. Sql-Connection is one of those classes. You could close SqlConnection like this:

```
public void ExecuteCommand( string connString,
  string commandString )
{
  SqlConnection myConnection = null;
  try {
```

```
  myConnection = new SqlConnection( connString );
  SqlCommand mySqlCommand = new SqlCommand( commandString,
    myConnection );

  myConnection.Open();
  mySqlCommand.ExecuteNonQuery();
}
finally
{
  if ( myConnection != null )
    myConnection.Close();
}
}
```

This version does close the connection, but that's not exactly the same as disposing of it. The `Dispose` method does more than free resources: It also notifies the Garbage Collector that the object no longer needs to be finalized. `Dispose` calls `GC.SuppressFinalize()`. `Close` typically does not. As a result, the object remains in the finalization queue, even though finalization is not needed. When you have the choice, `Dispose()` is better than `Close()`. You'll learn all the gory details in Item 18.

`Dispose()` does not remove objects from memory. It is a hook to let objects release unmanaged resources. That means you can get into trouble by disposing of objects that are still in use. Do not dispose of objects that are still being referenced elsewhere in your program.

In some ways, resource management can be more difficult in C# than it was in C++. You can't rely on deterministic finalization to clean up every resource you use. But a garbage-collected environment really is much simpler for you. The vast majority of the types you make use of do not implement `IDisposable`. Less than 100 classes in the .NET Framework implement `IDisposable`—that's out of more than 1,500 types. When you use the ones that do implement `IDisposable`, remember to dispose of them in all cases. You should wrap those objects in `using` clauses or `try/finally` blocks. Whichever you use, make sure that objects get disposed properly all the time, every time.

Item 16: Minimize Garbage

The Garbage Collector does an excellent job of managing memory for you, and it removes unused objects in a very efficient manner. But no matter how you look at it, allocating and destroying a heap-based object takes more processor time than not allocating and not destroying a heap-based object. You can introduce serious performance drains on your program by creating an excessive number of reference objects that are local to your methods.

So don't overwork the Garbage Collector. You can follow some simple techniques to minimize the amount of work that the Garbage Collector needs to do on your program's behalf. All reference types, even local variables, are allocated on the heap. Every local variable of a reference type becomes garbage as soon as that function exits. One very common bad practice is to allocate GDI objects in a Windows paint handler:

```
protected override void OnPaint( PaintEventArgs e )
{
  // Bad. Created the same font every paint event.
  using ( Font MyFont = new Font( "Arial", 10.0f ))
  {
    e.Graphics.DrawString( DateTime.Now.ToString(),
      MyFont, Brushes.Black, new PointF( 0,0 ));
  }
  base.OnPaint( e );
}
```

OnPaint() gets called frequently. Every time it gets called, you create another Font object that contains the exact same settings. The Garbage Collector needs to clean those up for you every time. That's incredibly inefficient.

Instead, promote the Font object from a local variable to a member variable. Reuse the same font each time you paint the window:

```
private readonly Font _myFont =
  new Font( "Arial", 10.0f );

protected override void OnPaint( PaintEventArgs e )
{
  e.Graphics.DrawString( DateTime.Now.ToString( ),
```

```
  _myFont, Brushes.Black, new PointF( 0,0 ));
    base.OnPaint( e );
}
```

Your program no longer creates garbage with every `paint` event. The Garbage Collector does less work. Your program runs just a little faster. When you elevate a local variable, such as a font, that implements `IDisposable` to a member variable, you need to implement `IDisposable` in your class. Item 18 explains how to properly do just that.

You should promote local variables to member variables when they are reference types (value types don't matter) and they will be used in routines that are called very frequently. The font in the `paint` routine makes an excellent example. Only local variables in routines that are frequently accessed are good candidates. Infrequently called routines are not. You're trying to avoid creating the same objects repeatedly, not turn every local variable into a member variable.

The static property `Brushes.Black`, used earlier illustrates another technique that you should use to avoid repeatedly allocating similar objects. Create static member variables for commonly used instances of the reference types you need. Consider the black brush used earlier as an example. Every time you need to draw something in your window using the color black, you need a black brush. If you allocate a new one every time you draw anything, you create and destroy a huge number of black brushes during the course of a program. The first approach of creating a black brush as a member of each of your types helps, but it doesn't go far enough. Programs might create dozens of windows and controls, and would create dozens of black brushes. The .NET Framework designers anticipated this and created a single black brush for you to reuse whenever you need it. The `Brushes` class contains a number of static `Brush` objects, each with a different common color. Internally, the `Brushes` class uses a lazy evaluation algorithm to create only those brushes you request. A simplified implementation looks like this:

```
private static Brush _blackBrush;
public static Brush Black
{
  get
  {
    if ( _blackBrush == null )
```

```
        _blackBrush = new SolidBrush( Color.Black );
        return _blackBrush;
    }
}
```

The first time you request a black brush, the Brushes class creates it. The Brushes class keeps a reference to the single black brush and returns that same handle whenever you request it again. The end result is that you create one black brush and reuse it forevermore. Furthermore, if your application does not need a particular resource—say, the lime green brush—it never gets created. The framework provides a way to limit the objects created to the minimum set you need to accomplish your goals. Copy that technique in your programs..

You've learned two techniques to minimize the number of allocations your program performs as it goes about its business. You can promote often-used local variables to member variables. You can provide a class that stores singleton objects that represent common instances of a given type. The last technique involves building the final value for immutable types. The System.String class is immutable: After you construct a string, the contents of that string cannot be modified. Whenever you write code that appears to modify the contents of a string, you are actually creating a new string object and leaving the old string object as garbage. This seemingly innocent practice:

```
string msg = "Hello, ";
msg += thisUser.Name;
msg += ". Today is ";
msg += System.DateTime.Now.ToString();
```

is just as inefficient as if you had written this:

```
string msg = "Hello, ";
// Not legal, for illustration only:
string tmp1 = new String( msg + thisUser.Name );
string msg = tmp1; // "Hello " is garbage.
string tmp2 = new String( msg + ". Today is " );
msg = tmp2; // "Hello <user>" is garbage.
string tmp3 = new String( msg + DateTime.Now.ToString( ) );
msg = tmp3;// "Hello <user>. Today is " is garbage.
```

The strings tmp1, tmp2, and tmp3, and the originally constructed msg ("Hello"), are all garbage. The += method on the string class creates a new string object and returns that string. It does not modify the existing string by concatenating the characters to the original storage. For simple constructs such as the previous one, you should use the `string.Format()` method:

```
string msg = string.Format ( "Hello, {0}. Today is {1}",
  thisUser.Name, DateTime.Now.ToString( ));
```

For more complicated string operations, you can use the `StringBuilder` class:

```
StringBuilder msg = new StringBuilder( "Hello, " );
msg.Append( thisUser.Name );
msg.Append( ". Today is " );
msg.Append( DateTime.Now.ToString());
string finalMsg = msg.ToString();
```

`StringBuilder` is the mutable string class used to build an immutable string object. It provides facilities for mutable strings that let you create and modify text data before you construct an immutable string object. Use `StringBuilder` to create the final version of a string object. More important, learn from that design idiom. When your designs call for immutable types (see Item 7), consider creating builder objects to facilitate the multiphase construction of the final object. That provides a way for users of your class to construct an object in steps, yet maintain the immutability of your type.

The Garbage Collector does an efficient job of managing the memory that your application uses. But remember that creating and destroying heap objects still takes time. Avoid creating excessive objects; don't create what you don't need. Also avoid creating multiple objects of reference types in local functions. Instead, consider promoting local variables to member variables, or create static objects of the most common instances of your types. Finally, consider creating mutable builder classes for immutable types.

Item 17: Minimize Boxing and Unboxing

Value types are containers for data. They are not polymorphic types. On the other hand, the .NET Framework was designed with a single reference type, `System.Object`, at the root of the entire object hierarchy. These two goals are at odds. The .NET Framework uses **boxing** and **unboxing** to bridge the gap between these two goals. Boxing places a value type in an untyped reference object to allow the value type to be used where a reference type is expected. Unboxing extracts a copy of that value type from the box. Boxing and unboxing are necessary for you to use value types where the System.Object type is expected. But boxing and unboxing are always performance-robbing operations. Sometimes, when boxing and unboxing also create temporary copies of objects, it can lead to subtle bugs in your programs. Avoid boxing and unboxing when possible.

Boxing converts a value type to a reference type. A new reference object, the box, is allocated on the heap, and a copy of the value type is stored inside that reference object. See Figure 2.3 for an illustration of how the boxed object is stored and accessed. The box contains the copy of the value type object and duplicates the interfaces implemented by the boxed value type. When you need to retrieve anything from the box, a copy of the value type gets created and returned. That's the key concept of boxing and unboxing: A copy of the object goes in the box, and another gets created whenever you access what's in the box.

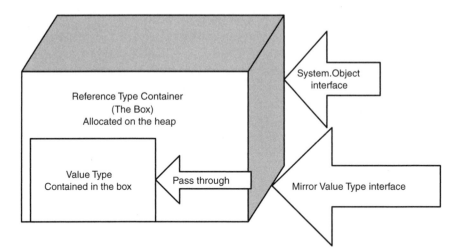

Figure 2.3   Value type in a box. To convert a value type into a *System.Object* reference, an unnamed reference type is created. The value type is stored inline inside the unnamed reference type. All methods that access the value type are passed through the box to the stored value type.

The insidious problem with boxing and unboxing is that it happens automatically. The compiler generates the boxing and unboxing statements whenever you use a value type where a reference type, such as

System.Object is expected. In addition, the boxing and unboxing operations occur when you use a value type through an interface pointer. You get no warnings—boxing just happens. Even a simple statement such as this performs boxing:

```
Console.WriteLine("A few numbers:{0}, {1}, {2}",
  25, 32, 50);
```

The referenced overload of Console.WriteLine takes an array of System.Object references. Ints are value types and must be boxed so that they can be passed to this overload of the WriteLine method. The only way to coerce the three integer arguments into System.Object is to box them. In addition, inside WriteLine, code reaches inside the box to call the ToString() method of the object in the box. In a sense, you have generated this construct:

```
int i =25;
object o = i; // box
Console.WriteLine(o.ToString());
```

Inside WriteLine, the following code executes:

```
object o;
int i = ( int )o; // unbox
string output = i.ToString( );
```

You would never write this code yourself. However, by letting the compiler automatically convert from a specific value type to System.Object, you did let it happen. The compiler was just trying to help you. It wants you to succeed. It happily generates the boxing and unboxing statements necessary to convert any value type into an instance of System.Object. To avoid this particular penalty, you should convert your types to string instances yourself before you send them to WriteLine:

```
Console.WriteLine("A few numbers:{0}, {1}, {2}",
  25.ToString(), 32.ToString(), 50.ToString());
```

This code uses the known type of integer, and value types (integers) are never implicitly converted to System.Object. This common example illustrates the first rule to avoid boxing: Watch for implicit conversions to System.Object. Value types should not be substituted for System.Object if you can avoid it.

Another common case in which you might inadvertently substitute a value type for System.Object is when you place value types in .NET 1.*x* collections. This incarnation of the .NET Framework collections store references to System.Object instances. Anytime you add a value type to a collection, it goes in a box. Anytime you remove an object from a collection, it gets copied from the box. Taking an object out of the box always makes a copy. That introduces some subtle bugs in your application. The compiler does not help you find these bugs. It's all because of boxing. Start with a simple structure that lets you modify one of its fields, and put some of those objects in a collection:

```
public struct Person
{
  private string _Name;

  public string Name
  {
    get
    {
      return _Name;
    }
    set
    {
      _Name = value;
    }
  }

  public override string ToString( )
  {
    Return _Name;
  }
}


// Using the Person in a collection:
ArrayList attendees = new ArrayList( );
Person p = new Person( "Old Name" );
attendees.Add( p );

// Try to change the name:
// Would work if Person was a reference type.
```

```
Person p2 = (( Person )attendees[ 0 ] );
p2.Name = "New Name";

// Writes "Old Name":
Console.WriteLine(
  attendees[ 0 ].ToString( ));
```

Person is a value type; it gets placed in a box before being stored in the ArrayList. That makes a copy. Then another copy gets made when you remove the Person object to access the Name property to change. All you did was change the copy. In fact, a third copy was made to call the ToString() function through the attendees[0] object.

For this and many other reasons, you should create immutable value types (see Item 7). If you must have a mutable value type in a collection, use the System.Array class, which is type safe.

If an array is not the proper collection, you can fix this error in C# 1.*x* by using interfaces. By coding to interfaces rather than the type's public methods, you can reach inside the box to make the change to the values:

```
public interface IPersonName
{
  string Name
  {
    get; set;
  }
}

struct Person : IPersonName
{
  private string _Name;

  public string Name
  {
    get
    {
      return _Name;
    }
    set
    {
      _Name = value;
```

```
      }
   }

   public override string ToString( )
   {
      return _Name;
   }
}


// Using the Person in a collection:
ArrayList attendees = new ArrayList( );
Person p = new Person( "Old Name" );
attendees.Add( p ); // box

// Try to change the name:
// Use the interface, not the type.
// No Unbox needed
(( IPersonName )attendees[ 0 ] ).Name = "New Name";

// Writes "New Name":
Console.WriteLine(
   attendees[ 0 ].ToString( )); // unbox
```

The box reference type implements all the interfaces implemented by the original object. That means no copy is made, but you call the IPerson-Name.Name method on the box, which forwards the request to the boxed value type. Creating interfaces on your value types enables you to reach inside the box to change the value stored in the collection. Implementing an interface is not really treating a value type polymorphically, which reintroduces the boxing penalty (see Item 20).

Many of these limitations change with the introduction of generics in C# 2.0 (see Item 49). Generic interfaces and generic collections will address the both the collection and the interface situations. Until then, though, avoid boxing. Yes, value types can be converted to System.Object or any interface reference. That conversion happens implicitly, complicating the task of finding them. Those are the rules of the environment and the language. The boxing and unboxing operations make copies where you might not expect. That causes bugs. There is also a performance cost to treating value types polymorphically. Be on the lookout for any constructs that convert value types to either `System.Object` or interface types: placing values in collections, calling methods defined in `System.Object`, and casts to `System.Object`. Avoid these whenever you can.

Item 18: Implement the Standard Dispose Pattern

We've discussed the importance of disposing of objects that hold unmanaged resources. Now it's time to cover how to write your own resource-management code when you create types that contain resources other than memory. A standard pattern is used throughout the .NET Framework for disposing of nonmemory resources. The users of your type will expect you to follow this standard pattern. The standard dispose idiom frees your unmanaged resources using the `IDisposable` interface when clients remember, and it uses the finalizer defensively when clients forget. It works with the Garbage Collector to ensure that your objects pay the performance penalty associated with finalizers only when necessary. This is the right way to handle unmanaged resources, so it pays to understand it thoroughly.

The root base class in the class hierarchy should implement the `IDispos-able` interface to free resources. This type should also add a finalizer as a defensive mechanism. Both of these routines delegate the work of freeing resources to a virtual method that derived classes can override for their own resource-management needs. The derived classes need override the virtual method only when the derived class must free its own resources and it must remember to call the base class version of the function.

To begin, your class must have a finalizer if it uses nonmemory resources. You should not rely on clients to always call the `Dispose()` method. You'll leak resources when they forget. It's their fault for not calling `Dis-pose`, but you'll get the blame. The only way you can guarantee that non-memory resources get freed properly is to create a finalizer. So create one.

When the Garbage Collector runs, it immediately removes from memory any garbage objects that do not have finalizers. All objects that have finalizers remain in memory. These objects are added to a finalization queue, and the Garbage Collector spawns a new thread to run the finalizers on those objects. After the finalizer thread has finished its work, the garbage objects can be removed from memory. Objects that need finalization stay in memory for far longer than objects without a finalizer. But you have no choice. If you're going to be defensive, you must write a finalizer when your type holds unmanaged resources. But don't worry about perform- ance just yet. The next steps ensure that it's easier for clients to avoid the performance penalty associated with finalization.

Implementing IDisposable is the standard way to inform users and the runtime system that your objects hold resources that must be released in a timely manner. The IDisposable interface contains just one method:

```
public interface IDisposable
{
  void Dispose( );
}
```

The implementation of your IDisposable.Dispose() method is resp- onsible for four tasks:

1. Freeing all unmanaged resources.
2. Freeing all managed resources (this includes unhooking events).
3. Setting a state flag to indicate that the object has been disposed. You need to check this state and throw ObjectDisposed exceptions in your public methods, if any get called after disposing of an object.
4. Suppressing finalization. You call GC.SuppressFinalize(this) to accomplish this task.

You accomplish two things by implementing IDisposable: You provide the mechanism for clients to release all managed resources that you hold in a timely fashion, and you give clients a standard way to release all unmanaged resources. That's quite an improvement. After you've imple- mented IDisposable in your type, clients can avoid the finalization cost. Your class is a reasonably well-behaved member of the .NET community.

But there are still holes in the mechanism you've created. How does a derived class clean up its resources and still let a base class clean up as well? If derived classes override finalize or add their own implementa- tion of IDisposable, those methods must call the base class; otherwise, the base class doesn't clean up properly. Also, finalize and Dispose share some of the same responsibilities: You have almost certainly dupli- cated code between the finalize method and the Dispose method. As you'll learn in Item 26, overriding interface functions does not work the way you'd expect. The third method in the standard Dispose pattern, a protected virtual helper function, factors out these common tasks and adds a hook for derived classes to free resources they allocate. The base class contains the code for the core interface. The virtual function provides the hook for derived classes to clean up resources in response to `Dispose()` or finalization:

```
protected virtual void Dispose( bool isDisposing );
```

This overloaded method does the work necessary to support both `finalize` and `Dispose`, and because it is virtual, it provides an entry point for all derived classes. Derived classes can override this method, provide the proper implementation to clean up their resources, and call the base class version. You clean up managed and unmanaged resources when `isDisposing` is `true`; clean up only unmanaged resources when `isDisposing` is `false`. In both cases, call the base class's `Dispose(bool)` method to let it clean up its own resources.

Here is a short sample that shows the framework of code you supply when you implement this pattern. The `MyResourceHog` class shows the code to implement `IDisposable`, a finalizer, and create the virtual `Dispose` method:

```
public class MyResourceHog : IDisposable
{
  // Flag for already disposed
  private bool _alreadyDisposed = false;

  // finalizer:
  // Call the virtual Dispose method.
  ~MyResourceHog()
  {
    Dispose( false );
  }

  // Implementation of IDisposable.
  // Call the virtual Dispose method.
  // Suppress Finalization.
  public void Dispose()
  {
    Dispose( true );
    GC.SuppressFinalize( true );
  }
```

```
// Virtual Dispose method
protected virtual void Dispose( bool isDisposing )
{
  // Don't dispose more than once.
  if ( _alreadyDisposed )
    return;
  if ( isDisposing )
  {
    // TODO: free managed resources here.
  }
  // TODO: free unmanaged resources here.
  // Set disposed flag:
  _alreadyDisposed = true;
  }
}
```

If a derived class needs to perform additional cleanup, it implements the protected Dispose method:

```
public class DerivedResourceHog : MyResourceHog
{
  // Have its own disposed flag.
  private bool _disposed = false;

  protected override void Dispose( bool isDisposing )
  {
    // Don't dispose more than once.
    if ( _disposed )
      return;
    if ( isDisposing )
    {
      // TODO: free managed resources here.
    }
    // TODO: free unmanaged resources here.

    // Let the base class free its resources.
    // Base class is responsible for calling
    // GC.SuppressFinalize( )
    base.Dispose( isDisposing );
```

```
    // Set derived class disposed flag:
    _disposed = true;
  }
}
```

Notice that both the base class and the derived class contain a flag for the disposed state of the object. This is purely defensive. Duplicating the flag encapsulates any possible mistakes made while disposing of an object to only the one type, not all types that make up an object.

You need to write `Dispose` and `finalize` defensively. Disposing of objects can happen in any order. You will encounter cases in which one of the member objects in your type is already disposed of before your `Dispose()` method gets called. You should not view that as a problem because the `Dispose()` method can be called multiple times. If it's called on an object that has already been disposed of, it does nothing. Finalizers have similar rules. Any object that you reference is still in memory, so you don't need to check null references. However, any object that you reference might be disposed of. It might also have already been finalized.

This brings me to the most important recommendation for any method associated with disposal or cleanup: You should be releasing resources only. Do not perform any other processing during a dispose method. You can introduce serious complications to object lifetimes by performing other processing in your `Dispose` or `finalize` methods. Objects are born when you construct them, and they die when the Garbage Collector reclaims them. You can consider them comatose when your program can no longer access them. If you can't reach an object, you can't call any of its methods. For all intents and purposes, it is dead. But objects that have finalizers get to breathe a last breath before they are declared dead. Finalizers should do nothing but clean up unmanaged resources. If a finalizer somehow makes an object reachable again, it has been *resurrected*. It's alive and not well, even though it has awoken from a comatose state. Here's an obvious example:

```
public class BadClass
{
  // Store a reference to a global object:
  private readonly ArrayList _finalizedList;
  private string _msg;
```

```
public BadClass( ArrayList badList, string msg )
{
  // cache the reference:
  _finalizedList = badList;
  _msg = (string)msg.Clone();
}

~BadClass()
{
  // Add this object to the list.
  // This object is reachable, no
  // longer garbage. It's Back!
  _finalizedList.Add( this );
}
}
```

When a BadClass object executes its finalizer, it puts a reference to itself on a global list. It has just made itself reachable. It's alive again! The number of problems you've just introduced will make anyone cringe. The object has been finalized, so the Garbage Collector now believes there is no need to call its finalizer again. If you actually need to finalize a resurrected object, it won't happen. Second, some of your resources might not be available. The GC will not remove from memory any objects that are reachable only by objects in the finalizer queue, but it might have already finalized them. If so, they are almost certainly no longer usable. Although the members that BadClass owns are still in memory, they will have likely been disposed of or finalized. There is no way in the language that you can control the order of finalization. You cannot make this kind of construct work reliably. Don't try.

I've never seen code that has resurrected objects in such an obvious fashion, except as an academic exercise. But I have seen code in which the finalizer attempts to do some real work and ends up bringing itself back to life when some function that the finalizer calls saves a reference to the object. The moral is to look very carefully at any code in a finalizer and, by extension, both Dispose methods. If that code is doing anything other than releasing resources, look again. Those actions likely will cause bugs in your program in the future. Remove those actions, and make sure that finalizers and Dispose() methods release resources and do nothing else.

In a managed environment, you do not need to write a finalizer for every type you create; you do it only for types that store unmanaged types or when your type contains members that implement IDisposable. Even if you need only the Disposable interface, not a finalizer, implement the entire pattern. Otherwise, you limit your derived classes by complicating their implementation of the standard Dispose idiom. Follow the standard Dispose idiom I've described. That will make life easier for you, for the users of your class, and for those who create derived classes from your types.

3 | Expressing Designs with C#

The C# language introduced new syntax to describe your designs. The techniques you choose communicate your design intent to the developers who maintain, extend, or use the software you develop. C# types all live inside the .NET environment. The environment makes some assumptions about the capabilities of all types as well. If you violate those assumptions, you increase the likelihood that your types won't function correctly.

These items are not a compendium of software design techniques—entire volumes have been written about software design. Instead, these items highlight how different C# language features can best express the intent of your software design. The C# language designers added language features to more clearly express modern design idioms. The distinctions among certain language features are subtle, and you often have many alternatives to choose from. More than one alternative might seem "best" at first; the distinctions show up only later, when you find that you must enhance an existing program. Make sure you understand these items well, and apply them carefully with an eye toward the most likely enhancements to the systems you are building.

Some syntax changes give you new vocabulary to describe the idioms you use everyday. Properties, indexers, events, and delegates are examples, as is the difference between classes and interfaces: Classes *define* types. Interfaces *declare* behavior. Base classes *declare* types and *define* common behavior for a related set of types. Other design idioms have changed because of the garbage collector. Still others have changed because most variables are reference types.

The recommendations in this chapter will help you pick the most natural expression for your designs. This will enable you to create software that is easier to maintain, easier to extend, and easier to use.

Item 19: Prefer Defining and Implementing Interfaces to Inheritance

Abstract base classes provide a common ancestor for a class hierarchy. An interface describes one atomic piece of functionality that can be implemented by a type. Each has its place, but it is a different place. Interfaces are a way to design by contract: A type that implements an interface must supply an implementation for expected methods. Abstract base classes provide a common abstraction for a set of related types. It's a cliché, but it's one that works: Inheritance means "is a," and interfaces means "behaves like." These clichés have lived so long because they provide a means to describe the differences in both constructs: Base classes describe what an object is; interfaces describe one way in which it behaves.

Interfaces describe a set of functionality, or a contract. You can create placeholders for anything in an interface: methods, properties,indexers, and events. Any type that implements the interface must supply concrete implementations of all elements defined in the interface. You must implement all methods, supply any and all property accessors and indexers, and define all events defined in the interface. You identify and factor reusable behavior into interfaces. You use interfaces as parameters and return values. You also have more chances to reuse code because unrelated types can implement interfaces. What's more, it's easier for other developers to implement an interface than it is to derive from a base class you've created.

What you can't do in an interface is provide implementation for any of these members. Interfaces contain no implementation whatsoever,and they cannot contain any concrete data members. You are declaring the contract that must be supported by all types that implement an interface.

Abstract base classes can supply some implementation for derived types, in addition to describing the common behavior. You can specify data members, concrete methods, implementation for virtual methods, properties, events, and indexers. A base class can provide implementation for some of the methods, thereby providing common implementation reuse. Any of the elements can be virtual, abstract, or nonvirtual. An abstract base class can provide an implementation for any concrete behavior; interfaces cannot.

This implementation reuse provides another benefit: If you add a method to the base class, all derived classes are automatically and implicitly enhanced. In that sense, base classes provide a way to extend the behavior of several types efficiently over time: By adding and implementing functionality in the base class, all derived classes immediately incorporate that behavior. Adding a member to an interface breaks all the classes that implement that interface. They will not contain the new method and will no longer compile. Each implementer must update that type to include the new member.

Choosing between an abstract base class and an interface is a question of how best to support your abstractions over time. Interfaces are fixed: You release an interface as a contract for a set of functionality that any type can implement. Base classes can be extended over time. Those extensions become part of every derived class.

The two models can be mixed to reuse implementation code while supporting multiple interfaces. One such example is System.Collections.CollectionBase.. This class provides a base class that you can use to shield clients from the lack of type safety in .NET collections. As such, it implements several interfaces on your behalf: IList, ICollection, and IEnumerable. In addition, it provides protected methods that you can override to customize the behavior for different uses. The IList interface contains the Insert() method to add a new object to a collection. Rather than provide your own implementation of Insert, you process those events by overriding the OnInsert() or OnInsertCcomplete() virtual methods of the CollectionBase class.

```
public class IntList : System.Collections.CollectionBase
{
  protected override void OnInsert( int index, object value )
  {
    try
    {
      int newValue = System.Convert.ToInt32( value );
      Console.WriteLine( "Inserting {0} at position {1}",
        index.ToString(), value.ToString());
        Console.WriteLine( "List Contains {0} items",
        this.List.Count.ToString());
    }
```

```
      catch( FormatException e )
      {
        throw new ArgumentException(
          "Argument Type not an integer",
          "value", e );
      }
    }

    protected override void OnInsertComplete( int index,
      object value )
    {
      Console.WriteLine( "Inserted {0} at position {1}",
        index.ToString( ), value.ToString( ));
      Console.WriteLine( "List Contains {0} items",
        this.List.Count.ToString( ) );
    }
  }


  public class MainProgram
  {
    public static void Main()
    {
      IntList l = new IntList();
      IList il = l as IList;
      il.Insert( 0,3 );
      il.Insert( 0, "This is bad" );
    }
  }
```

The previous code creates an integer array list and uses the IList interface pointer to add two different values to the collection. By overriding the OnInsert() method, the IntList class tests the type of the inserted value and throws an exception when the type is not an integer. The base class provides the default implementation and gives you hooks to specialize the behavior in your derived classes.

CollectionBase, the base class, gives you an implementation that you can use for your own classes. You need not write nearly as much code because you can make use of the common implementation provided. But the public API for IntList comes from the interfaces implemented by CollectionBase: the IEnumerable, ICollection, and IList interfaces. `CollectionBase` provides a common implementation for the interfaces that you can reuse.

That brings me to the topic of using interfaces as parameters and return values. An interface can be implemented by any number of unrelated types. Coding to interfaces provides greater flexibility to other developers than coding to base class types. That's important because of the single inheritance hierarchy that the .NET environment enforces.

These two methods perform the same task:

```
public void PrintCollection( IEnumerable collection )
{
  foreach( object o in collection )
  Console.WriteLine( "Collection contains {0}",
    o.ToString( ) );
}


public void PrintCollection( CollectionBase collection )
{
  foreach( object o in collection )
  Console.WriteLine( "Collection contains {0}",
    o.ToString( ) );
}
```

The second method is far less reusable. It cannot be used with `Arrays`, `ArrayLists`, `DataTables`, `Hashtables`, `ImageLists`, or many other collection classes. Coding the method using interfaces as its parameter types is far more generic and far easier to reuse.

Using interfaces to define the APIs for a class also provides greater flexibility. For example, many applications use a `DataSet` to transfer data between the components of your application. It's too easy to code that assumption into place permanently:

```
public DataSet TheCollection
{
  get { return _dataSetCollection; }
}
```

That leaves you vulnerable to future problems. At some point, you might change from using a `DataSet` to exposing one `DataTable`, using a

DataView, or even creating your own custom object. Any of those changes will break the code. Sure, you can change the parameter type, but that's changing the public interface to your class. Changing the public interface to a class causes you to make many more changes to a large system; you would need to change all the locations where the public property was accessed.

The second problem is more immediate and more troubling: The DataSet class provides numerous methods to change the data it contains. Users of your class could delete tables, modify columns, or even replace every object in the DataSet. That's almost certainly not your intent. Luckily, you can limit the capabilities of the users of your class. Instead of returning a reference to the DataSet type, you should return the interface you intend clients to use. The DataSet supports the IListSource interface, which it uses for data binding:

```
using System.ComponentModel;

public IListSource TheCollection
{
  get { return _dataSetCollection as IListSource; }
}
```

IListSource lets clients view items through the GetList() method. It also has a ContainsListCollection property so that users can modify the overall structure of the collection. Using the IListSource interface, the individual items in the DataSet can be accessed, but the overall structure of the DataSet cannot be modified. Also, the caller cannot use the DataSet's methods to change the available actions on the data by removing constraints or adding capabilities.

When your type exposes properties as class types, it exposes the entire interface to that class. Using interfaces, you can choose to expose only the methods and properties you want clients to use. The class used to implement the interface is an implementation detail that can change over time (see Item 23).

Furthermore, unrelated types can implement the same interface. Suppose you're building an application that manages employees, customers, and vendors. Those are unrelated, at least in terms of the class hierarchy. But they share some common functionality. They all have names, and you will likely display those names in Windows controls in your applications.

```csharp
public class Employee
{
  public string Name
  {
    get
    {
      return string.Format( "{0}, {1}", _last, _first );
    }
  }

  // other details elided.
}

public class Customer
{
  public string Name
  {
    get
    {
      return _customerName;
    }
  }

  // other details elided
}

public class Vendor
{
  public string Name
  {
    get
    {
      return _vendorName;
    }
  }
}
```

The `Employee`, `Customer`, and `Vendor` classes should not share a common base class. But they do share some properties: names (as shown earlier), addresses, and contact phone numbers. You could factor out those properties into an interface:

```
public interface IContactInfo
{
  string Name { get; }
  PhoneNumber PrimaryContact { get; }
  PhoneNumber Fax { get; }
  Address PrimaryAddress { get; }
}


public class Employee : IContactInfo
{
  // implementation deleted.
}
```

This new interface can simplify your programming tasks by letting you build common routines for unrelated types:

```
public void PrintMailingLabel( IContactInfo ic )
{
  // implementation deleted.
}
```

This one routine works for all entities that implement the `IContactInfo` interface. `Customer`, `Employee`, and `Vendor` all use the same routine—but only because you factored them into interfaces.

Using interfaces also means that you can occasionally save an unboxing penalty for structs. When you place a struct in a box, the box supports all interfaces that the struct supports. When you access the struct through the interface pointer, you don't have to unbox the struct to access that object. To illustrate, imagine this struct that defines a link and a description:

```
public struct URLInfo : IComparable
{
  private string URL;
  private string description;

  public int CompareTo( object o )
  {
    if (o is URLInfo)
```

```
    {
      URLInfo other = ( URLInfo ) o;
      return CompareTo( other );
    }
    else
      throw new ArgumentException(
        "Compared object is not URLInfo" );
  }

  public int CompareTo( URLInfo other )
  {
    return URL.CompareTo( other.URL );
  }
}
```

You can create a sorted list of URLInfo objects because URLInfo implements IComparable. The URLInfo structs get boxed when added to the list. But the Sort() method does not need to unbox both objects to call CompareTo(). You still need to unbox the argument (other), but you don't need to unbox the left side of the compare to call the IComparable.CompareTo() method.

Base classes describe and implement common behaviors across related concrete types. Interfaces describe atomic pieces of functionality that unrelated concrete types can implement. Both have their place. Classes define the types you create. Interfaces describe the behavior of those types as pieces of functionality. If you understand the differences, you will create more expressive designs that are more resilient in the face of change. Use class hierarchies to define related types. Expose functionality using interfaces implemented across those types.

Item 20: Distinguish Between Implementing Interfaces and Overriding Virtual Functions

At first glance, implementing an interface seems to be the same as overriding avirtual function. You provide a definition for a member that has been declared in another type. That first glance is very deceiving. Implementing an interface is very different from overriding a virtual function. Members declared in interfaces are not virtual—at least, not by default.

Derived classes cannot override an interface member implemented in a base class. Interfaces can be explicitly implemented, which hides them from a class's public interface. They are different concepts with different uses.

But you can implement interfaces in such a manner that derived classes can modify your implementation. You just have to create hooks for derived classes.

To illustrate the differences, examine a simple interface and implementation of it in one class:

```
interface IMsg
{
  void Message();
}


public class MyClass : IMsg
{
  public void Message()
  {
    Console.WriteLine( "MyClass" );
  }
}
```

The `Message()` method is part of `MyClass`'s public interface. `Message` can also be accessed through the `IMsg` point that is part of the `MyClass` type. Now let's complicate the situation a little by adding a derived class:

```
public class MyDerivedClass : MyClass
{
  public new void Message()
  {
    Console.WriteLine( "MyDerivedClass" );
  }
}
```

Notice that I had to add the new keyword to the definition of the previous `Message` method (see Item 29). `MyClass.Message()` is not virtual. Derived classes cannot provide an overridden version of `Message`. The `MyDerived` class creates anew `Message` method, but that method does not override `MyClass.Message`: It hides it. Furthermore, `MyClass.` `Message` is still available through the `IMsg` reference:

```
MyDerivedClass d = new MyDerivedClass( );
d.Message( ); // prints "MyDerivedClass".
IMsg m = d as IMsg;
m.Message( ); // prints "MyClass"
```

Interface methods are not virtual. When you implement an interface, you are declaring a concrete implementation of a particular contract in that type.

But you often want to create interfaces, implement them in base classes, and modify the behavior in derived classes. You can. You've got two options. If you do not have access to the base class, you can reimplement the interface in the derived class:

```
public class MyDerivedClass : MyClass, IMsg
{
  public new void Message()
  {
    Console.WriteLine( "MyDerivedClass" );
  }
}
```

The addition of the `IMsg` keyword changes the behavior of your derived class so that `IMsg.Message()` now uses the derived class version:

```
MyDerivedClass d = new MyDerivedClass( );
d.Message( ); // prints "MyDerivedClass".
IMsg m = d as IMsg;
m.Message( ); // prints "MyDerivedClass"
```

You still need the new keyword on the `MyDerivedClass.Message()` method. That's your clue that there are still problems (see Item 29). The base class version is still accessible through a reference to the base class:

```
MyDerivedClass d = new MyDerivedClass( );
d.Message( ); // prints "MyDerivedClass".
IMsg m = d as IMsg;
m.Message( ); // prints "MyDerivedClass"
MyClass b = d;
b.Message( ); // prints "MyClass"
```

The only way to fix this problem is to modify the base class, declaring that the interface methods should be virtual:

```
public class MyClass : IMsg
{
  public virtual void Message()
  {
    Console.WriteLine( "MyClass" );
  }
}

public class MyDerivedClass : MyClass
{
  public override void Message()
  {
    Console.WriteLine( "MyDerivedClass" );
  }
}
```

MyDerivedClass—and all classes derived from MyClass—can declare their own methods for Message(). The overridden version will be called every time: through the MyDerivedClass reference, through the IMsg reference, and through the MyClass reference.

If you dislike the concept of impure virtual functions, just make one small change to the definition of MyClass:

```
public abstract class MyClass, IMsg
{
  public abstract void Message();
}
```

Yes, you can implement an interface without actually implementing the methods in that interface. By declaring abstract versions of the methods in the interface, you declare that all types derived from your type must implement that interface. The IMsg interface is part of the declaration of MyClass, but defining the methods is deferred to each derived class.

Explicit interface implementation enables you to implement an interface, yet hide its members from the public interface of your type. Its use throws a few other twists into the relationships between implementing interfaces and overriding virtual functions. You use explicit interface implementation to limit client code from using the interface methods when a more appropriate version is available. The IComparable idiom in Item 26 shows this in detail.

Implementing interfaces allows more options than creating and overriding virtual functions. You can create sealed implementations, virtual implementations, or abstract contracts for class hierarchies. You can decide exactly how and when derived classes can modify the default behavior for members of any interface your class implements. Interface methods are not virtual methods, but a separate contract.

Item 21: Express Callbacks with Delegates

> Me: "Son, go mow the yard. I'm going to read for a while."
> Scott: "Dad, I cleaned up the yard."
> Scott: "Dad, I put gas in the mower."
> Scott: "Dad, the mower won't start."
> Me: "I'll start it."
> Scott: "Dad, I'm done."

This little exchange illustrates callbacks. I gave my son a task, and he (repeatedly) interrupted me with the status. I did not block my own progress while I waited for him to finish each part of the task. He was able to interrupt me periodically when he had an important (or even unimportant) status to report or needed my assistance. Callbacks are used to provide feedback from a server to a client asynchronously. They might involve multithreading, or they might simply provide an entry point for synchronous updates. Callbacks are expressed using delegates in the C# language.

Delegates provide type-safe callback definitions. Although the most common use of delegates is events, that should not be the only time you use this language feature. Any time you need to configure the communication between classes and you desire less coupling than you get from interfaces, a delegate is the right choice. Delegates let you configure the target at runtime and notify multiple clients. A delegate is an object that contains a reference to a method. That method can be either a static method or an instance method. Using the delegate, you can communicate with one or many client objects, configured at runtime.

Multicast delegates wrap all the functions that have been added to the delegate in a single function call. Two caveats apply to this construct: It is not safe in the face of exceptions, and the return value will be the return value of the last function invocation.

Inside a multicast delegate invocation, each target is called in succession. The delegate does not catch any exceptions. Therefore, any exception that the target throws ends the delegate invocation chain.

A similar problem exists with return values. You can define delegates that have return types other than `void`. You could write a callback to check for user aborts:

```
public delegate bool ContinueProcessing();

public void LengthyOperation( ContinueProcessing pred )
{
  foreach( ComplicatedClass cl in _container )
  {
    cl.DoLengthyOperation();
    // Check for user abort:
    if (false == pred())
      return;
  }
}
```

It works as a single delegate, but using it as a multicast is problematic:

```
ContinueProcessing cp = new ContinueProcessing (
  CheckWithUser );
cp += new ContinueProcessing( CheckWithSystem );
c.LengthyOperation( cp );
```

The value returned from invoking the delegate is the return value from the last function in the multicast chain. All other return values are ignored. The return from the `CheckWithUser()` predicate is ignored.

You address both issues by invoking each delegate target yourself. Each delegate you create contains a list of delegates. To examine the chain yourself and call each one, iterate the invocation list yourself:

```
public delegate bool ContinueProcessing();

public void LengthyOperation( ContinueProcessing pred )
{
  bool bContinue = true;
```

```
foreach( ComplicatedClass cl in _container )
{
  cl.DoLengthyOperation();
  foreach( ContinueProcessing pr in
    pred.GetInvocationList( ))

    bContinue &= pr();

  if (false == bContinue)
    return;
}
}
```

In this case, I've defined the semantics so that each delegate must be true for the iteration to continue.

Delegates provide the best way to utilize callbacks at runtime, with simpler requirements on client classes. You can configure delegate targets at runtime. You can support multiple client targets. Client callbacks should be implemented using delegates in .NET.

Item 22: Define Outgoing Interfaces with Events

Events define the outgoing interface for your type. Events are built on delegates to provide type-safe function signatures for event handlers. Add to this the fact that most examples that use delegates are events, and developers start thinking that events and delegates are the same things. In Item 21, I showed you examples of when you can use delegates without defining events. You should raise events when your type must communicate with multiple clients to inform them of actions in the system.

Consider a simple example. You're building a log class that acts as a dispatcher of all messages in an application. It will accept all messages from sources in your application and will dispatch those messages to any interested listeners. These listeners might be attached to the console, a database, the system log, or some other mechanism. You define the class as follows, to raise one event whenever a message arrives:

```
public class LoggerEventArgs : EventArgs
{
  public readonly string Message;
  public readonly int Priority;
```

```csharp
    public LoggerEventArgs ( int p, string m )
    {
      Priority = p;
      Message = m;
    }
}

// Define the signature for the event handler:
public delegate void AddMessageEventHandler( object sender,
  LoggerEventArgs msg );

public class Logger
{
  static Logger( )
  {
    _theOnly = new Logger( );
  }

  private Logger( )
  {
  }

  private static Logger _theOnly = null;
  public Logger Singleton
  {
    get
    {
      return _theOnly;
    }
  }

  // Define the event:
  public event AddMessageEventHandler Log;

  // add a message, and log it.
  public void AddMsg ( int priority, string msg )
  {
    // This idiom discussed below.
```

```
      AddMessageEventHandler l = Log;
      if ( l != null )
        l ( null, new LoggerEventArgs( priority, msg ) );
  }
}
```

The `AddMsg` method shows the proper way to raise events. The temporary variable to reference the log event handler is an important safeguard against race conditions in multithreaded programs. Without the copy of the reference, clients could remove event handlers between the `if` statement check and the execution of the event handler. By copying the reference, that can't happen.

I've defined `LoggerEventArgs` to hold the priority of an event and the message. The delegate defines the signature for the event handler. Inside the `Logger` class, the event field defines the event handler. The compiler sees the public event field definition and creates the `Add` and `Remove` operators for you. The generated code is exactly the same as though you had written the following:

```
public class Logger
{
  private AddMessageEventHandler _Log;

  public event AddMessageEventHandler Log
  {
    add
    {
      _Log = _Log + value;
    }
    remove
    {
      _Log = _Log - value;
    }
  }

    public void AddMsg (int priority, string msg)
    {
      AddMessageEventHandler l = _Log;
      if (l != null)
        l (null, new LoggerEventArgs (priority, msg));
```

```
      }
    }
  }
```

The C# compiler creates the add and remove accessors for the event. I find the public event declaration language more concise, easier to read and maintain, and more correct. When you create events in your class, declare public events and let the compiler create the add and remove properties for you. You can and should write these handlers yourself when you have additional rules to enforce.

Events do not need to have any knowledge about the potential listeners. The following class automatically routes all messages to the Standard Error console:

```
class ConsoleLogger
{
  static ConsoleLogger()
  {
    logger.Log += new AddMessageEventHandler( Logger_Log );
  }

  private static void Logger_Log( object sender,
    LoggerEventArgs msg )
  {
    Console.Error.WriteLine( "{0}:\t{1}",
      msg.Priority.ToString(),
      msg.Message );
  }
}
```

Another class could direct output to the system event log:

```
class EventLogger
{
  private static string eventSource;
  private static EventLog logDest;

  static EventLogger()
  {
    logger.Log +=new AddMessageEventHandler( Event_Log );
  }
```

```
public static string EventSource
{
  get
  {
    return eventSource;
  }

  set
  {
    eventSource = value;
    if ( ! EventLog.SourceExists( eventSource ) )
      EventLog.CreateEventSource( eventSource,
        "ApplicationEventLogger" );

    if ( logDest != null )
      logDest.Dispose( );
    logDest = new EventLog( );
    logDest.Source = eventSource;
  }
}

private static void Event_Log( object sender,
  LoggerEventArgs msg )
{
  if ( logDest != null )
    logDest.WriteEntry( msg.Message,
      EventLogEntryType.Information,
      msg.Priority );
}
}
```

Events notify any number of interested clients that something happened. The Logger class does not need any prior knowledge of which objects are interested in logging events.

The Logger class contained only one event. There are classes (mostly Windows controls) that have very large numbers of events. In those cases, the idea of using one field per event might be unacceptable. In some cases, only a small number of the defined events is actually used in any one application. When you encounter that situation, you can modify the design to create the event objects only when needed at runtime.

The core framework contains examples of how to do this in the Windows control subsystem. To show you how, add subsystems to the `Logger` class. You create an event for each subsystem. Clients register on the event that is pertinent to their subsystem.

The extended `Logger` class has a `System.ComponentModel.EventHandlerList` container that stores all the event objects that should be raised for a given system. The updated `AddMsg()` method now takes a string parameter that specifies the subsystem generating the log message. If the subsystem has any listeners, the event gets raised. Also, if an event listener has registered an interest in all messages, its event gets raised:

```
public class Logger
{
  private static System.ComponentModel.EventHandlerList
    Handlers = new System.ComponentModel.EventHandlerList();

  static public void AddLogger(
    string system, AddMessageEventHandler ev )
  {
    Handlers[ system ] = ev;
  }

  static public void RemoveLogger( string system )
  {
    Handlers[ system ] = null;
  }

  static public void AddMsg ( string system,
    int priority,  string msg )
  {
    if ( ( system != null ) && ( system.Length > 0 ) )
    {
      AddMessageEventHandler l =
        Handlers[ system ] as AddMessageEventHandler;

      LoggerEventArgs args = new LoggerEventArgs(
        priority, msg );
```

```
      if ( l != null )
        l ( null, args );

      // The empty string means receive all messages:
      l = Handlers[ "" ] as AddMessageEventHandler;
      if ( l != null )
        l( null, args );
    }
  }
}
```

This new example stores the individual event handlers in the `Event-HandlerList` collection. Client code attaches to a specific subsystem, and a new event object is created. Subsequent requests for the same subsystem retrieve the same event object. If you develop a class that contains a large number of events in its interface, you should consider using this collection of event handlers. You create event members when clients attach to the event handler on their choice. Inside the .NET Framework, the `System.Windows.Forms.Control` class uses a more complicated variation of this implementation to hide the complexity of all its event fields. Each event field internally accesses a collection of objects to add and remove the particular handlers. You can find more information that shows this idiom in the C# language specification (see Item 49).

You define outgoing interfaces in classes with events: Any number of clients can attach handlers to the events and process them. Those clients need not be known at compile time. Events don't need subscribers for the system to function properly. Using events in C# decouples the sender and the possible receivers of notifications. The sender can be developed completely independently of any receivers. Events are the standard way to broadcast information about actions that your type has taken.

Item 23: Avoid Returning References to Internal Class Objects

You'd like to think that a read-only property is read-only and that callers can't modify it. Unfortunately, that's not always the way it works. If you create a property that returns a reference type, the caller can access any public member of that object, including those that modify the state of the property. For example:

```
public class MyBusinessObject
{
  // Read Only property providing access to a
  // private data member:
  private DataSet _ds;
  public DataSet Data
  {
    get
    {
      return _ds;
    }
  }
}


// Access the dataset:
DataSet ds = bizObj.Data;
// Not intended, but allowed:
ds.Tables.Clear( ); // Deletes all data tables.
```

Any public client of `MyBusinessObject` can modify your internal dataset. You created properties to hide your internal data structures. You provided methods to let clients manipulate the data only through known methods, so your class can manage any changes to internal state. And then a read-only property opens a gaping hole in your class encapsulation. It's not a read-write property, where you would consider these issues, but a read-only property.

Welcome to the wonderful world of reference-based systems. Any member that returns a reference type returns a handle to that object. You gave the caller a handle to your internal structures, so the caller no longer needs to go through your object to modify that contained reference.

Clearly, you want to prevent this kind of behavior. You built the interface to your class, and you want users to follow it. You don't want users to access or modify the internal state of your objects without your knowledge. You've got four different strategies for protecting your internal data structures from unintended modifications: value types, immutable types, interfaces, and wrappers.

Value types are copied when clients access them through a property. Any changes to the copy retrieved by the clients of your class do not affect your object's internal state. Clients can change the copy as much as necessary to achieve their purpose. This does not affect your internal state.

Immutable types, such as System.String, are also safe. You can return strings, or any immutable type, safely knowing that no client of your class can modify the string. Your internal state is safe.

The third option is to define interfaces that allow clients to access a subset of your internal member's functionality (see Item 19). When you create your own classes, you can create sets of interfaces that support subsets of the functionality of your class. By exposing the functionality through those interfaces, you minimize the possibility that your internal data changes in ways you did not intend. Clients can access the internal object through the interface you supplied, which will not include the full functionality of the class. Exposing the IListsource interface pointer in the DataSet is one example of this strategy. The Machiavellian programmers out there can defeat that by guessing the type of the object that implements the interface and using a cast. But programmers who go to that much work to create bugs get what they deserve.

The System.Dataset class also uses the last strategy: wrapper objects. The DataViewManager class provides a way to access the DataSet but prevents the mutator methods available through the DataSet class:

```
public class MyBusinessObject
{
  // Read Only property providing access to a
  // private data member:
  private DataSet _ds;
  public DataView this[ string tableName ]
  {
    get
    {
      return _ds.DefaultViewManager.
        CreateDataView( _ds.Tables[ tableName ] );
    }
  }
}
```

```
// Access the dataset:
DataView list = bizObj[ "customers" ];
foreach ( DataRowView r in list )
  Console.WriteLine( r[ "name" ] );
```

The `DataViewManager` creates `DataViews` to access individual data tables in the `DataSet`. There is no way for the user of your class to modify the tables in your `DataSet` through the DataViewManager. Each `DataView` can be configured to allow the modification of individual data elements. But the client cannot change the tables or columns of data. Read/write is the default, so clients can still add, modify, or delete individual items.

Before we talk about how to create a completely read-only view of the data, let's take a brief look at how you can respond to changes in your data when you allow public clients to modify it. This is important because you'll often want to export a `DataView` to UI controls so that the user can edit the data (see Item 38). You've undoubtedly already used Windows forms data binding to provide the means for your users to edit private data in your objects. The `DataTable` class, inside the `DataSet`, raises events that make it easy to implement the observer pattern: Your classes can respond to any changes that other clients of your class have made. The `DataTable` objects inside your `DataSet` will raise events when any column or row changes in that table. The `ColumnChanging` and `RowChanging` events are raised before an edit is committed to the `DataTable`. The `ColumnChanged` and `RowChanged` events are raised after the change is committed.

You can generalize this technique anytime you want to expose internal data elements for modification by public clients, but you need to validate and respond to those changes. Your class subscribes to events generated by your internal data structure. Event handlers validate changes or respond to those changes by updating other internal state.

Going back to the original problem, you want to let clients view your data but not make any changes. When your data is stored in a `DataSet`, you can enforce that by creating a `DataView` for a table that does not allow any changes. The `DataView` class contains properties that let you customize support for add, delete, modification, or even sorting of the particular table. You can create an indexer to return a customized `DataView` on the requested table using an indexer:

```
public class MyBusinessObject
{
  // Read Only property providing access to a
  // private data member:
  private DataSet _ds;
  public IList this[ string tableName ]
  {
    get
    {
      DataView view =
        _ds.DefaultViewManager.CreateDataView
        ( _ds.Tables[ tableName ] );
      view.AllowNew = false;
      view.AllowDelete = false;
      view.AllowEdit = false;
      return view;
    }
  }
}


// Access the dataset:
    IList dv = bizOjb[ "customers" ];
    foreach ( DataRowView r in dv )
      Console.WriteLine( r[ "name" ] );
```

This final excerpt of the class returns the view into a particular data table through its `IList` interface reference. You can use the `IList` interface with any collection; it's not specific to the `DataSet`. You should not simply return the `DataView` object. Users could easily enable the editing and add/delete capability again. The view you are returning has been customized to disallow any modifications to the objects in the list. Returning the `IList` pointer keeps clients from modifying the rights they have been given to the `DataView` object.

Exposing reference types through your public interface allows users of your object to modify its internals without going through the methods and properties you've defined. That seems counterintuitive, which makes it a common mistake. You need to modify your class's interfaces to take into account that you are exporting references rather than values. If you simply return internal data, you've given access to those contained members. Your clients can call any method that is available in your members. You limit that access by exposing private internal data using interfaces, or wrapper objects. When you do want your clients to modify your internal data elements, you should implement the Observer pattern so that your objects can validate changes or respond to them.

Item 24: Prefer Declarative to Imperative Programming

Declarative programming can often be a simpler, more concise way to describe the behavior of a software program than imperative programming. **Declarative** programming means that you define the behavior of your program using declarations instead of by writing instructions. In C#, as in many other languages, most of your programming is **imperative**: You write methods that define the behavior of your programs. You practice declarative programming using attributes in C#. You attach attributes to classes, properties, data members, or methods, and the .NET runtime adds behavior for you. This declarative approach is simpler to implement and easier to read and maintain.

Let's begin with an obvious example that you've already used. When you wrote your first ASP.NET web service, the wizard generated this sequence of code:

```
[WebMethod]
public string HelloWorld()
{
    return "Hello World";
}
```

The VS .NET Web Service wizard added the [WebMethod] attribute to the HelloWorld() method. That declared HelloWorld as a web method. The ASP.NET runtime creates code for you in response to the presence of this attribute. The runtime created the Web Service Description Language (WSDL) document, which contains a description for the SOAP document that invokes the HelloWorld method. ASP.NET also adds support in the runtime to route SOAP requests to your `HelloWorld` method. In addition, the ASP.NET runtime dynamically creates HTML pages that enable you to test your new web service in IE. That's all in response to the presence of the `WebMethod` attribute. The attribute declared your intent, and the runtime ensured that the proper support was there. Using the attribute takes much less time and is much less error prone.

It's really not magic. The ASP.NET runtime uses reflection to determine which methods in your class are web methods. When they are found, the ASP.NET runtime can add all the necessary framework code to turn any function into a web method.

The `[WebMethod]` attribute is just one of many attributes that the .NET library defines that can help you create correct programs more quickly. A number of attributes help you create serializable types (see Item 25). As you saw in Item 4, attributes control conditional compilation. In those and other cases, you can create the code you need faster and with less chance for errors using declarative programming. You should use these .NET Framework attributes to declare your intent rather than write your own code. It takes less time, it's easier, and the compiler doesn't make mistakes.

If the predefined attributes don't fit your needs, you can create your own declarative programming constructs by defining custom attributes and using reflection. As an example, you can create an attribute and associated code to let users create types that define the default sort order using an attribute. A sample usage shows how adding the attribute defines how you want to sort a collection of customers:

```
[DefaultSort( "Name" )]
public class Customer
{
  public string Name
  {
    get { return _name; }
    set { _name = value; }
  }

  public decimal CurrentBalance
  {
    get { return _balance; }
  }
```

```
public decimal AccountValue
{
  get
  {
    return calculateValueOfAccount();
  }
}
}
```

The DefaultSort attribute e, the Name property. The implication is that any collection of Customers should be ordered by the customer name. The DefaultSort attribute is not part of the .NET Framework. To implement it, you need to create the DefaultSortAttribute class:

```
[AttributeUsage( AttributeTargets.Class |
  AttributeTargets.Struct )]
public class DefaultSortAttribute : System.Attribute
{
  private string _name;
  public string Name
  {
    get { return _name; }
    set { _name = value; }
  }

  public DefaultSortAttribute( string name )
  {
    _name = name;
  }
}
```

You must still write the code to sort a collection of objects based on the presence of the DefaultSort attribute. You'll use reflection to find the correct property and then compare values of that property in two different objects. The good news is that you need to write this code only once.

Next, you create a class that implements IComparer. (Comparers are discussed in more detail in Item 26.) IComparer has a version of CompareTo() that compares two objects of a given type, letting the target class, which implements IComparable, define the sort order. The constructor for the generic comparer finds the default sort property descriptor based on the type being compared. The `Compare` method sorts two objects of any type, using the default sort property:

```
internal class GenericComparer : IComparer
{
  // Information about the default property:
  private readonly PropertyDescriptor _sortProp;

  // Ascending or descending.
  private readonly bool _reverse = false;

  // Construct for a type
  public GenericComparer( Type t ) :
    this( t, false )
  {
  }

  // Construct for a type
  // and a direction
  public GenericComparer( Type t, bool reverse )
  {
    _reverse = reverse;
    // find the attribute,
    // and the name of the sort property:

    // Get the default sort attributes on the type:
    object [] a = t.GetCustomAttributes(
      typeof( DefaultSortAttribute ),
      false );

    // Get the PropertyDescriptor for that property:
    if ( a.Length > 0 )
    {
      DefaultSortAttribute sortName = a[ 0 ] as
        DefaultSortAttribute;
      string name = sortName.Name;

      // Initialize the sort property:
      PropertyDescriptorCollection props =
        TypeDescriptor.GetProperties( t );
```

```csharp
      if ( props.Count > 0 )
      {
        foreach ( PropertyDescriptor p in props )
        {
          if ( p.Name == name )
          {
            // Found the default sort property:
            _sortProp = p;
            break;
          }
        }
      }
    }
}

// Compare method.
int IComparer.Compare( object left,
  object right )
{
  // null is less than any real object:
  if (( left == null ) && ( right == null ))
    return 0;
  if ( left == null )
    return -1;
  if ( right == null )
    return 1;

  if ( _sortProp == null )
  {
    return 0;
  }

  // Get the sort property from each object:
  IComparable lField =
    _sortProp.GetValue( left ) as IComparable;
  IComparable rField =
    _sortProp.GetValue( right ) as IComparable;
  int rVal = 0;
  if ( lField == null )
    if ( rField == null )
```

```
        return 0;
      else
        return -1;
    rVal = lField.CompareTo( rField );
    return ( _reverse ) ? -rVal : rVal;
  }
}
```

The `Generic` comparer sorts any collection of `Customers` based on the property declared in the `DefaultSort` attribute:

```
CustomerList.Sort( new GenericComparer(
  typeof( Customer )));
```

The code to implement the `GenericComparer` makes use of advanced techniques, such as reflection (see Item 43). But you need to write it only once. From that point on, all you need to do is add the attribute to any class, and you can sort a collection of those objects using the generic comparer. If you change the parameter on the `DefaultSort` attribute, you change the class's behavior. You don't need to change any algorithms anywhere in your code.

This declarative idiom is useful to avoid writing repetitivecode when a simple declaration can specify your intent. Look at the `Generic-Comparer` class again. You could write different (and slightly simpler) versions of the sort algorithm for every type you created. The advantage to using declarative programming is that you can write one generic class and let a simple declaration create the behavior for each type. The key is that the behavior changes based on a single declaration, not based on any algorithm changes. The `GenericComparer` works for any type decorated with the `DefaultSort` attribute. If you need sorting functionality only once or twice in your application, write the simpler routines. However, if you might need the same behavior for many tens of different types in your program, the generic algorithm and the declarative solution will save you time and energy in the long run. You'd never write all the code generated by the `WebMethod` attribute. You should expand on that technique for your own algorithms. Item 42 discusses one example: how to use attributes to build add-on command handlers. Other examples might include anything from defining add-on packages to building dynamic web page UIs.

Declarative programming is a powerful tool. When you can use attributes to declare your intent, you save the possibility of logic mistakes in multiple similar hand-coded algorithms. Declarative programming creates more readable, cleaner code. That means fewer mistakes now and in the future. If you can use an attribute defined in the .NET Framework, do so. If not, consider the option of creating your own attribute definition so that you can use it to create the same behavior in the future.

Item 25: Prefer Serializable Types

Persistence is a core feature of a type. It's one of those basic elements that no one notices until you neglect to support it. If your type does not support serialization properly, you create more work for all developers who intend to use your types as a member or base class. When your type does not support serialization, they must work around it, adding their own implementation of a standard feature. It's unlikely that clients could properly implement serialization for your types without access to private details in your types. If you don't supply serialization, it's difficult or impossible for users of your class to add it.

Instead, prefer adding serialization to your types when practical. It should be practical for all types that do not represent UI widgets, windows, or forms. The extra perceived work is no excuse. .NET Serialization support is so simple that you don't have any reasonable excuse not to support it. In many cases, adding the `Serializable` attribute is enough:

```
[Serializable]
public class MyType
{
  private string _label;
  private int _value;
}
```

Adding the `Serializable` attribute works because all the members of this type are serializable: `string` and `int` both support NET serialization. The reason it's important for you to support serialization wherever possible becomes obvious when you add another field of a custom type:

```
[Serializable]
public class MyType
{
```

```
    private string      _label;
    private int         _value;
    private OtherClass  _object;
}
```

The `Serializable` attribute works here only if the `OtherClass` type supports .NET serialization. If `OtherClass` is not serializable, you get a runtime error and you have to write your own code to serialize `MyType` and the `OtherClass` object inside it. That's just not possible without extensive knowledge of the internals defined in `OtherClass`.

.NET serialization saves all member variables in your object to the output stream. In addition, the .NET serialization code supports arbitrary object graphs: Even if you have circular references in your objects, the `serialize` and `deserialize` methods will save and restore each actual object only once. The .NET Serialization Framework also will recreate the web of references when the web of objects is deserialized. Any web of related objects that you have created is restored correctly when the object graph is deserialized. A last important note is that the `Serializable` attribute supports both binary and SOAP serialization. All the techniques in this item will support both serialization formats. But remember that this works only if all the types in an object graph support serialization. That's why it's important to support serialization in all your types. As soon as you leave out one class, you create a hole in the object graph that makes it harder for anyone using your types to support serialization easily. Before long, everyone is writing their own serialization code again.

Adding the `Serializable` attribute is the simplest technique to support serializable objects. But the simplest solution is not always the right solution. Sometimes, you do not want to serialize all the members of an object: Some members might exist only to cache the result of a lengthy operation. Other members might hold on to runtime resources that are needed only for in-memory operations. You can manage these possibilities using attributes as well. Attach the `[NonSerialized]` attribute to any of the data members that should not be saved as part of the object state. This marks them as nonserializable attributes:

```
[Serializable]
public class MyType
{
  private string _label;
```

```
[NonSerialized]
private int _cachedValue;

private OtherClass  _object;
}
```

Nonserialized members add a little more work for you, you, the class designer. The serialization APIs do not initialize nonserialized members for you during the deserialization process. None of your types' constructors is called, so the member initializers are not executed, either. When you use the serializable attributes, nonserialized members get the default system-initialized value: 0 or null. When the default 0 initialization is not right, you need to implement the IDeserializationCallback interface to initialize these nonserializable members. IDeserializationCallback contains one method: OnDeserialization. The framework calls this method after the entire object graph has been deserialized. You use this method to initialize any nonserialized members in your object. Because the entire object graph has been read, you know that any function you might want to call on your object or any of its serialized members is safe. Unfortunately, it's not fool-proof. After the entire object graph has been read, the framework calls OnDeserialization on every object in the graph that supports the IDeserializationCallback interface. Any other objects in the object graph can call your object's public members when processing OnDeserialization. If they go first, your object's nonserialized members are null, or 0. Order is not guaranteed, so you must ensure that all your public methods handle the case in which nonserialized members have not been initialized.

So far, you've learned about why you should add serialization to all your types: Nonserializable types cause more work when used in types that should be serialized. You've learned about the simplest serialization methods using attributes, including how to initialize nonserialized members.

Serialized data has a way of living on between versions of your program. Adding serialization to your types means that one day you will need to read an older version. The code generated by the Serializable attribute throws exceptions when it finds fields that have been added or removed from the object graph. When you find yourself ready to support multiple versions and you need more control over the serialization process, use the ISerializable interface. This interface defines the hooks for you to customize the serialization of your types. The methods and storage that the ISerializable interface uses are consistent with the methods and storage that the default serialization methods use. That means you can use the serialization attributes when you create a class. If it ever becomes necessary to provide your own extensions, you then add support for the ISerializable interface.

As an example, consider how you would support MyType, version 2, when you add another field to your type. Simply adding a new field produces a new format that is incompatible with the previously stored versions on disk:

```
[Serializable]
public class MyType
{
  private string _label;

  [NonSerialized]
  private int _value;

  private OtherClass  _object;

  // Added in version 2
  // The runtime throws Exceptions
  // with it finds this field missing in version 1.0
  // files.
  private int  _value2;
}
```

You add support for ISerializable to address this behavior. The ISerializable interface defines one method, but you have to implement two. ISerializable defines the GetObjectData() method that is used to write data to a stream. In addition, you must provide a serialization constructor to initialize the object from the stream:

```
private MyType( SerializationInfo info,
  StreamingContext cntxt );
```

The serialization constructor in thefollowing class shows how to read a previous version of the type and read the current version consistently with the default implementation generated by adding the `Serializable` attribute:

```csharp
using System.Runtime.Serialization;
using System.Security.Permissions;

[Serializable]
public sealed class MyType : ISerializable
{
  private string _label;

  [NonSerialized]
  private int _value;

  private OtherClass  _object;

  private const int DEFAULT_VALUE = 5;
  private int  _value2;

  // public constructors elided.

  // Private constructor used only by the Serialization
        framework.
  private MyType( SerializationInfo info,
    StreamingContext cntxt )
  {
    _label = info.GetString( "_label" );
    _object = ( OtherClass )info.GetValue( "_object", typeof
      ( OtherClass ));
    try {
      _value2 = info.GetInt32( "_value2" );
    } catch ( SerializationException e )
    {
      // Found version 1.
      _value2 = DEFAULT_VALUE;
    }
  }

  [SecurityPermissionAttribute(SecurityAction.Demand,
    SerializationFormatter =true)]
```

```
void ISerializable.GetObjectData (SerializationInfo inf,
  StreamingContext cxt)
{
  inf.AddValue( "_label", _label );
  inf.AddValue( "_object", _object );
  inf.AddValue( "_value2", _value2 );
}
}
```

The serialization stream stores each item as a key/value pair. The code generated from the attributes uses the variable name as the key for each value. When you add the ISerializable interface, you must match the key name and the order of the variables. The order is the order declared in the class. (By the way, this fact means that rearranging the order of variables in a class or renaming variables breaks the compatibility with files already created.)

Also, I have demanded the SerializationFormatter security permission. GetObjectData could be a security hole into your class if it is not properly protected. Malicious code could create a StreamingContext, get the values from an object using GetObjectData, serialize modified versions to another SerializationInfo, and reconstitute a modified object. It would allow a malicious developer to access the internal state of your object, modify it in the stream, and send the changes back to you. Demanding the SerializationFormatter permission seals this potential hole. It ensures that only properly trusted code can access this routine to get at the internal state of the object (see Item 47).

But there's a downside to implementing the ISerializable interface. You can see that I made MyType sealed earlier. That forces it to be a leaf class. Implementing the ISerializable interface in a base class complicates serialization for all derived classes. Implementing ISerializable means that every derived class must create the protected constructor for deserialization. In addition, to support nonsealed classes, you need to create hooks in the GetObjectData method for derived classes to add their own data to the stream. The compiler does not catch either of these errors. The lack of a proper constructor causes the runtime to throw an exception when reading a derived object from a stream. The lack of a hook for GetObjectData() means that the data from the derived portion of the object never gets saved to the file. No errors are thrown. I'd like the recommendation to be "implement Serializable in leaf classes."

I did not say that because that won't work. Your base classes must be serializable for the derived classes to be serializable. To modify MyType so that
it can be a serializable base class, you change the serializable constructor
to protected and create a virtual method that derived classes can override to store their data:

```csharp
using System.Runtime.Serialization;
using System.Security.Permissions;

[Serializable]
public class MyType : ISerializable
{
  private string _label;

  [NonSerialized]
  private int _value;

  private OtherClass  _object;

  private const int DEFAULT_VALUE = 5;
  private int  _value2;

  // public constructors elided.

  // Protected constructor used only by the Serialization
      framework.
  protected MyType( SerializationInfo info,
    StreamingContext cntxt )
  {
    _label = info.GetString( "_label" );
    _object = ( OtherClass )info.GetValue( "_object", typeof
      ( OtherClass ));
    try {
      _value2 = info.GetInt32( "_value2" );
    } catch ( SerializationException e )
    {
      // Found version 1.
      _value2 = DEFAULT_VALUE;
    }
  }
```

```
[ SecurityPermissionAttribute( SecurityAction.Demand,
  SerializationFormatter =true ) ]
void ISerializable.GetObjectData(
  SerializationInfo inf,
  StreamingContext cxt )
{
  inf.AddValue( "_label", _label );
  inf.AddValue( "_object", _object );
  inf.AddValue( "_value2", _value2 );

  WriteObjectData( inf, cxt );
}


// Overridden in derived classes to write
// derived class data:
protected virtual void
  WriteObjectData(
  SerializationInfo inf,
  StreamingContext cxt )
{
}
}
```

A derived class would provide its own serialization constructor and override the `WriteObjectData` method:

```
public class DerivedType : MyType
{
  private int _DerivedVal;

  private DerivedType ( SerializationInfo info,
    StreamingContext cntxt ) :
      base( info, cntxt )
  {
    _DerivedVal = info.GetInt32( "_DerivedVal" );
  }

  protected override void WriteObjectData(
    SerializationInfo inf,
```

```
      StreamingContext cxt )
  {

    inf.AddValue( "_DerivedVal", _DerivedVal );

  }


}
```

The order of writing and retrieving values from the serialization stream must be consistent. I've chosen to read and write the base class values first because I believe it is simpler. If your read and write code does not serialize the entire hierarchy in the exact same order, your serialization code won't work.

The .NET Framework provides a simple, standard algorithm for serializing your objects. If your type should be persisted, you should follow the standard implementation. If you don't support serialization in your types, other classes that use your type can't support serialization, either. Make it as easy as possible for clients of your class. Use the default methods when you can, and implement the `ISerializable` interface when the default attributes don't suffice.

Item 26: Implement Ordering Relations with `IComparable` and `IComparer`

Your types need ordering relationships to describe how collections should be sorted and searched. The .NET Framework defines two interfaces that describe ordering relationships in your types: `IComparable` and `IComparer`.`IComparable` defines the natural order for your types. A type implements `IComparer` to describe alternative orderings. You can define your own implementations of the relational operators (<, >, <=, >=) to provide type-specific comparisons, to avoid some runtime inefficiencies in the interface implementations. This item discusses how to implement ordering relations so that the core .NET Framework orders your types through the defined interfaces and so that other users get the best performance from these operations.

The `IComparable` interface contains one method: `CompareTo()`. This method follows the long-standing tradition started with the C library function `strcmp`: Its return value is less than 0 if the current object is less than the comparison object, 0 if they are equal, and greater than 0 if the current object is greater than the comparison object. `IComparable` takes parameters of type `System.Object`. You need to perform runtime type checking on the argument to this function. Every time comparisons are performed, you must reinterpret the type of the argument:

```
public struct Customer : IComparable
{
  private readonly string _name;

  public Customer( string name )
  {
    _name = name;
  }

  #region IComparable Members
  public int CompareTo( object right )
  {
    if ( ! ( right is Customer ) )
      throw new ArgumentException( "Argument not a customer",
        "right" );
    Customer rightCustomer = ( Customer )right;
    return _name.CompareTo( rightCustomer._name );
  }
  #endregion
}
```

There's a lot to dislike about implementing comparisons consistent with the `IComparable` interface. You've got to check the runtime type of the argument. Incorrect code could legally call this method with anything as the argument to the `CompareTo` method. More so, proper arguments must be boxed and unboxed to provide the actual comparison. That's an extra runtime expense for each compare. Sorting a collection will make, on average N × log(n) comparisons of your object using the IComparable.Compare method. Each of those will cause three boxing and unboxing operations. For an array with 1,000 points, that will be more than 20,000 boxing and unboxing operations, on average: N × log(n) is almost 7,000, and there are 3 box and unbox operations per comparison. You must look for better alternatives. You can't change the definition of `IComparable.CompareTo()`. But that doesn't mean you're forced to live with the performance costs of a weakly typed implementation for all your users. You can create your own override of the `CompareTo` method that expects a `Customer` object:

```csharp
public struct Customer : IComparable
{
  private string _name;

  public Customer( string name )
  {
    _name = name;
  }

  #region IComparable Members
  // IComparable.CompareTo()
  // This is not type safe. The runtime type
  // of the right parameter must be checked.
  int IComparable.CompareTo( object right )
  {
    if ( ! ( right is Customer ) )
      throw new ArgumentException( "Argument not a customer",
        "right" );
    Customer rightCustomer = ( Customer )right;
    return CompareTo( rightCustomer );
  }

  // type-safe CompareTo.
  // Right is a customer, or derived from Customer.
  public int CompareTo( Customer right )
  {
    return _name.CompareTo( right._name );
  }

  #endregion
}
```

`IComparable.CompareTo()` is now an explicit interface implementation; it can be called only through an `IComparable` reference. Users of your customer struct will get the type-safe comparison, and the unsafe comparison is inaccessible. The following innocent mistake no longer compiles:

```
Customer c1;
Employee e1;
if ( c1.CompareTo( e1 ) > 0 )
  Console.WriteLine( "Customer one is greater" );
```

It does not compile because the arguments are wrong for the public `Customer.CompareTo(Customer right)` method. The `IComparable.CompareTo(object right)` method is not accessible. You can access the `IComparable` method only by explicitly casting the reference:

```
Customer c1;
Employee e1;
if ( ( c1 as IComparable ).CompareTo( e1 ) > 0 )
  Console.WriteLine( "Customer one is greater" );
```

When you implement `IComparable`, use explicit interface implementation and provide a strongly typed public overload. The strongly typed overload improves performance and decreases the likelihood that someone will misuse the `CompareTo` method. You won't see all the benefits in the `Sort` function that the .NET Framework uses because it will still access `CompareTo()` through the interface pointer (see Item 19), but code that knows the type of both objects being compared will get better performance.

We'll make one last small change to the `Customer` struct. The C# language lets you overload the standard relational operators. Those should make use of the type-safe `CompareTo()` method:

```
public struct Customer : IComparable
{
  private string _name;

  public Customer( string name )
  {
    _name = name;
  }

  #region IComparable Members
  // IComparable.CompareTo()
  // This is not type safe. The runtime type
```

```csharp
  // of the right parameter must be checked.
  int IComparable.CompareTo( object right )
  {
    if ( ! ( right is Customer ) )
      throw new ArgumentException( "Argument not a customer",
        "right");
    Customer rightCustomer = ( Customer )right;
    return CompareTo( rightCustomer );
  }

  // type-safe CompareTo.
  // Right is a customer, or derived from Customer.
  public int CompareTo( Customer right )
  {
    return _name.CompareTo( right._name );
  }

  // Relational Operators.
  public static bool operator < ( Customer left,
    Customer right )
  {
    return left.CompareTo( right ) < 0;
  }
  public static bool operator <=( Customer left,
    Customer right )
  {
    return left.CompareTo( right ) <= 0;
  }
  public static bool operator >( Customer left,
    Customer right )
  {
    return left.CompareTo( right ) > 0;
  }
  public static bool operator >=( Customer left,
    Customer right )
  {
    return left.CompareTo( right ) >= 0;
  }
  #endregion
}
```

That's all for the standard order of customers: by name. Later, you must create a report sorting all customers by revenue. You still need the normal comparison functionality defined by the `Customer` struct, sorting them by name. You can implement this additional ordering requirement by creating a class that implements the `IComparer` interface. `IComparer` provides the standard way to provide alternative orders for a type. Any of the methods inside the .NET FCL that work on `IComparable` types provide overloads that order objects through `IComparer`. Because you authored the `Customer` struct, you can create this new class (`Revenue-Comparer`) as a private nested class inside the `Customer` struct. It gets exposed through a static property in the `Customer` struct:

```
public struct Customer : IComparable
{
  private string _name;
  private double _revenue;

  // code from earlier example elided.

  private static RevenueComparer _revComp = null;

  // return an object that implements IComparer
  // use lazy evaluation to create just one.
  public static IComparer RevenueCompare
  {
    get
    {
      if ( _revComp == null )
        _revComp = new RevenueComparer();
      return _revComp;
    }
  }

  // Class to compare customers by revenue.
  // This is always used via the interface pointer,
  // so only provide the interface override.
  private class RevenueComparer : IComparer
  {
    #region IComparer Members
    int IComparer.Compare( object left, object right )
```

```
        {
          if ( ! ( left is Customer ) )
            throw new ArgumentException(
              "Argument is not a Customer",
              "left");
          if (! ( right is Customer) )
            throw new ArgumentException(
              "Argument is not a Customer",
              "right");
          Customer leftCustomer = ( Customer ) left;
          Customer rightCustomer = ( Customer ) right;

          return leftCustomer._revenue.CompareTo(
            rightCustomer._revenue);
        }
        #endregion
      }
    }
```

The last version of the Customer struct, with the embedded Revenue-Comparer, lets you order a collection of customers by name, the natural order for customers, and provides an alternative order by exposing a class that implements the IComparer interface to order customers by revenue. If you don't have access to the source for the Customer class, you can still provide an IComparer that orders customers using any of its public properties. You should use that idiom only when you do not have access to the source for the class, as when you need a different ordering for one of the classes in the .NET Framework.

Nowhere in this item did I mention Equals() or the == operator (see Item 9). Ordering relations and equality are distinct operations. You do not need to implement an equality comparison to have an ordering relation. In fact, reference types commonly implement ordering based on the object contents, yet implement equality based on object identity. CompareTo() returns 0, even though Equals() returns false. That's perfectly legal. Equality and ordering relations are not necessarily the same.

IComparable and IComparer are the standard mechanisms for providing ordering relations for your types. IComparable should be used for the most natural ordering. When you implement `IComparable`, you should overload the comparison operators (<, >, <=, >=) consistently with our `IComparable` ordering. `IComparable.CompareTo()` uses `System.Object` parameters, so you should also provide a type-specific overload of the `CompareTo()` method. `IComparer` can be used to provide alternative orderings or can be used when you need to provide ordering for a type that does not provide it for you.

Item 27: Avoid `ICloneable`

`ICloneable` sounds like a good idea: You implement the `ICloneable` interface for types that support copies. If you don't want to support copies, don't implement it. But your type does not live in a vacuum. Your decision to support `ICloneable` affects derived types as well. Once a type supports `ICloneable`, all its derived types must do the same. All its member types must also support `ICloneable` or have some other mechanism to create a copy. Finally, supporting deep copies is very problematic when you create designs that contain webs of objects. `ICloneable` finesses this problem in its official definition: It supports either a deep or a shallow copy. A shallow copy creates a new object that contains copies of all member variables. If those member variables are reference types, the new object *refers to* the same object that the original does. A deep copy creates a new object that copies all member variables as well. All reference types are cloned recursively in the copy. In built-in types, such as integers, the deep and shallow copies produce the same results. Which one does a type support? That depends on the type. But mixing shallow and deep copies in the same object causes quite a few inconsistencies. When you go wading into the `ICloneable` waters, it can be hard to escape. Most often, avoiding `ICloneable` altogether makes a simpler class. It's easier to use, and it's easier to implement.

Any value type that contains only built-in types as members does not need to support `ICloneable`; a simple assignment copies all the values of the struct more efficiently than `Clone()`. `Clone()` must box its return so that it can be coerced into a `System.Object` reference. The caller must perform another cast to extract the value from the box. You've got enough to do. Don't write a `Clone()` function that replicates assignment.

What about value types that contain reference types? The most obvious case is a value type that contains a string:

```
public struct ErrorMessage
{
  private int errCode;
  private int details;
  private string msg;

 // details elided
}
```

`string` is a special case because this class is immutable. If you assign an error message object, both error message objects refer to the same string. This does not cause any of the problems that might happen with a general reference type. If you change the `msg` variable through either reference, you create a new `string` object (see Item 7).

The general case of creating a struct that contains arbitrary reference variables is more complicated. It's also far more rare. The built-in assignment for the struct creates a shallow copy, with both structs referring to the same object. To create a deep copy, you need to clone the contained reference type, and you need to know that the reference type supported a deep copy with its `Clone()` method. In either way, you don't add support for `ICloneable` to a value type; the assignment operator creates a new copy of any value type.

That covers value types: There is never a good reason to support the `ICloneable` interface in value types. Now let's move on to reference types. Reference types should support the `ICloneable` interface to indicate that they support either shallow or deep copying. You should add support for `ICloneable` judiciously because doing so mandates that all classes derived from your type must also support `ICloneable`. Consider this small hierarchy:

```
class BaseType : ICloneable
{
  private string _label = "class name";
  private int [] _values = new int [ 10 ];

  public object Clone()
  {
```

```
    BaseType rVal = new BaseType( );
    rVal._label = _label;
    for( int i = 0; i < _values.Length; i++ )
      rVal._values[ i ] = _values[ i ];
    return rVal;
  }
}


class Derived : BaseType
{
  private double [] _dValues = new double[ 10 ];

  static void Main( string[] args )
  {
    Derived d = new Derived();
    Derived d2 = d.Clone() as Derived;

    if ( d2 == null )
      Console.WriteLine( "null" );
  }
}
```

If you run this program, you will find that the value of d2 is null. The Derived class does inherit ICloneable.Clone() from BaseType, but that implementation is not correct for the Derived type: It only clones the base type. BaseType.Clone() creates a BaseType object, not a Derived object. That is why d2 is null in the test program—it's not a Derived object. However, even if you could overcome this problem, BaseType.Clone() could not properly copy the _dValues array that was defined in Derived. When you implement ICloneable, you force all derived classes to implement it as well. In fact, you should provide a hook function to let all derived classes use your implementation (see Item 21). To support cloning, derived classes can add only member variables that are value types or reference types that implement ICloneable. That is a very stringent limitation on all derived classes. Adding ICloneable support to base classes usually creates such a burden on derived types that you should avoid implementing ICloneable in nonsealed classes.

When an entire hierarchy must implement ICloneable, you can create an abstract Clone() method and force all derived classes to implement it.

In those cases, you need to define a way for the derived classes to create copies of the base members. That's done by defining a protected copy constructor:

```
class BaseType
{
  private string _label;
  private int [] _values;

  protected BaseType( )
  {
    _label = "class name";
    _values = new int [ 10 ];
  }

  // Used by devived values to clone
  protected BaseType( BaseType right )
  {
    _label = right._label;
    _values = right._values.Clone( ) as int[ ] ;
  }
}

sealed class Derived : BaseType, ICloneable
{
  private double [] _dValues = new double[ 10 ];

  public Derived ( )
  {
    _dValues = new double [ 10 ];
  }

  // Construct a copy
  // using the base class copy ctor
  private Derived ( Derived right ) :
    base ( right )
    {
```

```
    _dValues = right._dValues.Clone( )
      as double[ ];
  }

  static void Main( string[] args )
  {
    Derived d = new Derived();
    Derived d2 = d.Clone() as Derived;
    if ( d2 == null )
      Console.WriteLine( "null" );
  }

  public object Clone()
  {
    Derived rVal = new Derived( this );
    return rVal;
  }
}
```

Base classes do not implement ICloneable; they provide a protected copy constructor that enables derived classes to copy the base class parts. Leaf classes, which should all be sealed, implement ICloneable when necessary. The base class does not force all derived classes to implement ICloneable, but it provides the necessary methods for any derived classes that want ICloneable support.

ICloneable does have its use, but it is the exception rather than rule. You should never add support for ICloneable to value types; use the assignment operation instead. You should add support for ICloneable to leaf classes when a copy operation is truly necessary for the type. Base classes that are likely to be used where ICloneable will be supported should create a protected copy constructor. In all other cases, avoid ICloneable.

Item 28: Avoid Conversion Operators

Conversion operators introduce a kind of **substitutability** between classes. Substitutability means that one class can be substituted for another. This can be a benefit: An object of a derived class can be substituted for an object of its base class, as in the classic example of the shape hierarchy. You create a `Shape` base class and derive a variety of customizations: `Rectangle`, `Ellipse`, `Circle`, and so on. You can substitute a `Circle` anywhere a `Shape` is expected. That's using polymorphism for substitutability. It works because a circle is a specific type of shape. When you create a class, certain conversions are allowed automatically. Any object can be substituted for an instance of `System.Object`, the root of the .NET class hierarchy. In the same fashion, any object of a class that you create will be substituted implicitly for an interface that it implements, any of its base interfaces, or any of its base classes. The language also supports a variety of numeric conversions.

When you define a conversion operator for your type, you tell the compiler that your type may be substituted for the target type. These substitutions often result in subtle errors because your type probably isn't a perfect substitute for the target type. Side effects that modify the state of the target type won't have the same effect on your type. Worse, if your conversion operator returns a temporary object, the side effects will modify the temporary object and be lost forever to the garbage collector. Finally, the rules for invoking conversion operators are based on the compile-time type of an object, not the runtime type of an object. Users of your type might need to perform multiple casts to invoke the conversion operators, a practice that leads to unmaintainable code.

If you want to convert another type into your type, use a constructor. This more clearly reflects the action of creating a new object. Conversion operators can introduce hard-to-find problems in your code. Suppose that you inherit the code for a library shown in Figure 3.1. Both the `Circle` class and the `Ellipse` class are derived from the `Shape` class. You decide to leave that hierarchy in place because you believe that, although the `Circle` and `Ellipse` are related, you don't want to have nonabstract leaf classes in your hierarchy, and several implementation problems occur when you try to derive the `Circle` class from the `Ellipse` class. However, you realize that every circle could be an ellipse. In addition, some ellipses could be substituted for circles.

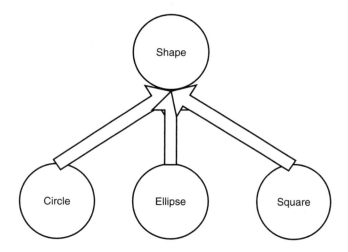

Figure 3.1 Basic shape hierarchy.

That leads you to add two conversion operators. Every `Circle` is an `Ellipse`, so you add an implicit conversion to create a new `Ellipse` from a `Circle`. An implicit conversion operator will be called whenever one type needs to be converted to another type. By contrast, an explicit conversion will be called only when the programmer puts a cast operator in the source code.

```
public class Circle : Shape
{
  private PointF _center;
  private float _radius;

  public Circle() :
    this ( PointF.Empty, 0 )
  {
  }

  public Circle( PointF c, float r )
  {
    _center = c;
    _radius = r;
  }
```

```
public override void Draw()
{
  //...
}

static public implicit operator Ellipse( Circle c )
{
  return new Ellipse( c._center, c._center,
    c._radius, c._radius );
}
}
```

Now that you've got the implicit conversion operator, you can use a `Circle` anywhere an `Ellipse` is expected. Furthermore, the conversion happens automatically:

```
public double ComputeArea( Ellipse e )
{
  // return the area of the ellipse.
}


// call it:
Circle c = new Circle( new PointF( 3.0f, 0 ), 5.0f );
ComputeArea( c );
```

This sample shows what I mean by substitutability: A circle has been substituted for an ellipse. The `ComputeArea` function works even with the substitution. You got lucky. But examine this function:

```
public void Flatten( Ellipse e )
{
  e.R1 /= 2;
  e.R2 *= 2;
}


// call it using a circle:
Circle c = new Circle( new PointF ( 3.0f, 0 ), 5.0f );
Flatten( c );
```

This won't work. The `Flatten()` method takes an ellipse as an argument. The compiler must somehow convert a circle to an ellipse. You've created an implicit conversion that does exactly that. Your conversion gets called, and the `Flatten()` function receives as its parameter the ellipse created by your implicit conversion. This temporary object is modified by the `Flatten()` function and immediately becomes garbage. The side effects expected from your `Flatten()` function occur, but only on a temporary object. The end result is that nothing happens to the circle, c.

Changing the conversion from implicit to explicit only forces users to add a cast to the call:

```
Circle c = new Circle( new PointF( 3.0f, 0 ), 5.0f );
Flatten( ( Ellipse ) c );
```

The original problem remains. You just forced your users to add a cast to cause the problem. You still create a temporary object, flatten the temporary object, and throw it away. The circle, c, is not modified at all. Instead, if you create a constructor to convert the `Circle` to an `Ellipse`, the actions are clearer:

```
Circle c = new Circle( new PointF( 3.0f, 0 ), 5.0f );
Flatten ( new Ellipse( c ));
```

Most programmers would see the previous two lines and immediately realize that any modifications to the ellipse passed to `Flatten()` are lost. They would fix the problem by keeping track of the new object:

```
Circle c = new Circle( new PointF( 3.0f, 0 ), 5.0f );
// Work with the circle.
// ...

// Convert to an ellipse.
Ellipse e = new Ellipse( c );
Flatten( e );
```

The variable e holds the flattened ellipse. By replacing the conversion operator with a constructor, you have not lost any functionality; you've merely made it clearer when new objects are created. (Veteran C++ programmers should note that C# does not call constructors for implicit or explicit conversions. You create new objects only when you explicitly use the new operator, and at no other time. There is no need for the explicit keyword on constructors in C#.)

Conversion operators that return fields inside your objects will not exhibit this behavior. They have other problems. You've poked a serious hole in the encapsulation of your class. By casting your type to some other object, clients of your class can access an internal variable. That's best avoided for all the reasons discussed in Item 23.

Conversion operators introduce a form of substitutability that causes problems in your code. You're indicating that, in all cases, users can reasonably expect that another class can be used in place of the one you created. When this substituted object is accessed, you cause clients to work with temporary objects or internal fields in place of the class you created. You then modify temporary objects and discard the results. These subtle bugs are hard to find because the compiler generates code to convert these objects. Avoid conversion operators.

Item 29: Use the new Modifier Only When Base Class Updates Mandate It

You use the new modifier on a class member to redefine a nonvirtual member inherited from a base class. Just because you can do something doesn't mean you should, though. Redefining nonvirtual methods creates ambiguous behavior. Most developers would look at these two blocks of code and immediately assume that they did exactly the same thing, if the two classes were related by inheritance:

```
object c = MakeObject( );

// Call through MyClass reference:
MyClass cl = c as MyClass;
cl.MagicMethod( );

// Call through MyOtherClass reference:
MyOtherClass cl2 = c as MyOtherClass;
cl2.MagicMethod( );
```

When the new modifier is involved, that just isn't the case:

```
public class MyClass
{
  public void MagicMethod( )
  {
    // details elided.
  }
}
```

```
public class MyOtherClass : MyClass
{
  // Redefine MagicMethod for this class.
  public new void MagicMethod( )
  {
    // details elided
  }
}
```

This kind of practice leads to much developer confusion. If you call the same function on the same object, you expect the same code to execute. The fact that changing the reference, the label, that you use to call the function changes the behavior feels very wrong. It's inconsistent. A MyOtherClass object behaves differently in response to how you refer to it. The new modifier does not make a nonvirtual method into a virtual method after the fact. Instead, it lets you add a different method in your class's naming scope.

Nonvirtual methods are statically bound. Any source code anywhere that references MyClass.MagicMethod() calls exactly that function. Nothing in the runtime looks for a different version defined in any derived classes. Virtual functions, on the other hand, are dynamically bound. The runtime invokes the proper function based on the runtime type of the object.

The recommendation to avoid using the new modifier to redefine nonvirtual functions should not be interpreted as a recommendation to make everything virtual when you define base classes. A library designer makes a contract when making a function virtual. You indicate that any derived class is expected to change the implementation of virtual functions. The set of virtual functions defines all behaviors that derived classes are expected to change. The "virtual by default" design says that derived classes can modify all the behavior of your class. It really says that you didn't think through all the ramifications of which behaviors derived classes might want to modify. Instead, spend the time to think through what methods and properties are intended as polymorphic. Make those—and only those—virtual. Don't think of it as restricting the users of your class. Instead, think of it as providing guidance for the entry points you provided for customizing the behavior of your types.

There is one time, and one time only, when you want to use the new modifier. You add new to incorporate a new version of a base class that contains a method name that you already use. You've already got code that depends on the name of the method in your class. You might already have other assemblies in the field that use this method. You've created the following class in your library, using BaseWidget that is defined in another library:

```
public class MyWidget : BaseWidget
{
  public void DoWidgetThings( )
  {
    // details elided.
  }
}
```

You finish your widget, and customers are using it. Then you find that the BaseWidget company has released a new version. Eagerly awaiting new features, you immediately purchase it and try to build your MyWidget class. It fails because the BaseWidget folks have added their own DoWidgetThings method:

```
public class BaseWidget
{
  public void DoWidgetThings()
  {
    // details elided.
  }
}
```

This is a problem. Your base class snuck a method underneath your class's naming scope. There are two ways to fix this. You could change that name of your DoWidgetThings method:

```
public class MyWidget : BaseWidget
{
  public void DoMyWidgetThings( )
  {
    // details elided.
  }
}
```

Or, you could use the new modifier:

```
public class MyWidget : BaseWidget
{
  public new void DoWidgetThings( )
  {
    // details elided.
  }
}
```

If you have access to the source for all clients of the MyWidget class, you should change the method name because it's easier in the long run. However, if you have released your MyWidget class to the world, that would force all your users to make numerous changes. That's where the new modifier comes in handy. Your clients will continue to use your DoWidgetThings() method without changing. None of them would be calling BaseWidget.DoWidgetThings() because it did not exist. The new modifier handles the case in which an upgrade to a base class now collides with a member that you previously declared in your class.

Of course, over time, your users might begin wanting to use the Base-Widget.DoWidgetThings() method. Then you are back to the original problem: two methods that look the same but are different. Think through all the long-term ramifications of the new modifier. Sometimes, the short-term inconvenience of changing your method is still better.

The new modifier must be used with caution. If you apply it indiscriminately, you create ambiguous method calls in your objects. It's for the special case in which upgrades in your base class cause collisions in your class. Even in that situation, think carefully before using it. Most importantly, don't use it in any other situations.

4 Creating Binary Components

Creating binary components has much in common with creating classes: You are trying to separate and partition functionality. The difference is that binary components enable you to deliver those discrete bits of functionality separately. You create component assemblies to simplify sharing logic, facilitate cross-language programming, and simplify deployment.

Assemblies are component packages in .NET. Each assembly can be released and upgraded independently. How easily you can upgrade a deployed application on an assembly-by-assembly basis depends on how well you minimize the coupling between assemblies. Minimizing coupling means more than just minimizing the compilation dependencies between assemblies. It also means building assemblies that you can easily upgrade in the field with new versions. This chapter is about creating assemblies that are easy to use, easy to deploy, and easy to upgrade.

The .NET environment is designed to support applications that consist of multiple binary components. Over time, you can upgrade those components independently, installing and upgrading one assembly in a multi-assembly application. You must have some understanding of how the CLR finds and loads assemblies to utilize this feature. You also must create components that conform to certain expectations if you are to make the most of this binary upgrade. The rest of this introduction explains these concepts.

The CLR loader does not load every referenced assembly when your program starts. Rather, the loader resolves assembly references when the runtime needs members in that assembly. This can be a method call or a data access request. The loader finds the referenced assembly, loads it, and JITs the necessary IL.

When the CLR needs to load an assembly, the first step is to determine what file gets loaded. The metadata for your assembly includes a record for each of the assemblies it references. This record is different for strong- and weak-named assemblies. A strong name consists of four items: the text name of the assembly, the version number, the culture attribute, and the public key token. If the requested assembly does not have a strong name, only the assembly name is part of the record. If you use strong names, your components will be less likely to be replaced by malicious components. Strong names also enable you to use config files to map the requested version to a new, improved version of a component.

After determining the correct assembly and version, the CLR determines whether the assembly is already loaded into the current application context. If so, that assembly is used. If not, the CLR continues by looking for the assembly. If the requested assembly has a strong name, the CLR first searches the Global Assembly Cache (GAC). If the requested assembly is not in the GAC, the loader checks for a codebase directory in the configuration files. If a codebase directory exists, only that directory is searched for the requested assembly., If the requested assembly is not found in the codebase directory, the load fails.

If there is no codebase directive, the loader searches a set of predefined directories:

- The application directory. This is the same location as the main application assembly.
- The culture directory. This is a subdirectory under the application directory. The subdirectory name matches the current culture.
- The assembly subdirectory. This subdirectory name matches the requested assembly name. These two can be combined in the form of [culture]/[assemblyname].
- The private binpath. This is a private directory defined in the application config file. This can also be combined with the culture and assembly path: [binpath]/[assemblyname], or [binpath]/[culture], or even [binpath]/[culture]/[assemblyname].

You should remember three items from this discussion. First, only strong-named assemblies can be stored in the GAC. Second, you can use configuration files to modify the default behavior to upgrade individual strong-named assemblies in your application. Third, strong-named assemblies provide greater application security by preventing malicious tampering.

This introduction into how the CLR loads assemblies should get you thinking about creating components that can be updated in the field. First, you should consider creating strong-named assemblies, with all the metadata records filled in. When you create projects in VS .NET, you should fill in all the attributes created in `assemblyInfo.cs`, including a complete version number. This makes it easier to upgrade the component in the field later. VS .NET creates three different sections in `assembly-Info.cs`. The first is mostly informational:

```
[assembly: AssemblyTitle("My Assembly")]
[assembly: AssemblyDescription
  ("This is the sample assembly")]
#if DEBUG
[assembly: AssemblyConfiguration("Debug")]
#else
[assembly: AssemblyConfiguration("Release")]
#endif
[assembly: AssemblyCompany("My company")]
[assembly: AssemblyProduct("It is part of a product")]
[assembly: AssemblyCopyright("Insert legal text here.")]
[assembly: AssemblyTrademark("More legal text")]
[assembly: AssemblyCulture("en-US")]
```

The last item, `AssemblyCulture` is filled in only for a localized assembly. If your assembly does not contain any localized resources, leave it blank. The string describing the culture conforms to the RFC 1766 standard.

The next section contains the version number. VS .NET writes this:

```
[assembly: AssemblyVersion("1.0.*")]
```

`AssemblyVersion` contains four portions: `Major.Minor.Build.Revision`. The asterisk tells the compiler to fill in the build and revision using the current date and time. The build number contains the number of days since January 1, 2000. The revision contains the number of seconds since midnight local time, divided by 2. This algorithm guarantees that the build and revision numbers continue to grow: Each new build has a greater number than before.

The good news about this algorithm is that no two builds have exactly the same version. The bad news is that you need to record the build and revision numbers after the fact for the builds that do get released. My preference is to let the compiler generate the build and the revision numbers for me. By recording the exact build number generated when I release the assembly, I know the final version number. I never forget to change versions when I release a new assembly. There are exceptions, though. COM components register themselves every time you build them. Letting the compiler automatically generate build numbers creates new Registry entries every build, which quickly fills the Registry with useless information.

The last section contains information about strong names:

```
[assembly: AssemblyDelaySign(false)]
[assembly: AssemblyKeyFile("")]
[assembly: AssemblyKeyName("")]
```

Consider generating a strong name for all your assemblies. Strong-named assemblies are safe from tampering and provide the support for upgrading independently of the other assemblies in an application. However, you should avoid strong names on ASP.NET applications; locally installed strong-named assemblies don't load properly. Also, strong-named assemblies must be decorated with the `AllowPartiallyTrustedCallers` attribute, or they cannot be accessed by non-strongly-named assemblies (see Item 47).

To upgrade a component in the field, the public and protected portions of the interface must be compatible at the IL level. That means no deleted methods, no modified parameters, and no changed return values. In short, none of the components that reference your component would need a recompile.

You add configuration information to change the referenced assembly. The configuration information can be stored in three different locations, depending on the component you want to upgrade. To configure a single application, you create an application config file, located in the same directory as the application. To configure all applications that use a single component, you create a publisher policy file in the GAC. Finally, to make a global configuration change, you can edit the `machine.config` file, located in the Config directory under the .NET runtime (see Item 37).

In practice, you will never modify the `machine.config` file toup grade your assemblies. This file contains information on a machine-wide basis. You will use the application config file to upgrade one application and then use a publisher policy file to upgrade a component shared by many applications.

The config files contain XML that describes the existing version and the upgraded version:

```
<dependentAssembly>
  <assemblyIdentity name="MyAssembly"
    publicKeyToken="a0231341ddcfe32b" culture="neutral" />
  <bindingRedirect oldVersion="1.0.1444.20531"
    newVersion="1.1.1455.20221" />
</dependentAssembly>
```

You use the config file to identify the assembly, the old version, and its upgraded version. When you install an upgraded assembly, you update or create the appropriate config file, and the applications use the new version.

Think of your software as a collection of assemblies: You want to be able to upgrade them independently. To update software by updating one assembly at a time, you need to do some upfront work so that your first installation contains the necessary information to support upgrades.

Item 30: Prefer CLS-Compliant Assemblies

The .NET environment is language agnostic: Developers can incorporate components written in different .NET languages without limitations. In practice, it's almost true. You must create assemblies that are compliant with the Common Language Subsystem (CLS) to guarantee that developers writing programs in other languages can use your components.

CLS compliance is a new twist on that least common denominator approach to interoperability. The CLS specification is a subset of operations that every language must support. To create a CLS-compliant assembly, you must create an assembly whose public interface is limited to those features in the CLS specification. Then any language supporting the CLS specification must be capable of using the component. This does not mean you must limit your entire programming palette to the CLS-compliant subset of the C# language, however.

To create a CLS-compliant assembly, you must follow two rules. First, the type of all parameters and return values from public and protected members must be CLS compliant. Second, any non-CLS-compliant public or protected member must have a CLS-compliant synonym.

The first rule is simple to follow: You can have it enforced by the compiler. Add the CLSCompliant attribute to your assembly:

```
[ assembly: CLSCompliant( true ) ]
```

The compiler enforces CLS compliance for the entire assembly. If you write a public method or property that uses a construct that is not compliant with CLS, it's an error. That's good because it makes CLS compliance an easy goal. After turning on CLS compliance, these two definitions won't compile because unsigned integers are not compliant with CLS:

```
// Not CLS Compliant, returns unsigned int:
public UInt32 Foo( )
{
  return _foo;
}

// Not CLS compliant, parameter is an unsigned int.
public void Foo2( UInt32 parm )
{
}
```

Remember that creating a CLS-compliant assembly affects only items that can be seen outside of the current assembly. Foo and Foo2 generate CLS compliance errors when declared either public or protected. However, if Foo and Foo2 were internal, or private, they could be included in a CLS-compliant assembly; CLS-compliant interfaces are required only for items that are exposed outside the assembly.

What about this property? Is it CLS compliant?

```
public MyClass TheProperty
{
  get { return _myClassVar; }
  set { _myClassVar = value; }
}
```

It depends. If MyClass is CLS compliant and indicates that it is CLS compliant, this property is CLS compliant. On the other hand, if MyClass is not marked as CLS compliant, this property is not CLS compliant. That means that the earlier TheProperty is CLS compliant only if MyClass resides in a CLS-compliant assembly.

You cannot build a CLS-compliant assembly if you have types in your public or protected interface that are not CLS compliant. If, as a component designer, you do not have an assembly marked as CLS compliant, you make it harder for users of your component to create CLS-compliant assemblies. They must hide your types and mirror the functionality in a CLS-compliant wrapper. Yes, this can be done. But, no, it's not a good way to treat the programmers who want to use your components. It's better to strive for CLS-compliant assemblies in all your work: This is the easiest way for clients to incorporate your work in their CLS-compliant assemblies.

The second rule is up to you: You need to make sure that you provide a language-agnostic way to perform all public and protected operations. You also need to make sure that you do not sneak a noncompliant object through your interface using polymorphism.

Operator overloading is a feature that some love and others hate. As such, not every language supports or allows operator overloading. The CLS standard does not take a pro or con stance on the concept of operator overloading. Instead, it defines a function name for each operator: op_equals is the function name created when you write an operator = function. op_add is the name for an overloaded addition operator. When you write an overloaded operator, the operator syntax can be used in languages that support overloaded operators. Developers using a language that does not support operator overloading must use the op_ function name. If you expect these programmers to use your CLS-compliant assembly, you should provide a more convenient syntax. That leads to this simple recommendation: Anytime you overload an operator, create a semantically equivalent function:

```
// Overloaded Addition operator, preferred C# syntax:
public static Foo operator+( Foo left, Foo right)
{
  // Use the same implementation as the Add method:
  return Foo.Add( left, right );
}


// Static function, desirable for some languages:
public static Foo Add( Foo left, Foo right)
{
  return new Foo ( left.Bar + right.Bar );
}
```

Finally, watch out for non-CLS types sneaking into an interface when you use polymorphic arguments. It's easy to do with event arguments. You can create a type that is not compliant with CLS and use it where a base type that is CLS-compliant is expected.

Suppose that you created this class derived from EventArgs:

```
internal class BadEventArgs : EventArgs
{
  internal UInt32 ErrorCode;
}
```

The BadEventArgs type is not CLS compliant; you should not use it with event handlers written in other languages. But polymorphism makes this easy to do. You can declare the event type to use the base class, EventArgs:

```
// Hiding the non-compliant event argument:
public delegate void MyEventHandler(
  object sender, EventArgs args );


public event MyEventHandler OnStuffHappens;


// Code to raise Event:
BadEventArgs arg = new BadEventArgs( );
arg.ErrorCode = 24;

// Interface is legal, runtime type is not:
OnStuffHappens( this, arg );
```

The interface declaration, which uses an EventArgs argument, is CLS compliant. However, the actual type you substituted in the event arguments was not. The end result is a type that some languages cannot use.

This discussion of CLS compliance ends with how CLS-compliant classes implement compliant or noncompliant interfaces. It can get complicated, but we'll simplify it. Understanding CLS compliance with interfaces also will help you fully understand what it means to be CLS compliant and how the environment views compliance.

This interface is CLS compliant if it is declared in a CLS-compliant assembly:

```
[ assembly:CLSCompliant( true ) ]
public interface IFoo
{
   void DoStuff( Int32 arg1, string arg2 );
}
```

You can implement that interface in any CLS-compliant class. However, if you declare this interface in an assembly that is not marked as CLS compliant, the IFoo interface is not CLS compliant. In other words, an interface is CLS compliant only if it is defined in a CLS-compliant assembly; conforming to the CLS spec is not enough. The reason is compiler performance. The compilers check CLS compliance on types only when the assembly being compiled is marked as CLS compliant. Similarly, the compilers assume that types declared in assemblies that are not CLS compliant actually are not CLS compliant. However, the members of this interface have CLS-compliant signatures. Even if IFoo is not marked as CLS compliant, you can implement IFoo in a CLS-compliant class. Clients of this class could access DoStuff through the class reference, but not through the IFoo reference.

Consider this small variation:

```
public interface IFoo2
{
   // Non-CLS compliant, Unsigned int
   void DoStuff( UInt32 arg1, string arg2 );
}
```

A class that publicly implements IFoo2 is not CLS compliant. To make a CLS-compliant class that implements IFoo2, you must use explicit interface implementation:

```
public class MyClass: IFoo2
{
   // explicit interface implementation.
   // DoStuff() is not part of MyClass's public interface
   void IFoo2.DoStuff( UInt32 arg1, string arg2 )
   {
      // content elided.
   }
}
```

`MyClass` has a CLS-compliant public interface. Clients expecting the `IFoo2` interface must access it through the non-CLS-compliant `IFoo2` pointer.

Complicated? No, not really. Creating a CLS-compliant type mandates that your public and protected interfaces contain only CLS-compliant types. It means that your base class must be CLS compliant. All interfaces that you implement publicly must be CLS compliant. If you implement a non-CLS compliant interface, you must hide it from your public interface using explicit interface implementation.

CLS compliance does not force you to adopt a least common denominator approach to your designs and implementations. It means carefully watching the publicly accessible interfaces of your assembly. For any public or protected class, any type mentioned in these constructs must be CLS compliant:

- Base classes
- Return values for public and protected methods and properties
- Parameters for public and protected methods and indexers
- Runtime event arguments
- Public interfaces, declared or implemented

The compiler tries to enforce a compliant assembly. That makes it easy for you to provide some minimum level of CLS support. With a bit of extra care, you can create an assembly that anyone using any language can use. The CLS specification tries to ensure that language interoperability is possible without sacrificing the constructs in your favorite language. You just need to provide alternatives in the interface.

CLS compliance requires you to spend a little time thinking about the public interfaces from the standpoint of other languages. You don't need to restrict all your code to CLS-compliant constructs; just avoid the non-compliant constructs in the interface. The payback of interlanguage operability is worth the extra time.

Item 31: Prefer Small, Simple Functions

As experienced programmers, in whatever language we favored before C#, we internalized several practices for developing more efficient code. Sometimes what worked in our previous environment is counterproductive in the .NET environment. This is very true when you try to hand-optimize algorithms for the C# compiler. Your actions often prevent the JIT compiler from more effective optimizations. Your extra work, in the name of performance, actually generates slower code. You're better off writing the clearest code you can create. Let the JIT compiler do the rest. One of the most common examples of premature optimizations causing problems is when you create longer, more complicated functions in the hopes of avoiding function calls. Practices such as hoisting function logic into the bodies of loops actually harm the performance of your .NET applications. It's counterintuitive, so let's go over all the details.

This chapter's introduction contains a simplified discussion of how the JIT compiler performs its work. The .NET runtime invokes the JIT compiler to translate the IL generated by the C# compiler into machine code. This task is amortized across the lifetime of your program's execution. Instead of JITing your entire application when it starts, the CLR invokes the JITer on a function-by-function basis. This minimizes the startup cost to a reasonable level, yet keeps the application from becoming unresponsive later when more code needs to be JITed. Functions that do not ever get called do not get JITed. You can minimize the amount of extraneous code that gets JITed by factoring code into more, smaller functions rather than fewer larger functions. Consider this rather contrived example:

```csharp
public string BuildMsg( bool takeFirstPath )
{
  StringBuilder msg = new StringBuilder( );
  if ( takeFirstPath )
  {
    msg.Append( "A problem occurred." );
    msg.Append( "\nThis is a problem." );
    msg.Append( "imagine much more text" );
  } else
  {
    msg.Append( "This path is not so bad." );
    msg.Append( "\nIt is only a minor inconvenience." );
    msg.Append( "Add more detailed diagnostics here." );
  }
  return msg.ToString( );
}
```

The first time `BuildMsg` gets called, both paths are JITed. Only one is needed. But suppose you rewrote the function this way:

```
public string BuildMsg( bool takeFirstPath )
{
  if ( takeFirstPath )
  {
    return FirstPath( );
  } else
  {
    return SecondPath( );
  }
}
```

Because the body of each clause has been factored into its own function, that function can be JITed on demand rather than the first time `BuildMsg` is called. Yes, this example is contrived for space, and it won't make much difference. But consider how often you write more extensive examples: an `if` statement with 20 or more statements in both branches of the `if` statement. You'll pay to JIT both clauses the first time the function is entered. If one clause is an unlikely error condition, you'll incur a cost that you could easily avoid. Smaller functions mean that the JIT compiler compiles the logic that's needed, not lengthy sequences of code that won't be used immediately. The JIT cost savings multiplies for long `switch` statements, with the body of each `case` statement defined inline rather than in separate functions.

Smaller and simpler functions make it easier for the JIT compiler to support enregistration. **Enregistration** is the process of selecting which local variables can be stored in registers rather than on the stack. Creating fewer local variables gives the JIT compiler a better chance to find the best candidates for enregistration. The simplicity of the control flow also affects how well the JIT compiler can enregister variables. If a function has one loop, that loop variable will likely be enregistered. However, the JIT compiler must make some tough choices about enregistering loop variables when you create a function with several loops. Simpler is better. A smaller function is more likely to contain fewer local variables and make it easier for the JIT compiler to optimize the use of the registers.

The JIT compiler also makes decisions about inlining methods. **Inlining** means to substitute the body of a function for the function call. Consider this example:

```
// readonly name property:
private string _name;
public string Name
{
  get
  {
    return _name;
  }
}


// access:
string val = Obj.Name;
```

The body of the property accessor contains fewer instructions than the code necessary to call the function: saving register states, executing method prologue and epilogue code, and storing the function return value. There would be even more work if arguments needed to be pushed on the stack as well. There would be far fewer machine instructions if you were to write this:

```
string val = Obj._name;
```

Of course, you would never do that because you know better than to create public data members (see Item 1). The JIT compiler understands your need for both efficiency and elegance, so it inlines the property accessor. The JIT compiler inlines methods when the speed or size benefits (or both) make it advantageous to replace a function call with the body of the called function. The standard does not define the exact rules for inlining, and any implementation could change in the future. Moreover, it's not your responsibility to inline functions. The C# language does not even provide you with a keyword to give a hint to the compiler that a method should be inlined. In fact, the C# compiler does not provide any hints to the JIT compiler regarding inlining. All you can do is ensure that your code is as clear as possible, to make it easier for the JIT compiler to make the best decision possible. The recommendation should be getting familiar by now: Smaller methods are better candidates for inlining. But remember that even small functions that are virtual or that contain try/catch blocks cannot be inlined.

Inlining modifies the principle that code gets JITed when it will be executed. Consider accessing the name property again:

```
string val = "Default Name";
if ( Obj != null )
  val = Obj.Name;
```

If the JIT compiler inlines the property accessor, it must JIT that code when the containing method is called.

It's not your responsibility to determine the best machine-level representation of your algorithms. The C# compiler and the JIT compiler together do that for you. The C# compiler generates the IL for each method, and the JIT compiler translates that IL into machine code on the destination machine. You should not be too concerned about the exact rules the JIT compiler uses in all cases; those will change over time as better algorithms are developed. Instead, you should be concerned about expressing your algorithms in a manner that makes it easiest for the tools in the environment to do the best job they can. Luckily, those rules are consistent with the rules you already follow for good software-development practices. One more time: smaller and simpler functions

Remember that translating your C# code into machine-executable code is a two-step process. The C# compiler generates IL that gets delivered in assemblies. The JIT compiler generates machine code for each method (or group of methods, when inlining is involved), as needed. Small functions make it much easier for the JIT compiler to amortize that cost. Small functions are also more likely to be candidates for inlining. It's not just smallness: Simpler control flow matters just as much. Fewer control branches inside functions make it easier for the JIT compiler to enregister variables. It's not just good practice to write clearer code; it's how you create more efficient code at runtime.

Item 32: Prefer Smaller, Cohesive Assemblies

This item should really be titled "Build Assemblies That Are the Right Size and Contain a Small Number of Public Types." But that's too wordy, so I titled it based on the most common mistake I see: developers putting everything but the kitchen sink in one assembly. That makes it hard to reuse components and harder to update parts of a system. Many smaller assemblies make it easier to use your classes as binary components.

The title also highlights the importance of cohesion. **Cohesion** is the degree to which the responsibilities of a single component form a meaningful unit. Cohesive components can be described in a single simple sentence. You can see this in many of the .NET FCL assemblies. Two examples are: *the* `System.Collections` *assembly provides data structures for storing sets of related objects* and *the* `System.Windows.Forms` *assembly provides classes that model Windows controls.* Web forms and Windows Forms are in different assemblies because they are not related. You should be able to describe your own assemblies in the same fashion using one simple sentence. No cheating: *The* `MyApplication` *assembly provides everything you need.* Yes, that's a single sentence. But it's also lazy, and you probably don't need all of that functionality in `My2ndApplication` (though you'd probably like to reuse some of it. That "some of it" should be packaged in its own assembly).

You should not create assemblies with only one public class. You do need to find the middle ground. If you go too far and create too many assemblies, you lose some benefits of encapsulation: You lose the benefits of internal types by not packaging related public classes in the same assembly (see Item 33). The JIT compiler can perform more efficient inlining inside an assembly than across assembly boundaries. This means that packaging related types in the same assembly is to your advantage. Your goal is to create the best-sized package for the functionality you are delivering in your component. This goal is easier to achieve with cohesive components: Each component should have one responsibility.

In some sense, an assembly is the binary equivalent of class. We use classes to encapsulate algorithms and data storage. Only the public interfaces are part of the official contract, so only the public interfaces are visible to users. In the same sense, assemblies provide a binary package for a related set of classes. Only public and protected classes are visible outside an assembly. Utility classes can be internal to the assembly. Yes, they are more visible than private nested classes, but you have a mechanism to share common implementation inside that assembly without exposing that implementation to all users of your classes. Partitioning your application into multiple assemblies encapsulates related types in a single package.

Second, using multiple assemblies makes a number of different deployment options easier. Consider a three-tiered application, in which part of the application runs as a smart client and part of the application runs on the server. You supply some validation rules on the client so that users get feedback as they enter or edit data. You replicate those rules on the server and combine them with other rules to provide more robust validation. The complete set of business rules is implemented at the server, and only a subset is maintained at each client.

Sure, you could reuse the source code and create different assemblies for the client and server-side business rules, but that would complicate your delivery mechanism. That leaves you with two builds and two installations to perform when you update the rules. Instead, separate the client-side validation from the more robust server-side validation by placing them in different assemblies. You are reusing binary objects, packaged in assemblies, rather than reusing object code or source code by compiling those objects into the multiple assemblies.

An assembly should contain an organized library of related functionality. That's an easy platitude, but it's much harder to implement in practice. The reality is that you might not know beforehand which classes will be distributed to both the server and client portions of a distributed application. Even more likely, the set of server- and client-side functionality will be somewhat fluid; you'll move features between the two locations. By keeping the assemblies small, you'll be more likely to redeploy more easily on both client and server. The assembly is a binary building block for your application. That makes it easier to plug a new component into place in a working application. If you make a mistake, make too many smaller assemblies rather than too few large ones.

I often use Legos as an analogy for assemblies and binary components. You can pull out one Lego and replace it easily; it's a small block. In the same way, you should be able to pull out one assembly and replace it with another assembly that has the same interfaces. The rest of the application should continue as if nothing happened. Follow the Lego analogy a little farther. If all your parameters and return values are interfaces, any assembly can be replaced by another that implements the same interfaces (see Item 19).

Smaller assemblies also let you amortize the cost of application startup. The larger an assembly is, the more work the CPU does to load the assembly and convert the necessary IL into machine instructions. Only the routines called at startup are JITed, but the entire assembly gets loaded and the CLR creates stubs for every method in the assembly.

Time to take a break and make sure we don't go to extremes. This item is about making sure that you don't create single monolithic programs, but that you build systems of binary, reusable components. You can take this advice too far. Some costs are associated with a large program built on too many small assemblies. You will incur a performance penalty when program flow crosses assembly boundaries. The CLR loader has a little more work to do to load many assemblies and turn IL into machine instructions, particularly resolving function addresses.

Extra security checks also are done across assembly boundaries. All code from the same assembly has the same level of trust (not necessarily the same access rights, but the same trust level). The CLR performs some security checks whenever code flow crosses an assembly boundary. The fewer times your program flow crosses assembly boundaries, the more efficient it will be.

None of these performance concerns should dissuade you from breaking up assemblies that are too large. The performance penalties are minor. C# and .NET were designed with components in mind, and the greater flexibility is usually worth the price.

So how do you decide how much code or how many classes go in one assembly? More important, how do you decide which code goesin an assembly? It depends greatly on the specific application, so there is not one answer. Here's my recommendation: Start by looking at all your public classes. Combine public classes with common base classes into assemblies. Then add the utility classes necessary to provide all the functionality associated with the public classes in that same assembly. Package related public interfaces into their own assemblies. As a final step, look for classes that are used horizontally across your application. Those are candidates for a broad-based utility assembly that contains your application's utility library.

The end result is that you create a component with a single related set of public classes and the utility classes necessary to support it. You create an assembly that is small enough to get the benefits of easy updates and easier reuse, while still minimizing the costs associated with multiple assemblies. Well-designed, cohesive components can be described in one simple sentence. For example, "`Common.Storage.dll` manages the offline data cache and all user settings" describes a component with low cohesion. Instead, make two components: "`Common.Data.dll` manages the offline data cache. `Common.Settings.dll` manages user settings." When you've split those up, you might need a third component: "`Common.Encrypted-Storage.dll` manages file system IO for encrypted local storage." You can update any of those three components independently.

Small is a relative term. `Mscorlib.dll` is roughly 2MB; `System.Web.RegularExpressions.dll` is merely 56KB. But both satisfy the core design goal of a small, reusable assembly: They contain a related set of classes and interfaces. The difference in absolute size has to do with the difference in functionality: `mscorlib.dll` contains all the low-level classes you need in every application. `System.Web.RegularExpressions.dll` is very specific; it contains only those classes needed to support regular expressions in Web controls. You will create both kinds of components: small, focused assemblies for one specific feature and larger, broad-based assemblies that contain common functionality. In either case, make them as small as what's reasonable, but not smaller.

Item 33: Limit Visibility of Your Types

Not everybody needs to see everything. Not every type you create needs to be public. You should give each type the least visibility necessary to accomplish your purpose. That's often less visibility than you think. Internal or private classes can implement public interfaces. All clients can access the functionality defined in the public interfaces declared in a private type.

Let's get right to the root cause: powerful tools and lazy developers. VS .NET is a great productivity tool. I use it or C# Builder for all my development simply because I get more done faster. One of the productivity enhancements lets you create a new class with two button clicks. If only it created exactly what I wanted. The class that VS.NET creates looks like this:

```csharp
public class Class2
{
  public Class2()
  {
    //
    // TODO: Add constructor logic here
    //
  }
}
```

It's a public class. It's visible to every piece of code that uses the assembly I'm creating. That's usually too much visibility. Many standalone classes that you create should be internal. You can further limit visibility by creating protected or private classes nested inside your original class. The less visibility there is, the less the entire system changes when you make updates later. The fewer places that can access a piece of code, the fewer places you must change when you modify it.

Expose only what needs to be exposed. Try implementing public interfaces with less visible classes. You'll find examples using the Enumerator pattern throughout the .NET Framework library. System.ArrayList contains a private class, ArrayListEnumerator, that implements the IEnumerator interface:

```
// Example, not complete source
public class ArrayList: IEnumerable
{
  private class ArraylistEnumerator : IEnumerator
  {
    // Contains specific implementation of
    // MoveNext( ), Reset( ), and Current.
  }

  public IEnumerator GetEnumerator()
  {
    return new ArrayListEnumerator( this );
  }

// other ArrayList members.
}
```

Client code, written by you, never needs to know about the class ArrayListEnumerator. All you need to know is that you get an object that implements the IEnumerator interface when you call the GetEnumerator function on an ArrayList object. The specific type is an implementation detail. The .NET Framework designers followed this same pattern with the other collection classes: Hashtable contains a private HashtableEnumerator, Queue contains a QueueEnumerator, and so on. The enumerator class being private gives many advantages. First, the ArrayList class can completely replace the type implementing

`IEnumerator`, and you'd be none the wiser. Nothing breaks. Also, the enumerator class need not be CLS compliant. It's not public (see Item 30.) Its public interface is compliant. You can use the enumerator without detailed knowledge about the class that implements it.

Creating internal classes is an often overlooked method of limiting the scope of types. By default, most programmers create public classes all the time, without any thought to the alternatives. It's that VS .NET wizard thing. Instead of unthinkingly accepting the default, you should give careful thought to where your new type will be used. Is it useful to all clients, or is it primarily used internally in this one assembly?

Exposing your functionality using interfaces enables you to more easily create internal classes without limiting their usefulness outside of the assembly (see Item 19). Does the type need to be public, or is an aggregation of interfaces a better way to describe its functionality? Internal classes allow you to replace the class with a different version, as long as it implements the same interfaces. As an example, consider a class that validates phone numbers:

```
public class PhoneValidator
{
  public bool ValidateNumber( PhoneNumber ph )
  {
    // perform validation.
    // Check for valid area code, exchange.
    return true;
  }
}
```

Months pass, and this class works fine. Then you get a request to handle international phone numbers. The previous `PhoneValidator` fails. It was codedto handle only U.S. phone numbers. You still need the U.S. Phone Validator, but now you need to use an international version in one installation. Rather than stick the extra functionality in this one class, you're better off reducing the coupling between the different items. You create an interface to validate any phone number:

```
public interface IPhoneValidator
{
  bool ValidateNumber( PhoneNumber ph );
}
```

Next, change the existing phone validator to implement that interface, and make it an internal class:

```
internal class USPhoneValidator : IPhoneValidator
{
  public bool ValidateNumber( PhoneNumber ph )
  {
    // perform validation.
    // Check for valid area code, exchange.
    return true;
  }
}
```

Finally, you can create a class for international phone validators:

```
internal class InternationalPhoneValidator : IPhoneValidator
{
  public bool ValidateNumber( PhoneNumber ph )
  {
    // perform validation.
    // Check international code.
    // Check specific phone number rules.
    return true;
  }
}
```

To finish this implementation, you need to create the proper class based on the type of the phone number. You can use the factory pattern for this purpose. Outside the assembly, only the interface is visible. The classes, which are specific for different regions in the world, are visible only inside the assembly. You can add different validation classes for different regions without disturbing any other assemblies in the system. By limiting the scope of the classes, you have limited the code you need to change to update and extend the entire system.

You could also create a public abstract base class for `PhoneValidator`, which could contain common implementation algorithms. The consumers could access the public functionality through the accessible base class. In this example, I prefer the implementation using public interfaces because there is little, if any, shared functionality. Other uses would be better served with public abstract base classes. Either way you implement it, fewer classes are publicly accessible.

Those classes and interfaces that you expose publicly to the outside world are your contract: You must live up to them. The more cluttered that interface is, the more constrained your future direction is. The fewer public types you expose, the more options you have to extend and modify any implementation in the future.

Item 34: Create Large-Grain Web APIs

The cost and inconvenience of a communication protocol dictates how you should use the medium. You communicate differently using the phone, fax, letters, and email. Think back on the last time you ordered from a catalog. When you order by phone, you engage in a question-and-answer session with the sales staff:

"Can I have your first item?"
"Item number 123-456."
"How many would you like?"
"Three."

This conversation continues until the sales staff has your entire order, your billing address, your credit-card information, your shipping address, and any other information necessary to complete the transaction. It's comforting on the phone to have this back-and-forth discussion. You never give long soliloquies with no feedback. You never endure long periods of silence wondering if the salesperson is still there.

Contrast that with ordering by fax. You fill out the entire document and fax the completed document to the company. One document, one transaction. You do not fill out one product line, fax it, add your address, fax again, add your credit number, and fax again.

This illustrates the common pitfalls of a poorly defined web method interface. Whether you use a web service or .NET Remoting, you must remember that the most expensive part of the operation comes when you transfer objects between distant machines. You must stop creating remote APIs that are simply a repackaging of the same local interfaces that you use. It works, but it reeks of inefficiency. It's using the phone call metaphor to process your catalog request via fax. Your application waits for the network each time you make a round trip to pass a new piece of information through the pipe. The more granular the API is, the higher percentage of time your application spends waiting for data to return from the server.

Instead, create web-based interfaces based on serializing documents or sets of objects between client and server. Your remote communications should work like the order form you fax to the catalog company: The client machine should be capable of working for extended periods of time without contacting the server. Then, when all the information to complete the transaction is filled in, the client can send the entire document to the server. The server's responses work the same way: When information gets sent from the server to the client, the client receives all the information necessary to complete all the tasks at hand.

Sticking with the customer order metaphor, we'll design a customer order-processing system that consists of a central server and desktop clients accessing information via web services. One class in the system is the customer class. If you ignore the transport issues, the customer class might look something like this, which allows client code to retrieve or modify the name, shipping address, and account information:

```
public class Customer
{
  public Customer( )
  {
  }

  // Properties to access and modify customer fields:
  public string Name
  {
    // get and set details elided.
  }

  public Address shippingAddr
  {
    // get and set details elided.
  }

  public Account creditCardInfo
  {
    // get and set details elided.
  }
}
```

The customer class does not contain the kind of API that should be called remotely. Calling a remote customer results in excessive traffic between the client and the server:

```
// create customer on the server.
Customer c = new Server.Customer( );
// round trip to set the name.
c.Name = dlg.Name.Text;
// round trip to set the addr.
c.shippingAddr = dlg.Addr;
// round trip to set the cc card.
c.creditCardInfo = dlg.credit;
```

Instead, you would create a local Customer object and transfer the Customer to the server after all the fields have been set:

```
// create customer on the client.
Customer c = new Customer( );
// Set local copy
c.Name = dlg.Name.Text;
// set the local addr.
c.shippingAddr = dlg.Addr;
// set the local cc card.
c.creditCardInfo = dlg.credit;
// send the finished object to the server. (one trip)
Server.AddCustomer( c );
```

The customer example illustrates an obvious and simple example: transfer entire objects back and forth between client and server. But to write efficient programs, you need to extend that simple example to include the right set of related objects. Making remote invocations to set a single property of an object is too small of a granularity. But one customer might not be the right granularity for transactions between the client and server, either.

To extend this example into the real-world design issues you'll encounter in your programs, we'll make a few assumptions about the system. This software system supports a major online vendor with more than 1 million customers. Imagine that it is a major catalog ordering house and that each customer has, on average, 15 orders in the last year. Each telephone operator uses one machine during the shift and must lookup or create customer records whenever he or she answers the phone. Your design task is to determine the most efficient set of objects to transfer between client machines and the server.

You can begin by eliminating some obvious choices. Retrieving every customer and every order is clearly prohibitive: 1 million customers and 15 million order records are just too much data to bring to each client. You've simply traded one bottleneck for another. Instead of constantly bombarding your server with every possible data update, you send the server a request for more than 15 million objects. Sure, it's only one transaction, but it's a very inefficient transaction.

Instead, consider how you can best retrieve a set of objects that can constitute a good approximation of the set of data that an operator must use for the next several minutes. An operator will answer the phone and be interacting with one customer. During the course of the phone call, that operator might add or remove orders, change orders, or modify a customer's account information. The obvious choice is to retrieve one customer, with all orders that have been placed by that customer. The server method would be something like this:

```
public OrderData FindOrders( string customerName )
{
  // Search for the customer by name.
  // Find all orders by that customer.
}
```

Or is that right? Orders that have been shipped and received by the customer are almost certainly not needed at the client machine. A better answer is to retrieve only the open orders for the requested customer. The server method would change to something like this:

```
public OrderData FindOpenOrders( string customerName )
{
  // Search for the customer by name.
  // Find all orders by that customer.
  // Filter out those that have already
  // been received.
}
```

You are still making the client machine create a new request for each customer phone call. Are there ways to optimize this communication channel more than including orders in the customer download? We'll add a few more assumptions on the business processes to give you some more ideas. Suppose that the call center is partitioned so that each working team receives calls from only one area code. Now you can modify your design to optimize the communication quite a bit more.

Each operator would retrieve the updated customer and order information for that one area code at the start of the shift. After each call, the client application would push the modified data back to the server, and the server would respond with all changes since the last time this client machine asked for data. The end result is that after every phone call, the operator sends any changes made and retrieves all changes made by any other operator in the same work group. This design means that there is one transaction per phone call, and each operator should always have the right set of data available when he or she answers a call. Now the server contains two methods that would look something like this:

```
public CustomerSet RetrieveCustomerData(
  AreaCode theAreaCode )
{
  // Find all customers for a given area code.
  // Foreach customer in that area code:
    // Find all orders by that customer.
    // Filter out those that have already
    // been received.
  // Return the result.
}


public CustomerSet UpdateCustomer( CustomerData
  updates, DataTime lastUpdate, AreaCode theAreaCode )
{
  // First, save any updates, marking each update
  // with the current time.

  // Next, get the updates:
  // Find all customers for a given area code.
  // Foreach customer in that area code:
    // Find all orders by that customer that have been
    // updated since the last time. Add those to the result.
  // Return the result.
}
```

But you might still be wasting some bandwidth. Your last design works best when every known customer calls every day. That's probably not true. If it is, your company has customer service problems that are far outside of the scope of a software program.

How can we further limit the size of each transaction without increasing the number of transactions or the latency of the service rep's responsiveness to a customer? You can make some assumptions about which customers in the database are going to place calls. You track some statistics and find that if customers go six months without ordering, they are very unlikely to order again. So you stop retrieving those customers and their orders at the beginning of the day. That shrinks the size of the initial transaction. You also find that any customer who calls shortly after placing an order is usually inquiring about the last order. So you modify the list of orders sent down to the client to include only the last order rather than all orders. This would not change the signatures of the server methods, but it would shrink the size of the packets sent back to the client.

This hypothetical discussion focused on getting you to think about the communication between remote machines: You want to minimize both the frequency and the size of the transactions sent between machines. Those two goals are at odds, and you need to make trade-offs between them. You should end up close to the center of the two extremes, but err toward the side of fewer, larger transactions.

5 | Working with the Framework

My friend and colleague Martin Shoemaker runs a great roundtable called "Do I Have to Write That .NET Code?" The answer is, hopefully, no. You should use all the tools at your disposal to avoid writing code that already exists and that you can use.

The .NET Framework is a rich class library. The more you learn about the framework, the less code you need to write yourself. The framework library will do more of the work for you. This chapter shows you some common techniques to get the most out of the .NET Framework. Other items help you choose the best option when multiple choices are available in the framework. You can write your classes and algorithms to utilize what's already there instead of fighting against it. The items in this chapter reflect the algorithms and classes that developers seem intent on building for themselves when they could easily use the .NET Framework. Sometimes it's because the framework isn't exactly what you need. In those cases, I show you how to extend the core functionality. Sometimes, it's because they don't understand how the core works. Sometimes, it's because they are overly concerned with performance.

Even with all the tools available in the framework, too many developers would rather create their own wheels. Don't write that code—especially if someone else already did.

Item 35: Prefer Overrides to Event Handlers

Many .NET classes provide two different ways to handle events from the system. You can attach an event handler, or you can override a virtual function in the base class. Why provide two ways of doing the same thing? Because different situations call for different methods, that's why. Inside derived classes, you should always override the virtual function. Limit your use of the event handlers to responding to events in unrelated objects.

You write a nifty Windows application that needs to respond to mouse down events. In your form class, you can choose to override the OnMouseDown() method:

```
public class MyForm : Form
{

  // Other code elided.

  protected override void OnMouseDown(
    MouseEventArgs e )
  {
    try {
      HandleMouseDown( e );
    } catch ( Exception e1 )
    {
      // add specific error handling here.
    }
    // *almost always* call base class to let
    // other event handlers process message.
    // Users of your class expect it.
    base.OnMouseDown( e );
  }
}
```

Or, you could attach an event handler:

```
public class MyForm : Form
{

  // Other code elided.

  public MyForm( )
  {
    this.MouseDown += new
      MouseEventHandler( this.MouseDownHandler );
  }

  private void MouseDownHandler( object sender,
    MouseEventArgs e )
  {
```

```
    try {
      HandleMouseDown( e );
    } catch ( Exception e1 )
    {
      // add specific error handling here.
    }
  }
}
```

The first method is preferred. If an event handler throws an exception, no other handlers in the chain for that event are called (see Item 21). Some other ill-formed code prevents the system from calling your event handler. By overriding the protected virtual function, your handler gets called first. The base class version of the virtual function is responsible for calling any event handlers attached to the particular event. That means that if you want the event handlers called (and you almost always do), you must call the base class. In some rare cases, you will want to replace the default behavior instead of calling the base class version so that none of the event handlers gets called. You can't guarantee that all the event handlers will be called because some ill-formed event handler might throw an exception, but you can guarantee that your derived class's behavior is correct.

Using the override is more efficient than attaching the event handler. I showed you in Item 22 how the `System.Windows.Forms.Control` class uses a sophisticated collection mechanism to store event handlers and map the appropriate handler to a particular event. The event-handling mechanism takes more work for the processor because it must examine the event to see if any event handlers have been attached. If so, it must iterate the entire invocation list. Each method in the event invocation list must be called. Determining whether there are event handlers and iterating each at runtime takes more execution time than invoking one virtual function.

If that's not enough for you, examine the first listing in this item again. Which is clearer? Overriding a virtual function has one function to examine and modify if you need to maintain the form. The event mechanism has two points to maintain: the event handler function and the code that wires up the event. Either of these could be the point of failure. One function is simpler.

Okay, I've been giving all these reasons to use the overrides and not use the event handlers. The .NET Framework designers must have added events for a reason, right? Of course they did. Like the rest of us, they're too busy to write code nobody uses. The overrides are for derived classes. Every other class must use the event mechanism. For example, you often add a button click handler in a form. The event is generated by the button, but the form object handles the event. You could define a custom button and override the click handler in that class, but that's way too much work to handle one event. It only moves the problem to your own class anyway: Somehow, your custom button must communicate to the form that the button was clicked. The obvious way to handle that is to create an event. So, in the end, you have created a new class to send an event to the form class. It would be simpler to just attach the form's event handler to the form in the first place. That's why the .NET Framework designers put those events in the forms in the first place.

Another reason for the event mechanism is that events are wired up at runtime. You have more flexibility using events. You can wire up different event handlers, depending on the circumstances of the program. Suppose that you write a drawing program. Depending on the state of the program, a mouse down might start drawing a line, or it might select an object. When the user switches modes, you can switch event handlers. Different classes, with different event handlers, handle the event depending on the state of the application.

Finally, with events, you can hook up multiple event handlers to the same event. Imagine the same drawing program again. You might have multiple event handlers hooked up on the MouseDown event. The first would perform the particular action. The second might update the status bar or update the accessibility of different commands. Multiple actions can take place in response to the same event.

When you have one function that handles one event in a derived class, the override is the better approach. It is easier to maintain, more likely to be correct over time, and more efficient. Reserve the event handlers for other uses. Prefer overriding the base class implementation to attaching an event handler.

Item 36: Leverage .NET Runtime Diagnostics

Problems happen. They don't always happen in the lab, on machines you can easily debug. The problems you can't fix always seem to occur on one user's machine in the field, with no debugging environment and no way to figure out the cause. Experienced developers have learned to build in the capability to capture as much information as possible from systems running in the field. The .NET Framework includes a set of classes that you can use to generate diagnostics. These are configurable at runtime or compile time. If you leverage them, you can more quickly find problems that occur only in the field. Using code already in the framework, you can send diagnostic messages to a file, to the system logger, or to a debugging terminal. In addition, you can specify the level of debugging output that your program produces. You should use these features early in your development and make sure that you can produce the output you need to fix unanticipated problems in the field. Don't write your own diagnostic library until you understand what's already provided.

The `System.Diagnostics.Debug`, `System.Diagnostics.Trace`, and `System.Diagnostics.EventLog` classes provide all the tools you need to create diagnostic information from a running program. The first two classes have almost identical capabilities. The difference is that the `Trace` class methods are controlled by the TRACE preprocessor symbol, and the `Debug` class methods are controlled by the DEBUG preprocessor symbol. When you create a project with VS .NET, the TRACE symbol is defined for both release and debug builds, while the DEBUG symbol is defined only for debug builds. You create all your release build diagnostics using the `Trace` class. The `EventLog` class provides entry points so that your application can write to the system event log. The `EventLog` class does not support runtime configuration, but you can wrap it to conform to the same interface illustrated shortly.

You can also control the diagnostic output at runtime. The .NET Framework uses an application-configuration file to control a variety of runtime settings. This file is an XML document, located in the same directory as the main executable. The file shares the same name as the executable, with `.config` appended. For example, `MyApplication.exe` would be controlled by the `MyApplication.exe.config` XML document. All the configuration information is contained in a configuration node:

```
<?xml version="1.0" encoding="utf-8" ?>
<configuration>

</configuration>
```

The .NET Framework uses predefined keys to control the behavior of framework classes. In addition, you can define your own configuration keys and values.

You combine the `Trace.WriteLineIf()` method and `TraceSwitches` to control the granularity of the output that your application generates. You turn off output by default so that you get the most performance possible out of your application. When you find problems, you can ratchet up the output to diagnose and correct any problems you find in the field. `WriteLineIf()` generates output only when an expression evaluates to `true`:

```
bool _printDiagnostics = true;
Trace.WriteLineIf( _printDiagnostics,
  "Printing Diagnostics Today", "MySubSystem" );
```

You create `TraceSwitches` to control the level of output. A `TraceSwitch` is a variable set using the application-configuration file to one of five states: `Off`, `Error`, `Warning`, `Info`, and `Verbose`. These states are part of an enumeration and have values from 0 to 4. You can create a switch for each subsystem to control its messages. To create the switch, declare a variable of the `TraceSwitch` class and construct it:

```
static private TraceSwitch librarySwitch = new
  TraceSwitch( "MyAssembly",
  "The switch for this assembly" );
```

The first parameter is the display name for the switch; the second parameter is the description. You set the value of the switch at runtime in the application configuration file. The following snippet sets the `librarySwitch` to `Info`:

```
<system.diagnostics>
  <switches>
    <add name="MyAssembly" value="3" />
  </switches>
</system.diagnostics>
```

If you edit the config file's value of the switch, you modify the output generated by all statements controlled by that switch.

One more task: You need to configure where your trace output goes. By default, one listener is connected to the `Trace` class: a `Default-TraceListener` object. The `DefaultTraceListener` sends messages to the debugger, and its `Fail` method (called when asserts fail) prints a diagnostic messages and terminates the program. In a production environment, you won't see any of the messages. You can configure a different listener in a production environment; you add listeners in the application configuration file. The following snippet adds a `TextWriterTraceListener` to your application:

```
<system.diagnostics>
  <trace autoflush="true" indentsize="0">
    <listeners>
      <add name="MyListener"
        type="System.Diagnostics.TextWriterTraceListener"
        initializeData="MyListener.log"/>
    </listeners>
  </trace>
</system.diagnostics>
```

This `TextWriterTraceListener` prints all diagnostic information to the `MyListener.log` file. The `name` attribute specifies the name for the listener. The type specifies the type of object to create as a listener; it must be derived from `System.Diagnostics.TraceListener`. On those rare occasions when the standard listener classes in the .NET Framework are not enough for you, create your own listener class. The `initializeData` value is a string that gets passed to the object's constructor. `TextWriter-TraceListeners` use this value for the filename.

You can extend these basics a bit to make it easier to create diagnostics for each assembly you distribute in your application. For each assembly you create, add a class to track the diagnostics generated by that assembly:

```
internal class MyAssemblyDiagnostics
{
  static private TraceSwitch myAssemblySwitch =
    new TraceSwitch( "MyAssembly",
    "The switch for this assembly" );

  internal static void Msg( TraceLevel l, object o )
  {
    Trace.WriteLineIf( myAssemblySwitch.Level >= l,
      o, "MyAssembly" );
  }
```

```
internal static void Msg( TraceLevel l, string s )
{
  Trace.WriteLineIf( myAssemblySwitch.Level >= l,
    s, "MyAssembly" );
}


// Add additional output methods to suit.
}
```

The MyAssemblyDiagnostices class creates diagnostic messages for the assembly, depending on a switch for that assembly. To generate a message, call either of the overloaded Msg routines:

```
public void Method1( )
{
  MyAssemblyDiagnostics.Msg( TraceLevel.Info,
    "Entering Method1." );

  bool rVal = DoMoreWork( );

  if( rVal == false )
  {
    MyAssemblyDiagnostics.Msg( TraceLevel.Warning,
      "DoMoreWork Failed in Method1" );
  }

  MyAssemblyDiagnostics.Msg( TraceLevel.Info,
    "Exiting Method1." );
}
```

You can also combine the assembly-specific switch with a global switch to control the entire application's output:

```
internal static void Msg( TraceLevel l, object o )
{
  Trace.WriteLineIf ( librarySwitch.Level >= l ||
    globalSwitch.Level >= l,
    o, "MyLibrary" );
}


internal static void Msg( TraceLevel l, string s )
{
```

```
Trace.WriteLineIf( librarySwitch.Level >= 1 ||
    globalSwitch.Level >= 1,
    s, "MyLibrary" );
}
```

This enables you to control application-wide diagnostics and more finely control an individual library's output. You can set the application-level diagnostics to the `Error` level to find errors anywhere in the application. When you have isolated the problem, you can raise the level of that one library's output to a higher level and find the exact source of the problem.

Diagnostic libraries are necessary to diagnose and maintain programs that have been distributed to the field. Don't write your own diagnostic library: The .NET FCL already has the core features you need. Use it to the fullest and then extend it for your own purposes, and you will capture all problems, even in production environments.

Item 37: Use the Standard Configuration Mechanism

In our quest to avoid hard-coding configuration and settings information, we have created many different strategies for storing configuration information. In our quest to get it right, we kept improving and changing our minds about where to put such information. INI files? That was so Windows 3.1. You were limited in the structure of your configuration information, and you had to contend with filename collisions with other applications. The Registry? Yes, this was a step in the right direction, but it had its limitations as well. Malicious programs could do serious damage to a machine writing the wrong things to the Registry. Because of the dangers inherent in writing to the Registry, a program must have administrative rights to write in parts of the Registry. Are all your users running as admins with the capability to edit the Registry? You hope not. If you use the Registry, users running as nonadmins will get exceptions and errors when they attempt to save or read their settings.

Thankfully, there are much better ways to store settings so that your program can adapt its behavior to your users' preferences, the install parameters, the machine settings, or just about anything else. The .NET Framework provides a standard set of locations that your application can use to store configuration information. These locations are specific to your application and will work when the user has limited privileges on the machine where the code executes.

Read-only information belongs in configuration files, XML files that control various types of behavior in the application. Defined schemas dictate all the elements and attributes that the .NET FCL parses from config files. These elements control settings such as the version of the framework being used, the level of debugging support (see Item 36), and the search path for assemblies. One section you must understand is the `appSettings` section, which applies to both web and desktop applications. The runtime reads this section when your application starts. It loads all the keys and values into a `NameValueCollection` owned by your application. This is your section. You add any values that your application needs to control its behavior. If you modify the config file, you modify the application's behavior.

ASP.NET applications have a little more flexibility than desktop applications do with respect to config files. Each virtual directory can have its own config file. The files are read in order for each virtual directory that is part of the URL. The most local wins. For example, the URL http://localhost/MyApplication/SubDir1/SubDir2/file.aspx could be controlled by four different config files. The `machine.config` file gets read first. Second is the `web.config` file in the MyApplication directory. Following is the `web.config` files in SubDir1 and SubDir2, in that order. Each can change values set by a previous config file or add its own key/value pairs. You can use this configuration inheritance to set up global application preferences and limit access to some private resources. Web applications can have different configurations for different virtual directories.

On the desktop, there is only one application configuration file for each app domain. The .NET runtime creates a default application domain for each executable that it loads, and reads one predefined config file into that domain. This default configuration file is located in the same directory as the executable and is called `<applicationname>.<ext>.config`. For example, `MyApp.exe` would have a config file named `MyApp.exe.config`. The `appsettings` section can be used to create your own key/value pairs for your application.

Config files are great to store information that controls the behavior of your application at runtime. But you will quickly notice that there are no APIs to write configuration information from your application. Configuration files are not the place for user settings of any sort. Don't go running for the Registry yet. Don't write your own from scratch. There is a better way for your .NET desktop applications.

You need to define the format for your configuration information and put that configuration information in the right location. You can easily store and retrieve these settings by defining a settings structure and adding public read/write properties for the global settings:

```
[ Serializable( ) ]
public struct GlobalSettings
{
  // Add public properties to store.
}
```

Use the XML serializer to save your settings:

```
XmlSerializer ser = new XmlSerializer(
  typeof( GlobalSettings ));
TextWriter wr = new StreamWriter( "data.xml" );
ser.Serialize( wr, myGlobalSettings );
wr.Close( );
```

Using XML format means that your settings will be easy to read, easy to parse, and easy to debug. You can use encrypted storage for these user settings, if necessary for your application. This example uses the XML serializer, not the object serializer for persistence (see Item 25). The XML serializer stores documents, not entire object trees. Configuration settings and user settings typically do not contain webs of objects, and the XML serializer is a simpler file format.

The only question remaining is where to store the information. You should put settings information in three different locations. Which you choose depends on when it should be used: Globally, per user, or per user and machine. All three locations are returned by different calls to by the `System.Environment.GetFolderPath()` method. You should append your application-specific directories on the end of the path returned by `GetFolderPath()`. Be extremely careful about writing information in the all-user or machine-wide directories. Doing so requires more privileges on the target machine.

`Environment.SpecialFolder.CommonApplicationData` returns the directory for storing information that is shared by all users on all machines. On a machine with a default installation, `GetFolderPath (SpecialFolder.CommonApplicationData)` returns `C:\Documents and Settings\All Users\Application Data`. Settings stored under this location should be used by all users, on all machines. When you create information that should go here, write it with the installer or an admin module. Avoid writing data here in your user programs. Chances are, your application does not have the necessary access rights on users' machines.

`Environment.SpecialFolders.ApplicationData` returns the directory for this user, shared by all machines in the network. On a default installation, `GetFolderPath(SpecialFolders.ApplicationData)` gives you `C:\Documents and Settings\<username>\Application Data`. Each user has his or her own application data directory. When the user logs into a domain, using this enumeration points to the network share that contains the user's global settings. Settings stored under this location are used by the current user, no matter what machine in the network he has logged in from.

`Environment.SpecialFolders.LocalApplicationData` returns the directory for storing information that is personal for this user—and only when logged in on this machine. A typical value returned by `GetFolderPath(SpecialFolders.LocalApplicationData)` is `C:\Documents and Settings\<username>\Local Settings\Application Data`.

These three different locations let you store settings that should apply to everyone, the given user, or the given user on the given machine. Exactly which you use depends on the application. But consider some obvious examples: The database connection is a global setting. It should be stored in the Common Application Data directory. A user's working context should be stored in the Application Data directory because it depends only on the user. Window locations should be in the Local Application Data directory because they depend on the user and properties of the machine (different machines might have different screen resolutions).

These special folders describe the top-level directory structure for user settings stored by all applications. In all cases, you should create subdirectories underneath these top-level structures. The .NET Framework's `System.Windows.Application` class defines properties that build common configuration paths for you. The `Application.Local-AppDataPath` property returns the path for `GetFolderPath(Special-Folders.CommonApplicationData)+"\\CompanyName\\ProductName\\ProductVersion"`. Similarly, `Application.UserDataPath` and `Application.LocalUserDataPath` produce pathnames underneath the user's data and local data directories for this company, application, and version. If you combine these locations, you can create configuration information for all your company's applications, for this application across all versions, and for this specific version.

Note that nowhere in those directories did I mention the application directory, under Program Files. You should not ever write data in any directory under Program Files or in the Windows system directory. Those locations require more security privileges, so you should not expect your users to have permission to write in them.

Where you store your application's settings has become more important as everyone from enterprise users to home users worries about the security of machines. Putting the information in the right location means that it is easier for your users to work with your application without compromising security. You can still provide your users with a personalized experience. Combine the right location with .NET serialization, and it's easy to have your application provide a personalized appearance for each user without compromising security.

Item 38: Utilize and Support Data Binding

Experienced Windows programmers are familiar with writing the code to place data values in controls and to store values from controls:

```
public Form1 : Form
{
  private MyType myDataValue;
  private TextBox textBoxName;

  private void InitializeComponent( )
  {
    textBoxName.Text = myDataValue.Name;
    this.textBoxName.Leave += new
      System.EventHandler( this.OnLeave );
  }

  private void OnLeave( object sender, System.EventArgs e )
  {
    myDataValue.Name = textBoxName.Text;
  }
}
```

It's simple, repetitive code—you know, the kind you hate to write because there must be a better way. There is. The .NET Framework supports **data binding**, which maps a property of an object to a property in the control:

```
textBoxName.DataBindings.Add ( "Text",
myDataValue, "Name" );
```

The previous code binds the "Text" property of the textBoxName control to the "Name" property of the myDataValue object. Internally, two objects, the BindingManager and the CurrencyManager, implement the transfer of data between the control and the data source. You've probably seen this construct in many samples, particularly with DataSets and DataGrids. You've also done simple binding to text boxes. You've likely only scratched the surface of the capabilities you get from data binding. You can avoid writing repetitive code by utilizing data binding more effectively.

A full treatment of data binding would span at least one book, if not two. Both Windows applications and web applications support data binding. Rather than write a complete treatise of data binding, I want to make sure you remember the key advantages of it. First, using data binding is much simpler than writing your own code. Second, you should use it for more than text items—other display properties can be bound as well. Third, on Windows forms, data binding handles synchronizing multiple controls that examine related data sources.

For example, suppose you get a requirement to display the text in red whenever the data shows an invalid value. You could write the following snippet:

```
if ( src.TextIsInvalid )
{
  textBox1.ForeColor = Color.Red;
} else
{
  textBox1.ForeColor = Color.Black;
}
```

That's well and good, but you need to call that snippet of code whenever the text in your source changes. That could be when the user edits the text or when the underlying data source changes. There are a lot of events to handle and many places that you might miss. Instead, use data binding. Add a property in your src object to return the proper foreground color.

Other logic will set the value of that variable to the proper color based on the state of the text message:

```
private Color _clr = Color.Black;
public Color ForegroundColor
{
  get
  {
    return _clr;
  }
}


private string _txtToDisplay;
public string Text
{
  get
  {
    return _txtToDisplay;
  }
  set
  {
    _txtToDisplay = value;
    UpdateDisplayColor( IsTextValid( ) );
  }
}


private void UpdateDisplayColor( bool bValid )
{
  _clr = ( bValid ) ? Color.Black : Color.Red;
}
```

Then simply add the binding to the text box:

```
textBox1.DataBindings.Add ("ForeColor",
src, "ForegroundColor");
```

When the data binding is configured, `textBox1` will draw its text in the correct color, based on the internal value of the source object. You've done more to decouple the control from the data source. Instead of having multiple event handlers and multiple locations where the display color changes, you have two. Your data source object keeps track of the properties that affect the proper display. Your form controls the data binding.

Although the samples I've shown are Windows forms, the same principle works for web applications: You can bind properties of data sources to a property in the web control as well:

```
<asp:TextBox id=TextBox1 runat="server"
  Text="<%# src.Text %>"
  ForeColor="<%# src.ForegroundColor %>">
```

This means that when you create the types that your application displays in its UI, you should add the necessary properties to create and update your UI in response to user needs.

What do you do if the objects you have don't support the properties you need? You wrap what you have and add what you need. Consider this data structure:

```
public struct FinancialResults
{
  public decimal Revenue
  {
    get { return _revenue; }
  }

  public int NumberOfSales
  {
    get { return _numSales; }
  }

  public decimal Costs
  {
    get { return _cost;}
  }

  public decimal Profit
  {
    get { return _revenue - _cost; }
  }
}
```

You have requirements to display these in a form with some special formatting notes. If the profit is negative, you must display the profit in red. If the number of sales drops below 100, it should be bold. If the cost is above 10,000, it should be bold. The developer who created the `Finan-cialResults` structure did not add UI capabilities into the structure. That was most likely the right choice. `FinancialResults` should limit its capabilities to storing the actual values. You can create a new type to include the UI formatting properties with the original store properties in the `FinancialResults` structure:

```
public struct FinancialDisplayResults
{
  private FinancialResults _results;
  public FinancialResults Results
  {
    get { return _results; }
  }

  public Color ProfitForegroundColor
  {
    get
    {
      return ( _results.Profit >= 0 ) ?
        Color.Black : Color.Red;
    }
  }

  // other formatting options elided
}
```

You have created a single data structure to facilitate data binding of your contained structure:

```
// Use the same datasource. That creates one Binding Manager
textBox1.DataBindings.Add ("Text",
  src, "Results.Profit");
textBox1.DataBindings.Add ("ForeColor",
  src, "ProfitForegroundColor");
```

I've created one read-only property that allows access to the core financial structure. That construct doesn't work if you intend to support read/write access to the data. The `FinancialResults` struct is a value type, which means that the `get` accessor does not provide access to the existing storage; it returns a copy. This idiom has happily returned a copy that cannot be modified using data binding. However, if you intended editing, the `FinancialResults` type would be a class, not a struct (see Item 6). As a reference type, your `get` accessor returns a reference to the internal storage and would support edits by the user. The internal structure would need to respond to changes made to the internal storage. The `FinancialResults` would raise events to notify other code of changes in state.

It's important to remember to use the data source for all related controls in the same form. Use the `DataMember` property to differentiate the property displayed in each control. You could have written the binding construct this way:

```
// Bad practice: creates two binding managers
textBox1.DataBindings.Add ("Text",
src.Results, "Profit");
textBox1.DataBindings.Add ("ForeColor",
src, "ProfitForegroundColor");
```

That would create two binding managers, one for the `src` object and one for the `src.Results` object. Each data source is managed by a different binding manager. If you want the binding manager to update all property changes when the data source changes, you need to make sure that the data sources match.

You can use data binding for almost any property of a Windows or web control. The values displayed in the control, the font, the read-only state, and even the location of the control can be the target of a binding operation. My advice is to create the class or struct that contains the values you need to display your data in the manner requested by your users. Then use data binding to update the controls.

In addition to simple controls, data binding often involves `DataSet`s and `DataGrid`s. It's very powerful: You bind the `DataGrid` to the `DataSet`, and all the values in the `DataSet` are displayed. If your `DataSet` has multiple tables, you can even navigate between tables. What's not to love?

Well, the problem arises if your data set does not contain the fields you want to display. In those cases, you must add a column to the `DataSet` that computes the value needed for the user interface. If the value can be computed using a SQL expression, the `DataSet` can compute the value for you. The following code adds a column n to the Employees data table that displays a formatted version of the name:

```
DataTable dt = data.Tables[ "Employees" ];
dt.Columns.Add( "EmployeeName",
  typeof( string ),
   "lastname + ', ' + firstname");
```

By adding columns to the DataSet, you can add columns to the Data-Grid. You build layers of objects on top of the stored data objects to create the data presentation you want to give the user.

All the items I showed you so far are string types. The framework does handle converting strings to numeric values: It tries to convert the user's input to the proper type. If that fails, the original value is restored. It works, but the user gets absolutely no feedback, their input is silently ignored. You add that feedback by processing the Parse event from the binding context. That event occurs when the binding manager updates the value in the data source from the value in the control. ParseEvent-Args gives you the text typed by the user and the desired type to convert the text. You can trap this event and perform your own notification, even going so far as to modify the value and update the text with your own value:

```
private void Form1_Parse( object sender, ConvertEventArgs e )
{
  try {
    Convert.ToInt32 ( e.Value );
  } catch
  {
    MessageBox.Show (
      string.Format( "{0} is not an integer",
        e.Value.ToString( ) ) );
    e.Value = 0;
  }
}
```

You might also want to handle the Format event. This is the hook that lets you format the data that comes from your data source and goes into the control. You can modify the Value field of ConvertEventArgs to format the string that should be displayed.

The .NET Framework provides the generic framework for you to support data binding. Your job is to provide the specific event handlers for your application and your data. Both the Windows Forms and Web forms subsystems contain rich data-binding capabilities. The library already contains all the tools you need, so your UI code should really be describing the data sources and properties to be displayed and what rules should be followed when you store those elements back in the data source. You concentrate on building the data types that describe the display parameters, and the Winforms and Webforms data binding does the rest. There is no way around writing the code that transfers values between the user controls and the data source objects. Somehow, data must get from your business objects to the controls that your users interact with. But by building layers of types and leveraging data-binding concepts, you write a lot less of it. The framework handles the transfers for you, in both Windows and web applications.

Item 39: Use .NET Validation

User input can come from a variety of locations: You must test input from data files as well as interactive controls. Writing user input validation is pedantic and error-prone but very necessary. Trusting user input can cause anything from exception conditions to SQL injection attacks. None of the options is pleasant. You know enough to be very skeptical of the validity of user input. Good. So does everyone else. That's why the .NET Framework has extensive capabilities that you can use to minimize the amount of code you need to write, yet still validate every piece of data that your users give you.

The .NET Framework provides different mechanisms to validate user input for web- and Windows-based applications. Web applications should get data validated at the browser, using JavaScript. The validation controls generate JavaScript in the HTML page. It's more efficient for your users: They do not need to have round-trips back to the server each time they change an entry. These web controls make extensive use of regular expressions to tentatively validate user input before the page is posted back to the server. Even so, you'll want to perform more extensive validation at the server, to prevent programmatic attacks. Windows applications use a different model. User input can be validated in C# code that runs in the same context as the application. The full gamut of Windows controls is available to you when you want to notify the user of invalid input. The general model uses exceptions in property accessors to indicate the invalid input. UI widgets catch those exceptions and display errors to the user.

You can use five web controls to handle most of the validation tasks in your ASP.NET applications. All five are controlled by properties that specify the field that should be validated and the conditions for valid input. `RequiredFieldValidator` forces the user to enter some value in a given field. `RangeValidator` mandates that a specific field supplies a value within a given range. This range could be the magnitude of a number or the length of a string value. `CompareValidator` lets you construct validation rules that relate two different fields in a web page. These three are relatively simple. The last two give you all the power you need to validate almost any user input you are expecting. The `RegularExpression` validator processes the user input using a regular expression. If the comparison returns a match, the user input is valid. Regular expressions are a very powerful language. You should be able to create a regular expression for any situation you have. Visual Studio .NET includes sample validation expressions that help get you started. There is a wealth of resources to help you learn all about regular expressions, and I strongly encourage you to do that. But I can't leave this topic without giving you a few of the most common constructs. Table 5.1 shows the most common regular expression elements you'll use for validating input in your applications.

Table 5.1   Common Regular Expression Constructs

Construct	Meaning
`[a-z]`	Matches any single lowercase letter. Anything inside square brackets matches a single character in the set.
`\d`	Any digit.
`^, $`	^ is the beginning of the line, and $ is the end.
`\w`	Matches any "word" character. It is shorthand for `[A-Za-z0-9]`.
`(?NamedGroup\d{4,16})`	Shows two different common elements. `?NamedGroup` defines a variable that references the match. `{4,16}` matches the preceding construct at least 4 times but no more than 16. This pattern matches a string of at least 4 but no more than 16 digits. If a match is found, the match can be referred to later as `NamedGroup`.
`(a|b|c)`	Matches any of **a**, **b**, or **c**. Options separated by vertical bars are `ORed`: The input string can contain any one of them.
`(?(NamedGroup)a|b)`	Alternation. This is the equivalent of the ternary operator in C#. It means "If NamedGroup exists, match a, else match b."

Using these constructs and regular expressions, you will find that you can validate just about anything that your users throw at you. If regular expressions aren't enough for you, you can add your own validator by deriving a new class from `CustomValidator`. This is quite a bit of work, and I avoid it whenever I can. You write a server validator function using C#, and then you also write a client-side validator function using ECMAscript. I hate writing anything twice. I also avoid writing anything in ECMAscript, so I like to stick to regular expressions.

For example, here is a regular expression that validates U.S. phone numbers. It accepts area codes with or without parentheses around them, as well as any number of whitespace between the area code, exchange, and number. A dash between the area code and the exchange is also optional:

```
((\(\s*\d{3}\s*\))|(\d{3}))-?\s*\d{3}\s*-\s*\d{4}
```

By examining each group of expressions, the logic is clear:

```
((\(\s*\d{3}\s*\))|(\d{3}))-?
```

This matches the area code. It allows either (xxx) or xxx, where xxx is three digits. Any amount of whitespace surrounding the digits is acceptable. The last two characters, - and ?, allow but do not demand a dash.

The remaining portion matches the xxx-xxxx portion of the phone number. \s matches any amount of whitespace. \d{3} matches three digits. \s*-\s* matches a dash surrounded by any number of whitespace. Finally, \d{4} matches exactly four digits.

Windows validation works somewhat differently. No precooked validators parse input for you. Instead, you need to write an event handler for the `System.Windows.Forms.Control.Validating` event. Or, if you are creating your own custom control, override the `OnValidating` method (see Item 35). A standard form for a validation event handler follows:

```
private void textBoxName_Validating( object sender,
  System.ComponentModel.CancelEventArgs e )
{
  string error = null;
  // Perform your test
  if ( textBoxName.Text.Length == 0 )
  {
    // If the test fails, set the error string
    // and cancel the validation event.
```

```
    error = "Please enter a name";
    e.Cancel = true;
  }
  // Update the state of an error provider with
  // the correct error text. Set to null for no
  // error.
  this.errorProviderAll.SetError( textBoxName, error );
}
```

You have a few more small tasks to make sure that no invalid input sneaks through. Every control contains a `CausesValidation` property. This property determines whether the control participates in validation. In general, you should leave it `true` for all of your controls, except for the Cancel button. If you forget, the user must create valid input to cancel from your dialog box. The second small task is to add an OK handler to force validation of all controls. Validation happens only when a user visits and leaves a control. If the user opens a form and immediately presses OK, none of your validation code executes. To fix that, you add an OK button handler to walk through all your controls and force them to validate. The following two routines show you how to do this correctly. The recursive routines handle those controls that are also containers for other controls: tab pages, group boxes, and panels:

```
private void buttonOK_Click( object sender,
  System.EventArgs e )
{
  // Validate everyone:
  // Here, this.DialogResult will be set to
  // DialogResult.OK
  ValidateAllChildren( this );
}


private void ValidateAllChildren( Control parent )
{
  // If validation already failed, stop checking.
  if( this.DialogResult == DialogResult.None )
    return;

  // For every control
  foreach( Control c in parent.Controls )
  {
```

```
    // Give it focus
    c.Focus( );

    // Try and validate:
    if (!this.Validate( ))
    {
      // when invalid, don't let the dialog close:
      this.DialogResult = DialogResult.None;
      return;
    }
    // Validate children
    ValidateAllChildren( c );
  }
}
```

This code handles most normal cases. A special shortcut applies to the DataGrid/DataSet combination. Assign the `ErrorProvider`'s `DataSource` and `DataMember` properties at design time:

```
ErrProvider.DataSource = myDataSet;
ErrProvider.DataMember = "Table1";
```

Or, at runtime, call the `BindToDataAndErrors` method to set both in one operation:

```
ErrProvider.BindToDataAndErrors(
  myDataSet, "Table1" );
```

Errors get displayed by setting the `DataRow.RowError` property and calling the `DataRow.SetColumnError` method to display specific errors. The `ErrorProvider` displays the red exclamation icon on the row and the specific cell in the `DataGrid`.

This whirlwind tour of the validation controls in the framework should help you efficiently create the validation you need in many applications. User input cannot be trusted: Users make mistakes, and occasionally malicious users try to break your application. By making the most use of the services already provided by the .NET Framework, you reduce the code you need to write. Validate all user input, but do it efficiently with the tools already provided.

Item 40: Match Your Collection to Your Needs

To the question of "Which collection is best?," the answer is "It depends." Different collections have different performance characteristics and are optimized for different actions. The .NET Framework supports many of the familiar collections: lists, arrays, queue, stack, and others. C# supports multidimensional arrays, which have performance characteristics that differ from either single-dimensional arrays or jagged arrays. The framework also includes many specialized collections; look through those before you build your own. You can find all the collections quickly because all collections implement the ICollection interface. The documentation for ICollection lists all classes that implement that interface. Those 20-odd classes are the collections at your disposal.

To pick the right collection for your proposed use, you need to consider the actions you'll most often perform on that collection. To produce a resilient program, you'll rely in the interfaces that are implemented by the collection classes so that you can substitute a different collection when you find that your assumptions about the usage of the collection were incorrect (see Item 19).

The .NET Framework has three different kinds of collections: arrays, arraylike collections, and hash-based containers. Arrays are the simplest and generally the fastest, so let's start there. This is the collection type you'll use most often.

Your first choice should often be the System.Array class—or, more correctly, a type-specific array class. The first and most significant reason for choosing the array class is that arrays are type-safe. All other collection classes store System.Object references, until C# 2.0 introduces generics (see Item 49). When you declare any array, the compiler creates a specific System.Array derivative for the type you specify. For example, this declaration creates an array of integers:

```
private int [] _numbers = new int[100];
```

The array stores integers, not System.Object. That's significant because you avoid the boxing and unboxing penalty when you add, access, or remove value types from the array (see Item 17). That initialization creates a single-dimensional array with 100 integers stored in it. All the memory occupied by the array has a 0 bit pattern stored in it. Arrays of value types are all 0s, and arrays of reference types are all null. Each item in the array can be accessed by its index:

```
int j = _numbers[ 50 ];
```

In addition to the array access, you can iterate the array using `foreach` or an enumerator (see Item 11):

```
foreach ( int i in _numbers )
  Console.WriteLine( i.ToString( ) );


// or:
IEnumerator it = _numbers.GetEnumerator( );
while( it.MoveNext( ))
{
  int i = (int) it.Current;
  Console.WriteLine( i.ToString( ) );
}
```

If you are storing a single sequence of like objects, you should store them in an array. But often, your data structures are more complicated collections. It's tempting to quickly fall back on the C-style jagged array, an array that contains other arrays. Sometimes, this is exactly what you need. Each element in the outer collection is an array along the inner direction:

```
public class MyClass
{
  // Declare a jagged array:
  private int[] [] _jagged;

  public MyClass()
  {
    // Create the outer array:
    _jagged = new int[5][];

    // Create each inner array:
    _jagged[0] = new int[5];
    _jagged[1] = new int[10];
    _jagged[2] = new int[12];
    _jagged[3] = new int[7];
    _jagged[4] = new int[23];
  }
}
```

Each inner single-dimension array can be a different size than the outer arrays. Use jagged arrays when you need to create differently sized arrays of arrays. The drawback to jagged arrays is that a column-wise traversal is inefficient. Examining the third column in each row of a jagged array requires two lookups for each access. There is no relationship between the locations of the element at row 0, column 3 and the element at row 1, column 3. Only multidimensional arrays can perform column-wise traversals more efficiently. Old-time C and C++ programmers made their own two- (or more) dimensional arrays by mapping them onto a single-dimension array. For old-time C and C++ programmers, this notation is clear:

```
double num = MyArray[ i * rowLength + j ];
```

The rest of the world would prefer this:

```
double num = MyArray[ i, j ];
```

But C and C++ did not support multidimensional arrays. C# does. Use the multidimensional array syntax: It's clearer to both you and the compiler when you mean to create a true multidimensional structure. You create multidimensional arrays using an extension of the familiar single-dimension array notation:

```
private int[ , ] _multi = new int[ 10, 10 ];
```

The previous declaration creates a two-dimensional array, a 10×10 array with 100 elements. The length of each dimension in a multidimensional array is always constant. The compiler utilizes this property to generate more efficient initialization code. Initializing the jagged array requires multiple initialization statements. In my simple example earlier, you need five statements. Larger arrays or arrays with more dimensions require more extensive initialization code. You must write code by hand. However, multidimensional arrays with more dimensions merely require more dimension specifiers in the initialization statement. Furthermore, the multidimensional array initializes all array elements more efficiently. Arrays of value types are initialized to contain a value at each valid index in the array. The contents of the value are all 0. Arrays of reference types contain null at each index in the array. Arrays of arrays contain null inner arrays.

Traversing multidimensional arrays is almost always faster than traversing jagged arrays, especially for by-column or diagonal traversals. The compiler can use pointer arithmetic on any dimension of the array. Jagged arrays require finding each correct value for each single-dimension array.

Multidimensional arrays can be used like any collection in many ways. Suppose you are building a game based on a checker board. You'd make a board of 64 Squares laid out in a grid:

```
private Square[ , ] _theBoard = new Square[ 8, 8 ];
```

This initialization creates the array storage for the Squares. Assuming that Square is a reference type, the Squares themselves are not yet created, and each array element is null. To initialize the elements, you must look at each dimension in the array:

```
for ( int i = 0; i < _theBoard.GetLength( 0 ); i++ )
  for( int j = 0; j < _theBoard.GetLength( 1 ); j++ )
    _theBoard[ i, j ] = new Square( );
```

But you have more flexibility in traversing the elements in a multidimensional array. You can get an individual element using the array indexes:

```
Square sq = _theBoard[ 4, 4 ];
```

If you need to iterate the entire collection, you can use an iterator:

```
foreach( Square sq in _theBoard )
  sq.PaintSquare( );
```

Contrast that with what you would write for jagged arrays:

```
foreach( Square[] row in _theBoard )
  foreach( Square sq in row )
    sq.PaintSquare( );
```

Every new dimension in a jagged array introduces another foreach statement. However, with a multidimensional array, a single foreach statement generates all the code necessary to check the bounds of each dimension and get each element of the array. The foreach statement generates specific code to iterate the array by using each array dimension. The foreach loop generates the same code as if you had written this:

```
for ( int i = _theBoard.GetLowerBound( 0 );
  i <= _theBoard.GetUpperBound( 0 ); i++ )
```

```
for( int j = _theBoard.GetLowerBound( 1 );
  j <= _theBoard.GetUpperBound( 1 ); j++ )
  _theBoard[ i, j ].PaintSquare( );
```

This looks inefficient, considering all those calls to `GetLowerBound` and `GetUpperBound` inside the loop statement, but it's actually the most efficient construct. The JIT compiler knows enough about the array class to cache the boundaries and to recognize that internal bounds checking can be omitted (see Item 11).

Two major disadvantages to the array class will make you examine the other collection classes in the .NET Framework. The first affects resizing the arrays: Arrays cannot be dynamically resized. If you need to modify the size of any dimension of an array, you must create a new array and copy all the existing elements to it. Resizing takes time: A new array must be allocated, and all the elements must be copied from the existing array into the new array. Although this copying and moving is not as expensive on the managed heap as it was in the C and C++ days, it still costs time. More important, it can result in stale data being used. Consider this code fragment:

```
private string [] _cities = new string[ 100 ];

public void SetDataSources( )
{
  myListBox.DataSource = _cities;
}

public void AddCity( string CityName )
{
  String[] tmp = new string[ _cities.Length + 1 ];
  _cities.CopyTo( tmp, 0 );
  tmp[ _cities.Length ] = CityName;

  _cities = tmp; // swap the storage.
}
```

Even after `AddCity` is called, the list box uses the old copy of the `_cities` array for its data source. Your new city never shows up in the list box.

The `ArrayList` class is a higher-level abstraction built on an array. The `ArrayList` collection mixes the semantics of a single-dimension array with the semantics of a linked list. You can perform inserts on an `ArrayList`, and you can resize an `ArrayList`. The `ArrayList` delegates almost all of its responsibilities to the contained array, which means that the `ArrayList` class has very similar performance characteristics to the `Array` class. The main advantage of `ArrayList` over `Array` is that `ArrayList` is easier to use when you don't know exactly how large your collection will be. `ArrayList` can grow and shrink over time. You still pay the performance penalty of moving and copying items, but the code for those algorithms has already been written and tested. Because the internal storage for the array is encapsulated in the `ArrayList` object, the problem of stale data does not exist: Clients point to the `ArrayList` object instead of the internal array. The `ArrayList` collection is the .NET Framework's version of the C++ Standard Library `vector` class.

The `Queue` and the `Stack` classes provide specialized interfaces on top of the `System.Array` class. The specific interfaces for those classes build custom interfaces for the first-in, first-out queue and the last-in, first-out stack. Always remember that these collections are built using a single-dimension array as their internal storage. The same performance penalty applies when you resize them.

The .NET collections don't contain a linked list structure. The efficiency of the garbage collector minimizes the times when a list structure is really the best choice. If you really need linked list behavior, you have two options. If you are using a list because you expect to add and remove items often, you can use the dictionary classes with null values. Simply store the keys. You can use the `ListDictionary` class, which implements a single linked list of key/value pairs. Or, you can use the `HybridDictionary` class, which uses the `ListDictionary` for small collections and switches to a `Hashtable` for larger collections. These collections and a host of others are in the `System.Collections.Specialized` namespace. However, if you want to use a list structure because of a user-controllable order, you can use the `ArrayList` collection. The `ArrayList` can perform inserts at any location, even though it uses an array as its internal storage.

Two other classes support dictionary-based collections: `SortedList` and `Hashtable`. Both contain key/value pairs. `SortedList` orders the keys, whereas `Hashtable` does not. `Hashtable` performs searches for a given key faster, but `SortedList` provides an ordered iteration of the elements by key. `Hashtable` finds keys using the hash value of the key object. It searches by a constant time operation, O(1), if the hash key is very efficient. The sorted list uses a binary search algorithm to find the keys. This is a logarithmic operation: O(ln n).

Finally, there is the BitArray class. As its name suggests, this holds bit values. The storage for the BitArray is an array of ints. Each int stores 32 binary values. This makes the BitArray class compact, but it can also decrease performance. Each get or set operation in the BitArray performs bit manipulations on the int value that stores the sought value and 31 other bits. BitArray contains methods that apply Boolean operations to many values at once: OR, XOR, AND, and NOT. These methods take a BitArray as a parameter and can be used to quickly mask multiple bits in the BitArray. The BitArray is the optimized container for bit operations; use it when you are storing a collection of bitflags that are often manipulated using masks. Do not use it as a substitute for a general-purpose array of Boolean values.

With the exception of the Array class, none of the collection classes in the 1.*x* release of C# is strongly typed. They all store references to Object. C# generics will contain new versions of all these topologies that are built on generics. That will be the best way to create type-safe collections. In the meantime, the current System.Collections namespace contains abstract base classes that you can use to build your own type-safe interfaces on top of the type-unsafe collections: CollectionBase and ReadOnlyCollectionBase provide base classes for a list or vector structure. DictionaryBase provides a base class for key/value pairs. The DictionaryBase class is built using a Hashtable implementation; its performance characteristics are consistent with the Hashtable.

Anytime your classes contain collections, you'll likely want to expose that collection to the users of your class. You do this in two ways: with indexers and the IEnumerable interface. Remember that, early in this item, I showed you that you can directly access items in an array using [ ] notation, and you can iterate the items in the array using foreach.

You can create multidimensional indexers for your classes. These are analogous to the overloaded operator [ ] that you could write in C++. As with arrays in C#, you can create multidimensional indexers:

```
public int this [ int x, int y ]
{
  get
```

```
  {
    return ComputeValue( x, y );
  }
}
```

Adding indexer support usually means that your type contains a collection. That means you should support the `IEnumerable` interface. `IEnumerable` provides a standard mechanism for iterating all the elements in your collection:

```
public interface IEnumerable
{
  IEnumerator GetEnumerator( );
}
```

The `GetEnumerator` method returns an object that implements the `IEnumerator` interface. The `IEnumerator` interface supports traversing a collection:

```
public interface IEnumerator
{
  object Current
  { get; }

  bool MoveNext( );

  void Reset( );
}
```

In addition to the `IEnumerable` interface, you should consider the `IList` or `ICollection` interfaces if your type models an array. If your type models a dictionary, you should consider implementing the `IDictionary` interface. You could create the implementations for these large interfaces yourself, and I could spend several more pages explaining how. But there is an easier solution: Derive your class from `CollectionBase` or `DictionaryBase` when you create your own specialized collections.

Let's review what we've covered. The best collection depends on the operations you perform and the overall goals of space and speed for your application. In most situations, the `Array` provides the most efficient container. The addition of multidimensional arrays in C# means that it is easier to model multidimensional structures clearly without sacrificing performance. When your program needs more flexibility in adding and removing items, use one of the more robust collections. Finally, implement indexers and the `IEnumerable` interface whenever you create a class that models a collection.

Item 41: Prefer `DataSets` to Custom Structures

`DataSets` have gotten a bad reputation for two reasons. First, XML serialized `DataSets` do not interact well with non-.NET code. Using `DataSets` as part of a web service API makes it more difficult to interact with systems that don't use the .NET Framework. Second, they are a very generic container. You can misuse a `DataSet` by circumventing some of the .NET Framework's type safety. But the `DataSet` still solves a large number of common requirements for modern systems. If you understand its strengths and avoid its weaknesses, you can make extensive use of the type.

The `DataSet` class is designed to be an offline cache of data stored in a relational database. You already know that it stores `DataTables`, which store rows and columns of data that can match the layout of a database. You know that the `DataSet` and its members support data binding. You might even have seen examples of how the `DataSet` supports relations between the `DataTables` it contains. It's even possible that you've seen examples of constraints that validate the data being placed in a `DataSet`.

But there's even more than that. `Datasets` also support transactions through the `AcceptChanges` and `RejectChanges` methods, and they can be stored as `DiffGrams` that contain the history of changes to the data. Multiple `Datasets` can be merged to provide a common storage repository. `DataSets` support views, which enable you to examine portions of your data that satisfy search criteria. You can create views that cross several tables.

Yet, some of us want to develop our own storage structures rather than use the `DataSet`. The `DataSet` is a general container. Performance suffers a little to support that generality. A `DataSet` is not a strongly typed container. The collection of `DataTables` is a dictionary. The collection of columns in a table is also a dictionary. Items are stored as `System.Object` references. That leads us to write these kinds of constructs:

```
int val = ( int )MyDataSet.Tables[ "table1" ].
  Rows[ 0 ][ "total" ];
```

To the strongly typed C# mind, this construct is troublesome. If you mistype `table1` or `total`, you get a runtime error. An access to the data element requires a cast. If you multiply these problems by the number of times you access the elements of a `DataSet`, you can really want to find a strongly typed solution. So we try typed `DataSets`. On the surface, it's what we want:

```
int val = MyDataSet.table1.
  Rows[ 0 ].total;
```

It's perfect—until you look inside the generated C# that comprises the typed `DataSet`. It wraps the existing `DataSet` and provides strongly typed access in addition to the weakly typed access in the `DataSet` class. Your clients can still access the weakly typed API. That's less than optimal.

Live with it. To illustrate how much you give up, I'll show you how some of the features inside the `DataSet` class are implemented, in the context of creating your own custom collection. You're thinking that it can't be that hard. You're thinking that you don't need all the features of the `DataSet`, so it won't take that long. Okay, fine, I'll play along.

Imagine that you need to create a collection that stores addresses. An individual item must support data binding, so you create a struct with public properties:

```
public struct AddressRecord
{
  private string _street;
  public string Street
  {
    get { return _street; }
    set { _street = value; }
  }

  private string _city;
  public string City
  {
    get { return _city; }
    set { _city = value; }
  }
```

```
    private string _state;
    public string State
    {
      get { return _state; }
      set { _state = value; }
    }

    private string _zip;
    public string Zip
    {
      get { return _zip; }
      set { _zip = value; }
    }
  }
```

Next, you need to create the collection. You want a type-safe collection, so you derive one from `CollectionsBase`:

```
public class AddressList : CollectionBase
{
}
```

`CollectionBase` supports the `IList` interface, so you can use it as a data-binding source. Now you discover your first serious problem: All your data-binding actions fail when your list of addresses is empty. That did not happen with the `Dataset`. Data binding consists of late-binding code built on reflection. The control uses reflection to load the first element in the list, and then uses reflection to determine its type and all the properties that are members of that type. That's how a `DataGrid` learns what columns to add. It finds all the public properties of the first element in the collection, and those are displayed. When the collection is empty, that won't work. You have two possible solutions to this problem. The first is the ugly but simple solution: Never allow an empty list. The second is the elegant but more time-consuming solution: Implement the `ITypedList` interface. `ITypedList` provides two methods that describe the types in the collection. `GetListName` returns a human-readable string that describes the list. `GetItemProperties` returns a list of `PropertyDescriptors` that describe each property that should form a column in the grid:

```
public class AddressList : CollectionBase
{
```

```
public string GetListName(
  PropertyDescriptor[ ] listAccessors )
{
  return "AddressList";
}

public PropertyDescriptorCollection
  GetItemProperties(
  PropertyDescriptor[ ] listAccessors)
{
  Type t = typeof( AddressRecord );
  return TypeDescriptor.GetProperties( t );
}
}
```

It's getting a little better. Now you have a collection that supports simple binding. You're missing a lot of features, though. The next requested feature is transaction support. If you had used a `DataSet`, your users would be able to cancel all changes to a single row in the `DataGrid` by pressing the Esc key. For example, a user could type the wrong city, press Esc, and have the original value restored. The `DataGrid` also supports error notification. You could attach a `ColumnChanged` event handler to perform any validation rules you need on a particular column For instance, the state code must be a two-letter abbreviation. Using the `DataSet` framework, that's coded like this:

```
ds.Tables[ "Addresses" ].ColumnChanged +=new
  DataColumnChangeEventHandler( ds_ColumnChanged );

private void ds_ColumnChanged( object sender,
  DataColumnChangeEventArgs e )
{
  if ( e.Column.ColumnName == "State" )
  {
    string newVal = e.ProposedValue.ToString( );
    if ( newVal.Length != 2 )
    {
      e.Row.SetColumnError( e.Column,
        "State abbreviation must be two letters" );
      e.Row.RowError = "Error on State";
    }
```

```
    else
    {
      e.Row.SetColumnError( e.Column,
        "" );
      e.Row.RowError = "";
    }
  }
}
```

To support both concepts on your custom collection, you have quite a bit more work ahead of you. You need to modify your `AddressRecord` structure to support two new interfaces, `IEditableObject` and `IDataError-Info`. `IEditableObject` provides transaction support for your object. `IDataErrorInfo` provides the error-handling routines. To support the transactions, you must modify your data storage to provide your own rollback capability. You might have errors on multiple columns, so your storage must also include a collection of errors for each column. Here's the updated listing for the `AddressRecord`:

```
public class AddressRecord : IEditableObject, IDataErrorInfo
{
    private struct AddressRecordData
    {
      public string street;
      public string city;
      public string state;
      public string zip;
    }

    private AddressRecordData permanentRecord;
    private AddressRecordData tempRecord;

    private bool _inEdit = false;
    private IList _container;

    private Hashtable errors = new Hashtable();

    public AddressRecord( AddressList container )
    {
      _container = container;
    }
```

```csharp
public string Street
{
  get
  {
    return ( _inEdit ) ? tempRecord.street :
      permanentRecord.street;
  }
  set
  {
    if ( value.Length == 0 )
      errors[ "Street" ] = "Street cannot be empty";
    else
    {
      errors.Remove( "Street" );
    }
    if ( _inEdit )
      tempRecord.street = value;
    else
    {
      permanentRecord.street = value;
      int index = _container.IndexOf( this );
      _container[ index ] = this;
    }
  }
}

public string City
{
  get
  {
    return ( _inEdit ) ? tempRecord.city :
      permanentRecord.city;
  }
  set
  {
    if ( value.Length == 0 )
      errors[ "City" ] = "City cannot be empty";
    else
    {
      errors.Remove( "City" );
```

```
      }
      if ( _inEdit )
        tempRecord.city = value;
      else
      {
        permanentRecord.city = value;
        int index = _container.IndexOf( this );
        _container[ index ] = this;
      }
    }
  }
}

public string State
{
  get
  {
    return ( _inEdit ) ? tempRecord.state :
      permanentRecord.state;
  }
  set
  {
    if ( value.Length == 0 )
      errors[ "State" ] = "City cannot be empty";
    else
    {
      errors.Remove( "State" );
    }
    if ( _inEdit )
      tempRecord.state = value;
    else
    {
      permanentRecord.state = value;
      int index = _container.IndexOf( this );
      _container[ index ] = this;
    }
  }
}

public string Zip
{
```

```
    get
    {
      return ( _inEdit ) ? tempRecord.zip :
        permanentRecord.zip;
    }
    set
    {
      if ( value.Length == 0 )
        errors["Zip"] = "Zip cannot be empty";
      else
      {
        errors.Remove ( "Zip" );
      }
      if ( _inEdit )
        tempRecord.zip = value;
      else
      {
        permanentRecord.zip = value;
        int index = _container.IndexOf( this );
        _container[ index ] = this;
      }
    }
  }
}
public void BeginEdit( )
{
  if ( ( ! _inEdit ) && ( errors.Count == 0 ) )
    tempRecord = permanentRecord;
  _inEdit = true;
}

public void EndEdit( )
{
  // Can't end editing if there are errors:
  if ( errors.Count > 0 )
    return;

  if ( _inEdit )
    permanentRecord = tempRecord;
  _inEdit = false;
}
```

```csharp
public void CancelEdit( )
{
  errors.Clear( );
  _inEdit = false;
}

public string this[string columnName]
{
  get
  {
    string val = errors[ columnName ] as string;
    if ( val != null )
      return val;
    else
      return null;
  }
}

public string Error
{
  get
  {
    if ( errors.Count > 0 )
    {
      System.Text.StringBuilder errString = new
        System.Text.StringBuilder();
      foreach ( string s in errors.Keys )
      {
        errString.Append( s );
        errString.Append( ", " );
      }
      errString.Append( "Have errors" );
      return errString.ToString( );
    }
    else
      return "";
  }
}
}
```

That's several pages of code—all to support features already implemented in the `DataSet`. In fact, this still doesn't have all the `DataSet` features working properly. Interactively adding new records to the collection and supporting transactions require some more hoops for `BeginEdit`, `CancelEdit`, and `EndEdit`. You need to detect when `CancelEdit` is called on a new object rather than a modified object. `CancelEdit` must remove the new object from the container if the object was created after that last `BeginEdit`. It requires more modification to the `AddressRecord` and a couple event handlers added to the `AddressList` class.

Finally, there's the `IBindingList` interface. This interface contains more than 20 methods and properties that controls query to describe the capabilities of the list. You must implement `IBindingList` for read-only lists or interactive sorting, or to support searching. That's before you get to anything involving navigation and hierarchies. I'm not even going to add an example of all that code.

Several pages later, ask yourself, do you still want to create your own specialized collection? Or do you want to use a `DataSet`? Unless your collection is part of a performance-critical set of algorithms or must have a portable format, use the `DataSet`—especially the typed `DataSet`. It will save you tremendous amounts of time. Yes, you can argue that the `DataSet` is not the best example of object-oriented design. Typed `DataSets` break even more rules. But this is one of those times when your productivity far outweighs what might be a more elegant hand-coded design.

Item 42: Utilize Attributes to Simplify Reflection

When you build systems that rely on reflection, you should define custom attributes for the types, methods, and properties you intend to use to make them easier to access. The custom attributes indicate how you intended the method to be used at runtime. Attributes can test some of the properties of the target. Testing these properties minimizes the likelihood of mistyping that can happen with reflection.

Suppose you need to build a mechanism to add menu items and command handlers to a running software system. The requirements are simple: Drop an assembly into a directory, and the program will find out about it and add new menu items for the new command. This is one of those jobs that is best handled with reflection: Your main program needs to interact with assemblies that have not yet been written. The new add-ins also don't represent a set of functionality that can be easily encoded in an interface.

Let's begin with the code you need to create the add-in framework. You need to load an assembly using the `Assembly.LoadFrom()` function. You need to find the types that might provide menu handlers. You need to create an object of the proper type. `Type.GetConstructor()` and `ConstructorInfo.Invoke()` are the tools for that. You need to find a method that matches the menu command event handler signature. After all those tasks, you need to figure out where on the menu to add the new text, and what the text should be.

Attributes make many of these tasks easier. By tagging different classes and event handlers with custom attributes, you greatly simplify your task of finding and installing those potential command handlers. You use attributes in conjunction with reflection to minimize the risks described in Item 43.

The first task is to write the code that finds and loads the add-in assemblies. Assume that the add-ins are in a subdirectory under the main executable directory. The code to find and load the assemblies is simple:

```
// Find all the assemblies in the Add-ins directory:
string AddInsDir = string.Format( "{0}/Addins",
  Application.StartupPath );
string[] assemblies = Directory.GetFiles( AddInsDir,
  "*.dll" );
foreach ( string assemblyFile in assemblies )
{
  Assembly asm = Assembly.LoadFrom( assemblyFile );
  // Find and install command handlers from the assembly.
}
```

Next, you need to replace that last comment with the code that finds the classes that implement command handlers and installs the handlers. After you load an assembly, you can use reflection to find all the exported types in an assembly. Use attributes to figure out which exported types contain command handlers and which methods are the command handlers. An attribute class marks the types that have command handlers:

```
// Define the Command Handler Custom Attribute:
[AttributeUsage( AttributeTargets.Class )]
```

```
public class CommandHandlerAttribute : Attribute
{
  public CommandHandlerAttribute( )
  {
  }
}
```

This attribute is all the code you need to write to mark each command. Always mark an attribute class with the `AttributeUsage` attribute; it tells other programmers and the compiler where your attribute can be used. The previous example states that the `CommandHandlerAttribute` can be applied only to classes; it cannot be applied on any other language element.

You call `GetCustomAttributes` to determine whether a type has the `CommandHandlerAttribute`. Only those types are candidates for add-ins:

```
// Find all the assemblies in the Add-ins directory:
string AddInsDir = string.Format( "{0}/Addins",
Application.StartupPath);
string[] assemblies = Directory.GetFiles( AddInsDir,
  "*.dll" );
foreach ( string assemblyFile in assemblies )
{
  Assembly asm = Assembly.LoadFrom( assemblyFile );
  // Find and install command handlers from the assembly.
  foreach( System.Type t in asm.GetExportedTypes( ))
  {
    if (t.GetCustomAttributes(
      typeof( CommandHandlerAttribute ), false ).Length > 0 )
    {
      // Found the command handler attribute on this type.
      // This type implements a command handler.
      // configure and add it.
    }
    // Else, not a command handler. Skip it.
  }
}
```

Now let's add another new attribute to find command handlers. A type might easily implement several command handlers, so you define a new attribute that add-in authors will attach to each command handler. This attribute will include parameters that define where to place menu items for new commands. Each event handler handles one specific command, which is located in a specific spot on the menu. To tag a command handler, you define an attribute that marks a property as a command handler and declares the text for the menu item and the text for the parent menu item. The DynamicCommand attribute is constructed with two parameters: the command text and the text of the parent menu. The attribute class contains a constructor that initializes the two strings for the menu item. Those strings are also available as read/write properties:

```
[AttributeUsage( AttributeTargets.Property ) ]
public class DynamicMenuAttribute : System.Attribute
{
  private string _menuText;
  private string _parentText;

  public DynamicMenuAttribute( string CommandText,
    string ParentText )
  {
    _menuText = CommandText;
    _parentText = ParentText;
  }

  public string MenuText
  {
    get { return _menuText; }
    set { _menuText = value; }
  }

  public string ParentText
  {
    get { return _parentText; }
    set { _parentText = value; }
  }
}
```

This attribute class is tagged so that it can be applied only to properties. The command handler must be exposed as a property in the class that provides access to the command handler. Using this technique simplifies finding the command handler code and attaching it to the program at startup.

Now you create an object of that type, find the command handlers, and attach them to new menu items. You guessed it—you use a combination of attributes and reflection to find and use the command handler properties:

```
// Expanded from the first code sample:
// Find the types in the assembly
foreach( Type t in asm.GetExportedTypes( ) )
{
  if (t.GetCustomAttributes(
    typeof( CommandHandlerAttribute ), false).Length > 0 )
  {
    // Found a command handler type:
    ConstructorInfo ci =
      t.GetConstructor( new Type[0] );
    if ( ci == null ) // No default ctor
      continue;
    object obj = ci.Invoke( null );
    PropertyInfo [] pi = t.GetProperties( );

    // Find the properties that are command
    // handlers
    foreach( PropertyInfo p in pi )
    {
      string menuTxt = "";
      string parentTxt = "";
      object [] attrs = p.GetCustomAttributes(
        typeof ( DynamicMenuAttribute ), false );
      foreach ( Attribute at in attrs )
      {
        DynamicMenuAttribute dym = at as
          DynamicMenuAttribute;
        if ( dym != null )
        {
```

```
            // This is a command handler.
            menuTxt = dym.MenuText;
            parentTxt = dym.ParentText;
            MethodInfo mi = p.GetGetMethod();
            EventHandler h = mi.Invoke( obj, null )
              as EventHandler;
            UpdateMenu( parentTxt, menuTxt, h );
          }
        }
      }
    }
}


private void UpdateMenu( string parentTxt, string txt,
  EventHandler cmdHandler )
{
  MenuItem menuItemDynamic = new MenuItem();
  menuItemDynamic.Index = 0;
  menuItemDynamic.Text = txt;
  menuItemDynamic.Click += cmdHandler;

  //Find the parent menu item.
  foreach ( MenuItem parent in mainMenu.MenuItems )
  {
    if ( parent.Text == parentTxt )
    {
      parent.MenuItems.Add( menuItemDynamic );
      return;
    }
  }
  // Existing parent not found:
  MenuItem newDropDown = new MenuItem();
  newDropDown.Text = parentTxt;
  mainMenu.MenuItems.Add( newDropDown );
  newDropDown.MenuItems.Add( menuItemDynamic );
}
```

Now you'll build a sample command handler. First, you tag the type with the `CommandHandler` attribute. As you see here, it is customary to omit `Attribute` from the name when attaching an attribute to an item:

```
[ CommandHandler ]
public class CmdHandler
{
  // Implementation coming soon.
}
```

Inside the `CmdHandler` class, you add a property to retrieve the command handler. That property should be tagged with the `DynamicMenu` attribute:

```
[DynamicMenu( "Test Command", "Parent Menu" )]
public EventHandler CmdFunc
{
  get
  {
    if ( theCmdHandler == null )
      theCmdHandler = new System.EventHandler
        (this.DynamicCommandHandler);
    return theCmdHandler;
  }
}


private void DynamicCommandHandler(
  object sender, EventArgs args )
{
  // Contents elided.
}
```

That's it. This example shows you how you can utilize attributes to simplify programming idioms that use reflection. You tagged each type that provided a dynamic command handler with an attribute. That made it easier to find the command handlers when you dynamically loaded the assembly. By applying `AttributeTargets` (another attribute), you limit where the dynamic command attribute can be applied. This simplifies the difficult task of finding the sought types in a dynamically loaded assembly: You greatly decrease the chance of using the wrong types. It's still not simple code, but it is a little more palatable than without attributes.

Attributes declare your runtime intent. Tagging an element with an attribute indicates its use and simplifies the task of finding that element at runtime. Without attributes, you need to define some naming convention to find the types and the elements that will be used at runtime. Any naming convention is a source of human error. Tagging your intent with attributes shifts more responsibilities from the developer to the compiler. The attributes can be placed only on a certain kind of language element. The attributes also carry syntactic and semantic information.

You use reflection to create dynamic code that can be reconfigured in the field. Designing and implementing attribute classes to force developers to declare the types, methods, and properties that can be used dynamically decreases the potential for runtime errors. That increases your chances of creating applications that will satisfy your users.

Item 43: Don't Overuse Reflection

Building binary components sometimes means utilizing late binding and reflection to find the code with the particular functionality you need. Reflection is a powerful tool, and it enables you to write software that is much more dynamic. Using reflection, an application can be upgraded with new capabilities by adding new components that were not available when the application was deployed. That's the upside.

With this flexibility comes increased complexity, and with increased complexity comes increased chance for many problems. When you use reflection, you circumvent C#'s type safety. Instead, the `Invoke` members use parameters and return values typed as `System.Object`. You must make sure the proper types are used at runtime. In short, using reflection makes it much easier to build dynamic programs, but it is also much easier to build broken programs. Often, with a little thought, you can minimize or remove the need for reflection by creating a set of interface definitions that express your assumptions about a type.

Reflection gives you the capability to create instances of objects, invoke members on those objects, and access data members in those objects. Those sound like normal everyday programming tasks. They are. There is nothing magic about reflection: It is a means of dynamically interacting with other binary components. In most cases, you don't need the flexibility of reflection because other alternatives are more maintainable.

Let's begin with creating instances of a given type. You can often accomplish the same result using a class factory. Consider this code fragment, which creates an instance of MyType by calling the default constructor using reflection:

```
// Usage:Create a new object using reflection:
Type t = typeof( MyType );
MyType obj = NewInstance( t ) as MyType;


// Example factory function, based on Reflection:
object NewInstance( Type t )
{
  // Find the default constructor:
  ConstructorInfo ci = t.GetConstructor( new Type[ 0 ] );
  if ( ci != null )
    // Invoke default constructor, and return
    // the new object.
    return ci.Invoke( null );

  // If it failed, return null.
  return null;
}
```

The code examines the type using reflection and invokes the default constructor to create the object. If you need to create a type at runtime without any previous knowledge of the type, this is the only option. This is brittle code that relies on the presence of a default constructor. It still compiles if you remove the default constructor from MyType. You must perform runtime testing to catch any problems that arise. A class factory function that performed the same operations would not compile if the default constructor was removed:

```
public MyType NewInstance( )
{
  return new MyType();
}
```

You should create static factory functions instead of relying on reflection to instantiate objects. If you need to instantiate objects using late binding, create factory functions and tag them as such with attributes (see Item 42).

Another potential use of reflection is to access members of a type. You can use the member name and the type to call a particular function at runtime:

```
// Example usage:
Dispatcher.InvokeMethod( AnObject, "MyHelperFunc" );

// Dispatcher Invoke Method:
public void InvokeMethod ( object o, string name )
{
  // Find the member functions with that name.
  MemberInfo[] myMembers = o.GetType( ).GetMember( name );
  foreach( MethodInfo m in myMembers )
  {
    // Make sure the parameter list matches:
    if ( m.GetParameters( ).Length == 0 )
      // Invoke:
      m.Invoke( o, null );
  }
}
```

Runtime errors are lurking in the previous code. If the name is typed wrong, the method won't be found. No method will be called.

It's also a simple example. Creating a more robust version of `Invoke-Method` would need to check the types of all proposed parameters against the list of all parameters returned by the `GetParameters()` method. That code is lengthy enough and ugly enough that I did not even want to waste the space to show it to you. It's that bad.

The third use of reflection is accessing data members. The code is similar to accessing member functions:

```
// Example usage:
object field = Dispatcher.RetrieveField ( AnObject,
  "MyField" );

// elsewhere in the dispatcher class:
public object RetrieveField ( object o, string name )
{
  // Find the field.
  FieldInfo myField = o.GetType( ).GetField( name );
```

```
  if ( myField != null )
    return myField.GetValue( o );
  else
    return null;
}
```

As with the method invocation, using reflection to retrieve a data member involves querying the type for a field with a name that matches the requested field. If one is found, the value can be retrieved using the FieldInfo structure. This construct is rather common in the framework. DataBinding makes use of reflection to find the properties that are the targets of binding operation. In those cases, the dynamic nature of data binding outweighs the possible costs.

So, if reflection is such a painful process, you need to look for better and simpler alternatives. You have three options. The first is interfaces. You can define interfaces for any contract that you expect classes or structs to implement (see Item 19). That would replace all the reflection code with a few far clearer lines of code:

```
IMyInterface foo = obj as IMyInterface;
if ( foo != null)
{
  foo.DoWork( );
  foo.Msg = "work is done.";
}
```

If you combine interfaces with a factory function tagged with an attribute, almost any system you thought deserved a solution based on reflection gets much more simple:

```
public class MyType : IMyInterface
{
  [FactoryFunction]
  public static IMyInterface
    CreateInstance( )
  {
    return new MyType( );
  }

  #region IMyInterface
  public string Msg
```

```
  {
    get
    {
      return _msg;
    }
    set
    {
      _msg = value;
    }
  }
  public void DoWork( )
  {
    // details elided.
  }
  #endregion
}
```

Contrast this code with the reflection-based solution shown earlier. Even these simple examples have glossed over some of the weakly typed issues common to all the reflection APIs: The return values are all typed as objects. If you want to get the proper type, you need to cast or convert the type. Those operations could fail and are inherently dangerous. The strong type checking that the compiler provides when you create interfaces is much clearer and more maintainable.

Reflection should be used only when the invocation target can't be cleanly expressed using an interface. .NET data binding works with any public property of a type. Limiting it to an interface definition would greatly limit its reach. The menu handler sample allows any function (either instance or static) to implement the command handler. Using an interface would limit that functionality to instance methods only. Both FxCop and NUnit (see Item 48) make extensive use of reflection. They use reflection because the nature of the problems they address are best handled using it. FxCop examines all your code to evaluate it against a set of known rules. That requires reflection. NUnit must call test code you've written. It uses reflection to determine what code you've written to unit test your code. An interface cannot express the full set of methods used to test any code you might write. NUnit does use attributes to find tests and test cases to make its job easier (see Item 42).

When you can factor out the methods or properties that you intend to invoke using interfaces, you'll have a cleaner, more maintainable system. Reflection is a powerful late-binding mechanism. The .NET Framework uses it to implement data binding for both Windows- and web-based controls. However, in many less general uses, creating code using class factories, delegates, and interfaces will produce more maintainable systems.

Item 44: Create Complete Application-Specific Exception Classes

Exceptions are the mechanism of reporting errors that might be handled at a location far removed from the location where the error occurred. All the information about the error's cause must be contained in the exception object. Along the way, you might want to translate a low-level error to more of an application-specific error, without losing any information about the original error. You need to be very thoughtful about when you create your own specific exception classes in your C# applications.

The first step is to understand when and why to create new exception classes, and how to construct informative exception hierarchies. When developers using your libraries write `catch` clauses, they differentiate actions based on the specific runtime type of the exception. Each different exception class can have a different set of actions taken:

```
try {
  Foo( );
  Bar( );
} catch( MyFirstApplicationException e1 )
{
  FixProblem( e1 );
} catch( AnotherApplicationException e2 )
{
  ReportErrorAndContinue( e2 );
} catch( YetAnotherApplicationException e3 )
{
  ReportErrorAndShutdown( e3 );
} catch( Exception e )
{
  ReportGenericError( e );
}
```

```
finally
{
  CleanupResources( );
}
```

Different `catch` clauses can exist for different runtime types of exceptions. You, as a library author, must create or use different exception classes when `catch` clauses might take different actions. If you don't, your users are left with only unappealing options. You can punt and terminate the application whenever an exception gets thrown. That's certainly less work, but it won't win kudos from users. Or, they can reach into the exception to try to determine whether the error can be corrected:

```
try {
  Foo( );
  Bar( );
} catch( Exception e )
{
  switch( e.TargetSite.Name )
  {
    case "Foo":
      FixProblem( e );
      break;
    case "Bar":
      ReportErrorAndContinue( e );
      break;
    // some routine called by Foo or Bar:
    default:
      ReportErrorAndShutdown( e );
      break;
  }
} finally
{
  CleanupResources( );
}
```

That's far less appealing than using multiple `catch` clauses. It's very brittle code: If you change the name of a routine, it's broken. If you move the error-generating calls into a shared utility function, it's broken. The deeper into the call stack that an exception is generated, the more fragile this kind of construct becomes.

Before going any deeper into this topic, let me add two disclaimers. First, exceptions are not for every error condition you encounter. There are no firm guidelines, but I prefer throwing exceptions for error conditions that cause long-lasting problems if they are not handled or reported immediately. For example, data integrity errors in a database should generate an exception. The problem only gets bigger if it is ignored. Failure to correctly write the user's window location preferences is not likely to cause far-reaching consequences. A return code indicating the failure is sufficient.

Second, writing a `throw` statement does not mean it's time to create a new exception class. My recommendation on creating more rather than fewer Exception classes comes from normal human nature: People seem to gravitate to overusing `System.Exception` anytime they throw an exception. That provides the least amount of helpful information to the calling code. Instead, think through and create the necessary exceptions classes to enable calling code to understand the cause and provide the best chance of recovery.

I'll say it again: The reason for different exception classes—in fact, the only reason—is to make it easier to take different actions when your users write `catch` handlers. Look for those error conditions that might be candidates for some kind of recovery action, and create specific exception classes to handle those actions. Can your application recover from missing files and directories? Can it recover from inadequate security privileges? What about missing network resources? Create new exception classes when you encounter errors that might lead to different actions and recovery mechanisms.

So now you are creating your own exception classes. You do have very specific responsibilities when you create a new exception class. You should always derive your exception classes from the `System.ApplicationException` class, not the `System.Exception` class. You will rarely add capabilities to this base class. The purpose of different exception classes is to have the capability to differentiate the cause of errors in `catch` clauses.

But don't take anything away from the exception classes you create, either. The `ApplicationException` class contains four constructors:

```
// Default constructor
public ApplicationException( );
```

```
// Create with a message.
public ApplicationException( string );

// Create with a message and an inner exception.
public ApplicationException( string, Exception );

// Create from an input stream.
protected ApplicationException(
  SerializationInfo, StreamingContext );
```

When you create a new exception class, create all four of these constructors. Different situations call for the different methods of constructing exceptions. You delegate the work to the base class implementation:

```
public class MyAssemblyException :
  ApplicationException
{
  public MyAssemblyException( ) :
    base( )
  {
  }

  public MyAssemblyException( string s ) :
    base( s )
  {
  }

  public MyAssemblyException( string s,
    Exception e) :
    base( s, e )
  {
  }

  protected MyAssemblyException(
    SerializationInfo info, StreamingContext cxt ) :
    base( info, cxt )
  {
  }
}
```

The constructors that take an exception parameter deserve a bit more discussion. Sometimes, one of the libraries you use generates an exception. The code that called your library will get minimal information about the possible corrective actions when you simply pass on the exceptions from the utilities you use:

```
public double DoSomeWork( )
{
  // This might throw an exception defined
  // in the third party library:
  return ThirdPartyLibrary.ImportantRoutine( );
}
```

You should provide your own library's information when you generate the exception. Throw your own specific exception, and include the original exception as its `InnerException` property. You can provide as much extra information as you can generate:

```
public double DoSomeWork( )
{
  try {
    // This might throw an exception defined
    // in the third party library:
    return ThirdPartyLibrary.ImportantRoutine( );
  } catch( Exception e )
    {
      string msg =
        string.Format("Problem with {0} using library",
          this.ToString( ));
      throw new DoingSomeWorkException( msg, e );
    }
  }
}
```

This new version creates more information at the point where the problem is generated. As long as you have created a proper `ToString()` method (see Item 5), you've created an exception that describes the complete state of the object that generated the problem. More than that, the inner exception shows the root cause of the problem: something in the third-party library you used.

This technique is called exception translation, translating a low-level exception into a more high-level exception that provides more context about the error. The more information you generate when an error occurs, the easier it will be for users to diagnose and possibly correct the error. By creating your own exception types, you can translate low-level generic problems into specific exceptions that contain all the application-specific information that you need to fully diagnose and possibly correct the problem.

Your application will throw exceptions—hopefully not often, but it will happen. If you don't do anything specific, your application will generate the default .NET Framework exceptions whenever something goes wrong in the methods you call on the core framework. Providing more detailed information will go a long way to enabling you and your users to diagnose and possibly correct errors in the field. You create different exception classes when different corrective actions are possible and only when different actions are possible. You create full-featured exception classes by providing all the constructors that the base exception class supports. You use the `InnerException` property to carry along all the error information generated by lower-level error conditions.

6 | Miscellaneous

Some items don't fit convenient categories. But that does not limit their importance. Understanding code access security is important for everyone, as is understanding exception-handling strategies. Other recommendations are constantly changing because C# is a living language, with an active community and an evolving standard. It pays to look forward to these changes and prepare for them; they will impact your future work.

Item 45: Prefer the Strong Exception Guarantee

When you throw an exception, you've introduced a disruptive event into the application. Control flow has been compromised. Expected actions did not occur. Worse, you've left the cleanup operation to the programmer writing the code that eventually catches the exception. The actions available when you catch exceptions are directly related to how well you manage program state when an exception gets thrown. Thankfully, the C# community does not need to create its own strategies for exception safety; the C++ community did all the hard work for us. Starting with Tom Cargill's article "Exception Handling: A False Sense of Security," and continuing with writings by Herb Sutter, Scott Meyers, Matt Austern, Greg Colvin, and Dave Abrahams, the C++ community developed a series of best practices that we can adapt to C# applications. The discussions on exception handling occurred over the course of 6 years, from 1994 to 2000. They discussed, debated, and examined many twists on a difficult problem. We should leverage all that hard work in C#.

Dave Abrahams defined three exception-safe guarantees: the basic guarantee, the strong guarantee, and the no-throw guarantee. Herb Sutter discussed these guarantees in his book *Exceptional C++* (Addison-Wesley, 2000). The basic guarantee states that no resources are leaked and all objects are in a valid state after your application throws an exception. The strong exception guarantee builds on the basic guarantee and adds that if an exception occurs, the program state did not change. The no-throw guarantee states that an operation never fails, from which it follows that a method does not ever throw exceptions. The strong exception guarantee provides the best trade-off between recovering from exceptions and simplifying exception handling.

The basic guarantee happens almost by default in .NET and C#. The environment handles memory management. The only way you can leak resources due to exceptions is to throw an exception while you own a resource that implements IDisposable. Item 18 explains how to avoid leaking resources in the face of exceptions.

The strong guarantee states that if an operation terminates because of an exception, program state remains unchanged. Either an operation completes or it does not modify program state; there is no middle ground. The advantage of the strong guarantee is that you can more easily continue execution after catching an exception when the strong guarantee is followed. Anytime you catch an exception, whatever operation was attempted did not occur. It did not start, and it did not make some changes. The state of the program is as though you did not start the action.

Many of the recommendations I made earlier will help ensure that you meet the strong exception guarantee. Data elements that your program uses should be stored in immutable value types (see Items 6 and 7). If you combine those two items, any modification to program state can easily take place after performing any operation that might throw an exception. The general guideline is to perform any data modifications in the following manner:

1. Make defensive copies of data that will be modified.
2. Perform any modifications to these defensive copies of the data. This includes any operations that might throw an exception.
3. Swap the temporary copies back to the original. This operation cannot throw an exception.

As an example, the following code updates an employee's title and pay using defensive copy:

```
public void PhysicalMove( string title, decimal newPay )
{
  // Payroll data is a struct:
  // ctor will throw an exception if fields aren't valid.
```

```
PayrollData d = new PayrollData( title, newPay,
  this.payrollData.DateOfHire );

// if d was constructed properly, swap:
this.payrollData = d;
}
```

Sometimes, the strong guarantee is just too inefficient to support, and sometimes you cannot support the strong guarantee without introducing subtle bugs. The first and simplest case is looping constructs. When the code inside a loop modifies the state of the program and might throw an exception, you are faced with a tough choice: You can either create a defensive copy of all the objects used in the loop, or you can lower your expectations and support only the basic exception guarantee. There are no hard and fast rules, but copying heap-allocated objects in a managed environment is not as expensive as it was in native environments. A lot of time has been spent optimizing memory management in .NET. I prefer to support the strong exception guarantee whenever possible, even if it means copying a large container: The capability to recover from errors outweighs the small performance gain from avoiding the copy. In special cases, it doesn't make sense to create the copy. If any exceptions would result in terminating the program anyway, it makes no sense to worry about the strong exception guarantee. The larger concern is that swapping reference types can lead to program errors. Consider this example:

```
private DataSet _data;
public IListSource MyCollection
{
  get
  {
    return _data;
  }
}

public void UpdateData( )
{
  // make the defensive copy:
  DataSet tmp = _data.Clone( ) as DataSet;

  using ( SqlConnection myConnection =
    new SqlConnection( connString ))
```

```
  {
    myConnection.Open();

    SqlDataAdapter ad = new SqlDataAdapter( commandString,
      myConnection );

    // Store data in the copy
    ad.Fill( tmp );

    // it worked, make the swap:
    _data = tmp;
  }
}
```

This looks like a great use of the defensive copy mechanism. You've created a copy of the DataSet. Then you grab new data from the database and fill the temporary DataSet. Finally, you swap the temporary storage back. It looks great. If anything goes wrong trying to retrieve the data, you have not made any changes.

There's only one problem: It doesn't work. The MyCollection property returns a reference to the _data object (see Item 23). All the clients of this class are left holding references to the original DataSet after you call UpdateData. They are looking at the old view of the data. The swap trick does not work for reference types—it works only for value types. Because it is a common operation, there is a specific fix for DataSets. Use the Merge method:

```
private DataSet _data;
public IListSource MyCollection
{
  get
  {
    return _data;
  }
}

public void UpdateData( )
{
  // make the defensive copy:
  DataSet tmp = new DataSet( );
```

```
using ( SqlConnection myConnection =
  new SqlConnection( connString ))
{
  myConnection.Open();

  SqlDataAdapter ad = new SqlDataAdapter( commandString,
    myConnection);

  ad.Fill( tmp );

  // it worked, merge:
  _data.Merge( tmp );
}
}
```

Merging the changes into the current `DataSet` lets all clients keep a valid reference, and the internal contents of the `DataSet` are updated.

In the general case, you cannot fix the problem of swapping reference types while still ensuring that all clients have the current copy of the object. Swapping works for value types only. That should be sufficient, if you're following the advice of Item 6.

Last, and most stringent, is the no-throw guarantee. The no-throw guarantee is pretty much what it sounds like: A method satisfies the no-throw guarantee if it is guaranteed to always run to completion and never let an exception leave a method. This just isn't practical for all routines in large programs. However, in a few locations, methods must enforce the no-throw guarantee. Finalizers and `Dispose` methods must not throw exceptions. In both cases, throwing an exception can cause more problems than any other alternative. In the case of a finalizer, throwing an exception terminates the program without further cleanup.

In the case of a `Dispose` method throwing an exception, the system might now have two exceptions running through the system. The .NET environment loses the first exception and throws the new exception. You can't catch the initial exception anywhere in your program; it was eaten by the system. This greatly complicates your error handling. How can you recover from an error you don't see?

The last location for the no-throw guarantee is in delegate targets. When a delegate target throws an exception, none of the other delegate targets

gets called from the same multicast delegate. The only way around this is to ensure that you do not throw any exceptions from a delegate target. Let's state that again: Delegate targets (including event handlers) should not throw exceptions. Doing so means that the code raising the event cannot participate in the strong exception guarantee. But here, I'm going to modify that advice. Item 21 showed that you can invoke delegates so that you can recover from exceptions. Not everyone does, though, so you should avoid throwing exceptions in delegate handlers. Just because you don't throw exceptions in delegates does not mean that others follow that advice; do not rely on the no-throw guarantee for your own delegate invocations. It's that defensive programming: You should do the best you can because other programmers might do the worst they can.

Exceptions introduce serious changes to the control flow of an application. In the worst case, anything could have happened—or not happened. The only way to know what has and hasn't changed when an exception is thrown is to enforce the strong exception guarantee. Then an operation either completes or does not make any changes. Finalizers, `Dispose()`, and delegate targets are special cases and should complete without allowing exceptions to escape under any circumstances. As a last word, watch carefully when swapping reference types; it can introduce numerous subtle bugs.

Item 46: Minimize Interop

One of the smartest moves Microsoft made when designing .NET was to realize that no one would adopt the platform if there wasn't a way to integrate their existing code assets into new .NET development. Microsoft knew that without a way to leverage existing code, adoption would slow down. But that doesn't make interop easy or efficient. Interop works, but that's the only good thing that can be said about it. All the interop strategies are forced to provide some marshalling when the flow of control passes between the native and the managed boundaries. Also, interop strategies force you, the developer, to declare the method parameters by hand. Finally, the CLR cannot perform optimizations across an interop boundary. Nothing would be better for a developer than to ignore all the investment in native code and COM objects. But the world doesn't always work that way. Most of us need to add new features to existing applications, enhance and update existing tools, or otherwise make new managed applications interact with old legacy applications. Using some kind of interop is often the only practical way to slowly replace legacy systems. Therefore, it's important to understand the costs associated with the different interop strategies. These costs are paid in terms of both development schedules and runtime performance. Sometimes, the best choice is to rewrite the legacy code. Other times, you need to pick the correct interop strategy.

Before I discuss the interop strategies that are available to you, I need to spend a paragraph discussing the "just throw it out" strategy. Chapter 5, "Working with the Framework," showed you some of the classes and techniques that are already built for you and delivered in the .NET Framework. More often than you would think, you can identify the classes and algorithms that represent your core functionality and rewrite only those in C#. The rest of the existing codebase can be replaced by the functionality delivered in the .NET Framework. It doesn't work everywhere or every time, but it should be seriously considered as a migration strategy. All of Chapter 5 could be taken as a recommendation to follow the "throw it out" strategy. This one item is dedicated to interop. Interop is painful.

For the rest of this item, let's assume that you've determined that the full rewrite isn't practical. Several different strategies will let you access native code from .NET code. You need to understand the cost and inefficiencies inherent in crossing the boundary between managed and unmanaged code. There are three tolls to pay using interop. The first toll is paid by marshalling data back and forth between the managed heap and the native heap. The second toll is the thunking cost of moving between managed code and unmanaged code. You and your users pay these performance tolls. The third toll is yours alone: the amount of work you need to perform to manage this mixed environment. The third toll is the biggest, so your design decisions should minimize that cost.

Let's begin by discussing the performance costs associated with interop and how to minimize that cost. Marshalling is the single biggest factor. As with the web services and remoting, you need to strive for a chunky API rather than a chatty API. You accomplish this differently when you interact with unmanaged code. You create a chunky interop API by modifying the existing unmanaged to add a new, more interop-friendly API. A common COM practice is to declare many properties that clients can set, changing the internal state or the behavior of the object. Setting each property marshals data back and forth across the boundary. (It also thunks each time as it crosses the interop boundary.) That is very ineffi-cient. Unfortunately, the COM object or unmanaged library might not be under your control. When that happens, you need to work harder. In this case, you can create a very thin unmanaged C++ library that exposes the type's capabilities using the chunkier API that you need. That's going to increase your development time (that third toll again).

When you wrap a COM object, make sure that you modify the data types to provide a better marshalling strategy between the managed and unmanaged sections of your code. Some types can be marshaled much more efficiently than others. Try to limit the data types passed between the managed and unmanaged layers of your code to blittable types. A **blit-table** type is one in which the managed and unmanaged representations of the type are the same. The contents can be copied without regard to the internal structure of the object. In some cases, the unmanaged code can use the managed memory. The blittable types are listed here:

```
System.Byte
System.SByte
System.Int16
System.UInt16
System.Int32
System.UInt32
System.Int64
System.UInt64
System.UIntPtr
```

In addition, any one-dimensional array of a blittable type is blittable. Finally, any formatted type that contains only blittable types is blittable. A **formatted** type is a struct that explicitly defines its layout using StructLayoutAttribute:

```
[ StructLayout( LayoutKind.Sequential ) ]
public struct Point3D
{
  public int X;
  public int Y;
  public int Z;
}
```

When you use only blittable types between the unmanaged and managed layers of your code, you minimize how much information must be copied. You also optimize any copy operations that must occur.

If you can't restrict your data types to the blittable types, you can use InAttribute and OutAttribute to control when copies are made. Similar to COM, these attributes control which direction the data is copied. In/Out parameters are copied both ways; In parameters and Out parameters are copied only once. Make sure you apply the most restrictive In/Out combination to avoid more copying than necessary.

Finally, you can increase performance by declaring how data should be marshaled. This is most common with strings. Marshalling strings uses BSTRs by default. That's a safe strategy, but it is the least efficient. You can save extra copying operations by modifying the default marshalling scheme by applying the MarshalAs attribute. The following declaration marshals the string as a LPWStr, or wchar*:

```
public void SetMsg(
  [ MarshalAs( UnmanagedType.LPWStr ) ] string msg );
```

That's the short story for handling data between managed and unmanaged layers: Data gets copied and possibly translated between managed and unmanaged types. You can minimize the copy operations in three ways. The first is by limiting the parameters and return values to blittable types. That's the preferred solution. When you can't do that, apply the In and Out attributes to minimize the copy and transfer operations that must occur. As a final optimization, some types can be marshaled in more than one manner, so pick the most optimal manner for your use.

Now let's move on to how you can transfer program control between managed and unmanaged components. You have three options: COM interop, Platform Invoke (P/Invoke), and managed C++. Each has its own advantages and disadvantages.

COM interop is the easiest way to leverage those COM components you are already using. But COM interop is the least efficient way to access native code in .NET. Unless you already have a significant investment in COM components, don't go down this path. Don't look at this path—don't even think about it. Using COM interop if you don't have COM components means learning COM as well as all the interop rules. This is no time to start understanding IUnknown. Those of us who did are trying to purge it from our memories as quickly as possible. Using COM interop also means that you pay the runtime cost associated with the COM subsystem. You also have to consider what it means in terms of the differences between the CLR's object lifetime management and the COM version of object lifetime management. You can defer to the CLR, in which case every COM object you import has a finalizer, which calls `Release()` on that COM interface. Or, you can explicitly release the COM object yourself by using `ReleaseCOMObject`. The first approach introduces runtime inefficiencies in your program (see Item 15). The second introduces headaches in your programmers. Using `ReleaseCOMObject` means you are diving down into the management issues already solved by the CLR's COM interop layer. You're taking over, and you think you know best. The CLR begs to differ, and it releases COM objects, unless you tell it correctly that you have done so. This is tricky, at best, because COM expects programmers to call `Release()` on each interface, and your managed code is dealing with objects. In short, you need to know which interfaces have been `AddRef`'d on an object and release only those. Let the CLR manage COM lifetimes for you, and pay the performance costs. You're a busy developer. Learning to mix COM resource management in .NET is more than you should take on (that third toll).

Your second option is to use P/Invoke. This is the most efficient way to call any of the Win32 APIs because you avoid the overhead associated with COM. The bad news is that you need to hand-code the interface to each method that you call using P/Invoke. The more methods you invoke, the more method declarations you must hand-code. This P/Invoke declaration tells the CLR how to access the native method. This extra work explains why every example of P/Invoke (including the following one) uses `MessageBox`:

```
public class PInvokeMsgBox
{
    [ DllImport( "user32.dll" ) ]
    public static extern int MessageBoxA(
        int h, string m, string c, int type );

    public static int Main()
    {
        return MessageBoxA( 0,
          "P/InvokeTest",
          "It is using Interop", 0 );
    }
}
```

The other major drawback to P/Invoke is that it is not designed for object-oriented languages. If you need to import a C++ library, you must specify the decorated names in your import declarations. Suppose that instead of the Win32 MessageBox API, you wanted to access one of the two `AfxMessageBox` methods in the MFC C++ DLL. You'd need to create a P/Invoke declaration for one of these two methods:

```
?AfxMessageBox@@YGHIII@Z
?AfxMessageBox@@YGHPBDII@Z
```

These two decorated names match these two methods:

```
int AfxMessageBox( LPCTSTR lpszText,
  UINT nType, UINT nIDHelp );
int AFXAPI AfxMessageBox( UINT nIDPrompt,
  UINT nType, UINT nIDHelp);
```

Even after just a few overloaded methods, you quickly realize that this is not a productive way to provide interoperability. In short, use P/Invoke only to access C-style Win32 methods (more toll in developer time).

Your last option is to mix managed and unmanaged code using the /CLR switch on the Microsoft C++ compiler. If you compile all your native code using /CLR, you create an MSIL-based library that uses the native heap for all data storage. That means this C++ library cannot be called directly from C#. You must build a managed C++ library on top of your legacy code to provide the bridge between the unmanaged and managed types, providing the marshalling support between the managed and unmanaged heaps. This managed C++ library contains managed classes, whose data members are on the managed heap. These classes also contain references to the native objects:

```
// Declare the managed class:
public __gc class ManagedWrapper : public IDisposable
{
private:
  NativeType* _pMyClass;

public:
  ManagedWrapper( ) :
    _pMyClass( new NativeType( ) )
  {
  }
```

```
// Dispose:
virtual void Dispose( )
{
  delete _pMyClass;
  _pMyClass = NULL;
  GC::SuppressFinalize( this );
}

~ManagedWrapper( )
{
  delete _pMyClass;
}

// example property:
__property System::String* get_Name( )
{
  return _pMyClass->Name( );
}
__property void set_Name( System::String* value )
{
  char* tmp  = new char [ value->Length + 1 ];
  for (int i = 0 ; i < value->Length; i++ )
    tmp[ i ] = ( char )value->Chars[ i ];
  tmp[ i ] = 0;
  _pMyClass->Name( tmp );
  delete [] tmp;
}

// example method:
void DoStuff( )
{
  _pMyClass->DoStuff( );
}

// other methods elided...
}
```

Again, this is not the most productive programming tool we've ever used. This is repetitive code, and the entire purpose is to handle the marshalling and thunking between managed and unmanaged data. The advantages are that you have complete control over how you expose your methods and properties from your native code. The disadvantage is that you have to write all this code with one part of your head writing .NET code and another part writing C++. It's easy to make simple mistakes as you shift between the two. You must remember to delete unmanaged objects. Managed objects are not your responsibility. It slows down your developer time to constantly check which is correct.

Using the /CLR switch sounds like magic, but it's not the magic bullet for all interop scenarios. Templates and exception handling are handled quite differently in C++ and C#. Well-written, efficient C++ does not necessarily translate into the best MSIL constructs. More importantly, C++ code compiled with the /CLR switch is not verifiable. As I said earlier, this code uses the native heap: It accesses native memory. The CLR cannot verify this code as safe. Programs that call this code must have been granted security permission to access unsafe code. Even so, the /CLR strategy is the best way to leverage your existing C++ code (not COM objects) in .NET. Your program does not incur the thunking cost because your C++ libraries are now in MSIL, not native CPU instructions.

Interop is painful. Seriously consider rewriting native applications before you use interop. It is often easier and faster. Unfortunately for many developers, interop is necessary. If you have existing COM objects written in any language, use COM interop. If you have existing C++ code, the /CLR switch and managed C++ provide the best strategy to access your existing native codebase from new development created in C#. Pick the strategy that takes the least time. It might be the "just throw it out" strategy.

Item 47: Prefer Safe Code

The .NET runtime has been designed so that malicious code cannot infiltrate and execute on a remote machine. Yet some distributed systems rely on downloading and executing code from remote machines. If you might be delivering your software via the Internet or an intranet, or running it directly from the web, you need to understand the restrictions that the

CLR will place on your assemblies. If the CLR does not fully trust an assembly, it limits the allowed actions. This is called **code access security (CAS)**. On another axis, the CLR enforces **role-based security**, in which code might or might not execute based on a particular user account's privileges.

Security violations are runtime conditions; the compiler cannot enforce them. Furthermore, they are far less likely to show up on your development machine; code that you compile is loaded from your hard drive and, therefore, has a higher trust level. Discussing all the implications of the .NET Security model fills volumes, but you can take a small set of reasonable actions to enable your assemblies to interact with the .NET security model more easily. These recommendations apply only if you are creating library components, or components and programs that might be delivered across the web.

Throughout this discussion, remember that .NET is a managed environment. The environment guarantees a certain amount of safety. The bulk of the .NET Framework library is granted full trust through the .NET config policy when it is installed. It is verifiably safe, which means that the CLR can examine the IL and ensure that it does not perform any potentially dangerous actions, such as accessing raw memory. It does not assert any particular security rights needed to access local resources. You should try to follow that same example. If your code does not need any particular security rights, avoid using any of the CAS APIs to determine your access rights; all you do is decrease performance.

You will use the CAS APIs to access a small set of protected resources that demand increased privileges. The most common protected resources are unmanaged memory and the file system. Other protected resources include databases, network ports, the Windows Registry, and the printing subsystem. In each case, attempting to access those resources fires exceptions when the calling code does not have the proper permissions. Furthermore, accessing those resources might cause the runtime to perform a security stack walk to ensure that all assemblies in the current call stack have the proper permissions. Let's look at memory and the file system, discussing the best practices for a secure and safe program.

You can avoid unmanaged memory access by creating verifiably safe assemblies whenever possible. A safe assembly is one that does not use any pointers to access either the managed or unmanaged heaps. Whether you knew it or not, almost all the C# code that you create is safe. Unless you turn on the /unsafe C# compiler option, you've created verifiably safe code. /unsafe allows the use of pointers, which the CLR cannot verify.

The reasons to use unsafe code are few, with the most common being performance. Pointers to raw memory are faster than safe reference checks. In a typical array, they can be up to 10 times faster. But when you use unsafe constructs, understand that unsafe code anywhere in an assembly affects the entire assembly. When you create unsafe code blocks, consider isolating those algorithms in their own assembly (see Item 32). This limits the affect that unsafe code has on your entire application. If it's isolated, only callers who need the particular feature are affected. You can still use the remaining safe functionality in more restrictive environments. You might also need unsafe code to deal with P/Invoke or COM interfaces that require raw pointers. The same recommendation applies: Isolate it. Unsafe code should affect its own small assembly and nothing else.

The advice for memory access is simple: Avoid accessing unmanaged memory whenever possible.

The next most common security concern is the file system. Programs store data, often in files. Code that has been downloaded from the Internet does not have access to most locations on the file system—that would be a huge security hole. Yet, not accessing the file system at all would make it far more difficult to create usable programs. This problem is solved by using isolated storage. Isolated storage can be thought of as a virtual directory that is isolated based on the assembly, the application domain, and the current user. Optionally, you can use a more general isolated storage virtual directory that is based on the assembly and the current user.

Partially trusted assemblies can access their own specific isolated storage area, but nowhere else on the file system. The isolated storage directory is hidden from other assemblies and other users. You use isolated storage through the classes in the System.IO.IsolatedStorage namespace. The IsolatedStorageFile class contains methods very similar to the System.IO.File class. In fact, it is derived from the System.IO.FileStream class. The code to write to isolated storage is almost the same as writing to any file:

```
IsolatedStorageFile iso =
  IsolatedStorageFile.GetUserStoreForDomain( );
```

```
IsolatedStorageFileStream myStream = new
  IsolatedStorageFileStream( "SavedStuff.txt",
  FileMode.Create, iso );
StreamWriter wr = new StreamWriter( myStream );
// several wr.Write statements elided
wr.Close();
```

Reading is equally familiar to anyone who has used file I/O:

```
IsolatedStorageFile isoStore =
  IsolatedStorageFile.GetUserStoreForDomain( );

string[] files = isoStore.GetFileNames( "SavedStuff.txt" );
if ( files.Length > 0 )
{
  StreamReader reader = new StreamReader( new
    IsolatedStorageFileStream( "SavedStuff.txt",
    FileMode.Open,isoStore ) );

  // Several reader.ReadLines( ) calls elided.

  reader.Close();
}
```

You can use isolated storage to persist reasonably sized data elements that enable partially trusted code to save and load information from a carefully partitioned location on the local disk. The .NET environment defines limits on the size of isolated storage for each application. This prevents malicious code from consuming excessive disk space, rendering a system unusable. Isolated storage is hidden from other programs and other users. Therefore, it should not be used for deployment or configuration settings that an administrator might need to manipulate. Even though it is hidden, however, isolated storage is not protected from unmanaged code or from trusted users. Do not use isolated storage for high-value secrets unless you apply additional encryption.

To create an assembly that can live within the possible security restrictions on the file system, isolate the creation of your storage streams. When your assembly might be run from the Web or might be accessed by code run from the web, consider isolated storage.

You might need other protected resources as well. In general, access to those resources is an indication that your program needs to be fully trusted. The only alternative is to avoid the protected resource entirely. Consider the Windows Registry, for example. If your program needs to access the Registry, you must install your program to the end user's computer so that it has the necessary privileges to access the Registry. You simply can't safely create a Registry editor that runs from the web. That's the way it should be.

The .NET Security model means that your program's actions are checked against its rights. Pay attention to the rights your program needs, and try to minimize them. Don't ask for rights you don't need. The fewer protected resources your assembly needs, the less likely it will generate security exceptions. Avoid using secure resources, and consider alternatives whenever possible. When you do need higher security permissions for some algorithms, isolate that code in its own assembly.

Item 48: Learn About Tools and Resources

These are exciting times for C# and .NET. These tools are still new enough that the entire community is learning how best to use them. Several resources are available to help you improve your knowledge and build a larger community of knowledge for .NET and C#. These are the tools that I use daily and recommend to other C# developers. The full set of C# best practices is still being written. Keep up, and get involved.

The first tool that should be in every C# developer's toolbox is **NUnit**, available on the web at www.nunit.org. NUnit is an automated unit-test tool, functionally similar to JUnit. Like most developers, I hate writing tests and testing my code. NUnit makes that process so efficient that using it regularly ensures that you will be in the habit of testing all your C# classes. Whenever I make a class library project, I add an NUnit test project and include executing the tests as part of the automated build. I add new configurations that include build and test, which run the tests on every compile. Then I can switch the active configuration to control whether unit tests are run as part of the regular build process. By default, I run them. I switch to the other configuration when I'm running tests that require the UI.

In addition to using NUnit, you can learn several interesting techniques by examining the NUnit source code. NUnit uses some advanced reflection idioms to load and test your assemblies. It uses attributes to find test suites, test cases, and expected results from each test case (see Item 42). It's a great example of how to use these techniques to build a tool that configures itself dynamically, and it can be used in a wide variety of ways.

Next is **FXCop**, a free tool available at GotDotNet (www.gotdotnet.com). FXCop analyzes the IL in your assembly against a set of rules and best practices, and reports violations. Each rule has a reliability metric and a reason for the rule. As with all the recommendations in this book, the rule documentation has a brief justification for the advice. You can then determine whether the advice fits your particular problem space. You can also configure whether each rule is applied in your project. I disagree with some of the FXCop rules, and I've said as much earlier in this book. However, like NUnit, FXCop can become part of your regular build process. Each build can have a post-build step that analyzes the code using FXCop with your chosen rules. Figure 6.1 shows a sample output from FXCop. Although some of the recommendations are not to my liking (such as the one that every assembly should be COM visible), it's a useful tool because it makes you think about many decisions you might have made by default.

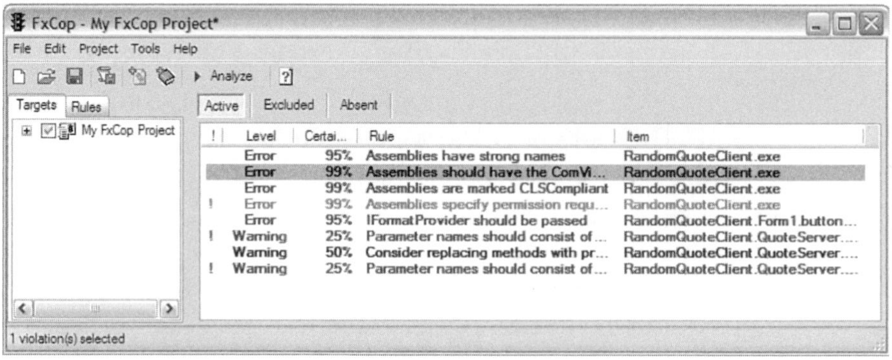

Figure 6.1   FXCop analyzing a project.

IldAsm is an IL disassembler. In different locations in this book, I've shown the IL that the compiler generates for different C# constructs. Although I don't believe that many people are choosing to write IL in favor of any high-level language, you should be familiar with it. Knowing the IL that gets generated from different C# constructs will help you be a better developer. You can examine the IL for your own assemblies or for assemblies in the .NET Framework by using IldAsm, which comes with the .NET Framework SDK. The IL is available to all developers. IldAsm lets you see the intermediate language for your assemblies. However, a better way to learn about the .NET Framework assemblies you use is to get the source.

Those are the tools that are part of your regular toolbox. But having the tools is only one way to improve your skill. A variety of online resources and communities enables you to participate and learn and increase your knowledge of C# and the .NET Framework. First and foremost is the Got-DotNet site (www.gotdotnet.com), the official site of the .NET team. The C# team has a page on the MSDN site, currently located at msdn.microsoft.com/vcsharp/ (it moves occasionally as the MSDN site gets reorganized). If your work is primarily web-based, try www.asp.net, the site for the ASP.NET team. If your work is Windows Forms–based, try www.windowsforms.net, the official site of the Windows forms team. These sites contain reference implementations of many common idioms that you will want to make use of in your applications. They all come with source components, so you can examine and modify them as you need to for your purposes. The last and most important location to become familiar with is the MS Patterns & Practices page. This page is currently located at www.microsoft.com/resources/practices/. From this location, you will find common patterns and starter code for those best practices. This area continues to be updated with more sample code and libraries that will help you solve common programming problems. At this writing, you can use 10 different application blocks to implement common programming requirements; I'm sure there are already more by the time you read this.

I also recommend subscribing to the C# Team FAQ: http://blogs.msdn.com/csharpfaq. In addition to that one, several of the C# team members have blogs where they discuss C# issues. You can find the up-to-date list at http://msdn.microsoft.com/vcsharp/team/blogs/.

If you want to learn more and get an even deeper understanding of the language and the environment, examine the shared source CLI (code-named rotor). This includes the core .NET Framework and a C#

compiler. You can read the source code to gain an even deeper understanding of each feature in the C# language and the .NET Framework. Not every assembly in the commercial .NET Framework is available in the shared source version: For example, the Windows-specific code is not delivered with the shared source code. However, what is delivered is a rich subset that you can use to learn much about the inner workings of the CLR and the C# language.

The C# compiler delivered with the shared source CLI is written in C++, as is part of the low-level CLR code. You need to have a strong background in C++ and a strong understanding of compiler design to understand it thoroughly. Modern-language compilers are intricate pieces of software, but the CLR source is a valuable tool to understand how the core features in the .NET Framework are implemented.

This is intentionally a small list. I've only touched the surface of the many resources that are available to you from Microsoft, online at other sites, and in books. The more you use these tools, the more knowledgeable you will be. The entire C# and .NET community is moving forward. Because it's moving forward quickly, the list of resources changes constantly. Learn and contribute yourself.

Item 49: Prepare for C# 2.0

C# 2.0, available in 2005, will have some major new features in the C# language. Some of today's best practices will change with the tools that will be available in the next release. Although you might not be using these features just yet, you should prepare for them.

When Visual Studio .NET 2005 is released, you will get a new, upgraded C# language. The additions to the language are sure to make you a more productive developer: You'll be able to write more reusable code and higher-level constructs in fewer lines of source. All in all, you'll get more done faster.

C# 2.0 has four major new features: generics, iterators, anonymous methods, and partial types. The focus of these new features is to increase your productivity as a C# developer. This item discusses three of those features and how you should prepare for them now.

Generics will have more impact on how you develop software than any of the other new features in C#. The generics feature is not specific to C#. To implement C# generics, Microsoft is extending the CLR and Microsoft Intermediate Language (MSIL) as well as the C# language. C#, Managed C++, and VB .NET will be capable of creating generics. J# will be capable of consuming them.

Generics provide "parametric polymorphism," which is a fancy way of saying you that create a series of similar classes from a single source. The compiler generates different versions when you provide a specific type for a generic parameter. You use generics to build algorithms that are parameterized with respect to the structures they act upon. You can find great candidates for generics in the .NET Collections namespace: `HashTables`, `ArrayLists`, `Queue`, and `Stack` all can store different object types without affecting their implementation. These collections are such good candidates that the 2.0 release of the .NET Framework will include the `System.Collections.Generic` namespace containing generic counterparts for all the current collection classes. C# 1.0 stores reference to the `System.Object` type. Although the current design is reusable for all types, it has many deficiencies and is not type-safe. Consider this code:

```
ArrayList myIntList = new ArrayList( );
myIntList.Add(32 );
myIntList.Add(98.6 );
myIntList.Add("Bill Wagner" );
```

This compiles just fine, but it almost certainly is not the intent. Did you really create a design that calls for a container that holds totally disparate items? Or were you working around a limitation in the language? This practice means that when you remove items from the collection, you must add extra code to determine what kind of objects were put on the list in the first place. In all cases, you need to cast items from `System.Object` to the particular type you placed on the list.

But that's not all. Value types pay a particular penalty when they are placed in these 1.0-style collections. Anytime you put a value type in a collection, you must store it in a box. You pay again to remove the item from the box when you access an element in the collection. This penalty is small, but with large collections of thousands of items, it adds up quickly. Generics remove this penalty by generating specific object code for each value type.

Those of you familiar with C++ templates will have no trouble working with C# generics because the syntax is very similar. The inner workings for generics, however, are quite different. Let's look at one simple example to see how generics work and how they are implemented. Consider this portion of a list class:

```
public class List
{
  internal class Node
  {
    internal object val;
    internal Node next;
  }
  private Node first;


  public void AddHead( object t )
  {
    // ...
  }

  public object Head()
  {
    return first.val;
  }

}
```

This code stores `System.Object` references in its collection. Anytime you use it, you must add casts on the objects accessed from the collection. But using C# generics, you define the same class like this:

```
public class List < ItemType >
{
  private class Node < ItemType >
  {
    internal ItemType val;
    internal Node < ItemType > next;
  }
```

```
private Node < ItemType > first;

public void AddHead( ItemType t )
{
  // ...
}

public ItemType Head( )
{
  return first.val;
}
}
```

You replace `object` with `ItemType`, the parameter type in the class definition. The C# compiler replaces `ItemType` with the proper type when you instantiate the list. For example, take a look at this code:

```
List < int > intList = new List < int >();
```

The MSIL generated specifies that `intList` stores integers—and only integers. Generics have several advantages over the implementations you can create today. For starters, the C# compiler reports compile-time errors if you attempt anything but an integer in the collection; today, you need to catch those errors by testing the code at runtime.

In C# 1.0, you pay the boxing and unboxing penalty whenever you move a value type into or out of a collection that stores `System.Object` references. Using generics, the JIT compiler creates a specific instance of the collection that stores a particular value type; you don't need to box or unbox the items. But there's more to it. The C# designers want to avoid the code bloat often associated with C++ templates. To save space, the JIT compiler generates only one version of the type for all reference types. This provides a size/speed trade-off whereby value types get a specific version of each type (avoiding boxing), and reference types share a single runtime version storing `System.Object` (avoiding code bloat). The compiler still reports errors when the wrong reference type is used with these collections.

To implement generics, the CLR and the MSIL language undergo some changes. When you compile a generic class, MSIL contains placeholders for each parameterized type. Consider these two method declarations in MSIL:

```
.method public AddHead (!0 t) {
 }

.method public !0 Head () {
}
```

!0 is a placeholder for a type to be created when a particular instantiation is declared and created. Here's one possible replacement:

```
.method public AddHead (System.Int32 t) {
 }

.method public System.Int32 Head () {
}
```

Similarly, variable instantiations contain the specific type. The previous declaration for a list of integers becomes this:

```
.locals (class List<int>)
newobj void List<int>::.ctor ()
```

This illustrates the way the C# compiler and the JIT compiler work together for generics. The C# compiler generates MSIL that contains placeholders for each type parameter. The JIT compiler turns these placeholders into specific types—either System.Object for all reference types, or specific value types for each value type. Each variable instantiation of a generic type includes type information so the C# compiler can enforce type safety.

Constraint definitions for generics will have a large impact on how you prepare for generics. Remember that a specific instantiation of a generic runtime class does not get created until the CLR loads and creates that instantiation at runtime. To generate MSIL for all possible instantiations of a generic class, the compiler needs to know the capabilities of the parameterized type in the generic classes you create. The C# solution for this problem is constraints. Constraints declare expected capabilities on the parameterized type. Consider a generic implementation of a binary tree.

Binary trees store objects in sorted order; therefore, a binary tree can store only types that implement `IComparable`. You can specify this requirement using constraints:

```
public class BinaryTree < ValType > where
  ValType : IComparable < ValType >
{
}
```

Using this definition, any instantiation of `BinaryTree` using a class that does not support the `IComparable` interface won't compile. You can specify multiple constraints. Suppose that you want to limit your `BinaryTree` to objects that support `ISerializable`. You simply add more constraints. Notice that interfaces and constraints can be generic types as well:

```
public class BinaryTree < ValType > where
      ValType : IComparable < ValType > ,
  ValType : ISerializable
{
}
```

You can specify one base class and any number of interfaces as a set of constraints for each parameterized type. In addition, you can specify that a type must have a parameterless constructor.

Constraints also provide one more advantage: The compiler assumes that the objects in your generic class support any interfaces (or base class methods) specified in the constraint list. In the absence of any constraints, the compiler assumes only the methods defined in `System.Object`. You would need to add casts to use any other method. Whenever you use a method that is not defined in `System.Object`, you should document those requirements in a set of constraints.

Constraints point out yet another reason to use interfaces liberally (see Item 19): It will be relatively easy to define constraints if you have defined your functionality using interfaces.

Iterators are a new syntax to create a common idiom using much less code. Imagine that you create some specialized new container class. To support your users, you need to create methods that support traversing this collection and returning the objects in the collection.

Today, you would do this by creating a class that implements IEnumerator. IEnumerator contains two methods—Reset and MoveNext—and one property: Current. In addition, you would add IEnumerable to the list of implemented interfaces on your collection, and its GetEnumerator method would return an IEnumerator for your collection. By the time you're done, you have written an extra class with at least three functions, as well as some state management and another method in your main class. To illustrate this, you must write this page of code today to handle list enumeration:

```
public class List : IEnumerable
{
  internal class ListEnumerator : IEnumerator
  {
    List theList;
    int pos = -1;

    internal ListEnumerator( List l )
    {
      theList = l;
    }

    public object Current
    {
      get
      {
        return theList [ pos ];
      }
    }

    public bool MoveNext( )
    {
      pos++;
      return pos < theList.Length;
    }

    public void Reset( )
    {
      pos = -1;
    }
  }
```

```
public IEnumerator GetEnumerator()
{
  return new ListEnumerator( this );
}


// Other methods removed.
}
```

C# 2.0 adds new syntax in the `yield` keyword that lets you write these iterators more concisely. Here is the C# 2.0 version of the previous code:

```
public class List
{
  public object iterate()
  {
    int i=0;
    while ( i < theList.Length ( ) )
      yield theList [ i++ ];
  }


// Other methods removed.
}
```

The `yield` statement lets you replace roughly 30 lines of code with only 6. This means fewer bugs, less development time, and less source code to maintain—all good things.

Internally, the compiler generates the MSIL that corresponds to those 30 lines of code in today's version. The compiler does it so you don't have to. The compiler generates a class that implements the `IEnumerator` interface and adds it to your list of supported interfaces.

The last major new feature is **partial types**. Partial types let you split a C# class implementation into more than one source file. You rarely, if ever, will use this feature yourself to create multiple source files in your daily development. Microsoft proposed this change to C# to support IDEs and code generators. Today, you get a region in your form classes that contains all the code created by the VS .NET designer. In the future, these tools should create partial classes and place the code in a separate file.

To use this feature, you add the `partial` keyword to your class declaration:

```
public partial class Form1
{
  // Wizard Code:
  private void InitializeComponent()
  {
    // wizard code...
  }
}

// In another file:
public partial class Form1
{
  public void Method ()
  {
    // etc...
  }
}
```

Partial types do have some limitations. They are a source-only feature—there is no difference in the MSIL generated from a single source file and one generated from multiple files. You also need to compile all files that form a complete type into the same assembly, and there is no automated way to ensure that you have added all the source files that form a complete class definition to your builds. You can introduce any number of problems when you split your class definition into multiple files, so I recommend that you use this feature only when IDEs generate the source using partial types. This includes forms, as I've shown earlier. VS .NET also generates partial types for typed `DataSets` (see Item 41) and web service proxies, so you can add your own members to those classes.

I did not cover a number of C# 2.0 features because their addition will have less of an impact on how you write code today. You can make it easier to use your types with generics by defining interfaces to describe behavior: Those interfaces can be used as constraints. The new iterator syntax will provide a more efficient way to implement enumerations. You can easily replace nested enumerators with this new syntax quickly. However, custom external classes will not be so easy to replace. Develop your code now with an eye toward where you will leverage these features, and it will be easier to upgrade your existing code with new C# 2.0 features with minimal work.

Item 50: Learn About the ECMA Standard

The ECMA standard is the official word on how every feature in the C# language behaves. ECMA-334 defines the 1.0 standard for the C# language. You can learn about the C# 2.0 proposals from the book *The C# Programming Language*, by Anders Hejlsberg, Scott Wiltamuth, and Peter Golde (Addison-Wesley, 2003). This book is a language reference, not a tutorial. It explains in very pedantic detail exactly how each feature of the language works. Each language feature is annotated so that you can better understand the justification of each language feature. While I was working on this book, I constantly had this reference open on my desk.

If you are a serious C# programmer, you should understand the language, including the rationale behind different features. It will make your job easier if you know when to apply each feature in your own work. You will have a better understanding of any subtle differences in different language expressions.

In addition to the C# language, you should understand the Common Language Runtime (CLR) thoroughly. The CLR and Common Language Infrastructure (CLI) standards are defined in ECMA-335, the CLR standard. As with C#, this is version 1.0 of the standard. *The Common Language Infrastructure Annotated Standard*, by James Miller and Susann Ragsdale (Addison-Wesley, 2003), explains the CLI version 2.0. This reference includes the Common Language Subsystem (CLS), which will help you understand the rules behind CLS compliance. This also helps you understand the ECMA standard for the .NET runtime and infrastructure.

Both the C# and CLR committees continue to publish working documents on the discussion and progress of the 2.0 version of the C# language and the CLR. The discussions are a valuable way to understand how C# will grow and change over time.

In addition, a deeper understanding of the current standard and the proposed enhancements will help you create code that stands the test of time. By understanding the features that will be added to the language and the environment, you are in a better position to create software that lasts longer into the future. You can anticipate the future modifications that might be necessary.

Software changes over time. C# will grow and change, probably for some time and for several revisions after 2.0. This is a tool that you use every day, for most of your day. Learn the official definitions, and stay on top of them.

Index

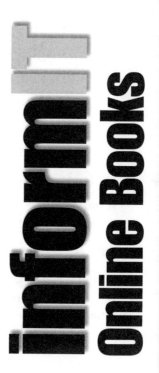